Organ Literature:
A Comprehensive Survey

Volume I: Historical Survey

by

Corliss Richard Arnold

Second Edition

The Scarecrow Press, Inc.
Metuchen, N.J., and London
1984

Library of Congress Cataloging in Publication Data

Arnold, Corliss Richard.
   Organ literature.

   Bibliography: v. 2, p.
   Includes index (v. 1)
   Contents: v. 1. Historical survey -- v. 2. Biographical
catalog.
   1. Organ music--History and criticism. I. Title.
ML600.A76 1984   786.5'09   83-20075
ISBN 0-8108-1662-8 (v. 1)
ISBN 0-8108-1663-6 (v. 2)

To Betty

PRELUDE

The inspiration and need for an organized, comprehensive introduction to the vast literature for the organ and its development (a field which has often been ignored by general music historians) grew from a course on organ literature taught at Michigan State University. The purpose of this book is to provide such an introduction.

The text discusses organ composition styles and their development in a general, non-detailed fashion according to various geographical areas and periods. Charts give a view of the entire school of composers and show how important relationships (such as those of teacher, student, and contemporaries) occurred during the same period. The historical background pages provide a few key items to establish an historical setting for each chapter. Several maps help to clarify geographical relationships within schools. The bibliographies (to each chapter as well as a general one at the end of the book) and the Appendix devoted to Bach should prove helpful in guiding serious organists, students, teachers, and performers to sources for more detailed study.

In the Biographical Catalog of Organ Literature the reader will be able to find a brief biographical sketch and ready references to published organ music under the composer's name.

I have written this book in the sincere hope that it will become a valuable handbook for my organist-colleagues.

February 1972
Corliss R. Arnold
Sac. Mus. Doc. , F. A. G. O.
Assoc. Prof. of Music
Michigan State University
East Lansing, Michigan

PRELUDE (1983)

Ten years have elapsed since the first edition of the Survey was published. Organists in many countries, organ teachers and students have been enthusiastic about the value of this encyclopedia-handbook of organ literature.

The second edition contains much more information gleaned from many sources. New features are the list of chorale title translations with their appropriate liturgical settings and the list of new books and periodical literature about organ music. The charts of various national schools of organ composers have been greatly enlarged to include the organ composers added to the biographical catalog. The catalog is more than twice as large as the first because of the new composers, new editions and new publications which merit attention. I appreciate receiving biographical information not given in these volumes because it is often very difficult to acquire.

I wish to acknowledge the cooperation of the staff of Malecki Music House, Grand Rapids, and the staff of the Library of Congress. I am especially grateful to Dr. D. DeWitt Wasson who allowed me to study his large personal library of organ music. I must also offer my warm appreciation to the staff of Scarecrow Press for their unfailing courtesy and understanding. And, most of all, I am deeply grateful to my family for their patience and sacrifice during the enormous amount of time needed to prepare these volumes.

July 1983   Corliss R. Arnold
                                   Professor of Music
                                   Michigan State University
                                   East Lansing, Michigan 48824

v

ACKNOWLEDGMENTS

It would have been impossible to complete the task of writing so large a book as this without the assistance of many friends and acquaintances. Colleagues at Michigan State University, who helped in a number of different ways, were Dr. Paul A. Varg, former Dean of the College of Arts and Letters, Dr. Hans Nathan, Dr. William Hughes, Dr. Theodore Johnson, and Dr. John Curry. Dr. C. William Young of Wayne State University read the manuscript and offered many helpful suggestions.

Friends in Europe who helped in my research were Mr. John B. Ferguson, M. B. E., F. L. A., Director, Books Department, British Council, London; Mrs. Christine England, A. L. A., Librarian at the British Council Library, Paris; Mr. Jack Dove, F. L. A., F. R. C. O., A. R. C. M., F. R. S. A., Borough Librarian and Curator, Hove Central Library, Hove, England, and the Music Librarian at Hove, Mr. Phil Green; Mr. L. Fenton of British and Continental Music Agencies Ltd., London; Mr. Julian Mitchell-Dawson of J. & W. Chester Ltd., London; M. Jean Bonfils, organist, musicologist, teacher, prominent music editor, Paris; M. E. Ploix and M. Jean Leguy of the firm E. Ploix, Paris; and Professor Grethe Kroghe of the Royal Conservatory of Music, Copenhagen.

Last, and certainly not least, I am grateful to my family whose patience over a long period of time permitted me to finish this arduous effort.

C. R. A.

TABLE OF CONTENTS

Volume I

HISTORICAL SURVEY

1. TABLATURES, MANUSCRIPTS, AND EARLIEST
    PUBLISHED ORGAN MUSIC IN WESTERN EUROPE:
    1300-1600

    The history of music for the organ is inextricably
associated with the development of the organ in its many
stages. Before considering music written for the organ,
therefore, it might be wise to review a few of the mile-
stones in the history of this, the oldest of keyboard instruments.

    All knowledge about the organ up until the fourteenth
century is based upon written descriptions, pictures, carv-
ings, and preserved fragments of the instruments themselves. A Greek named Ktesibios, who lived in Alexandria,
built an organ called a hydraulis about 250 B. C. Pressure
was provided by water, which was pumped by hand. This
instrument became popular in Rome where it was used for
entertainment at feasts and gladitorial combats. Two widely separated historical facts illustrate that organ building
during the first millenium after Christ took place mainly in
the Byzantine Empire. The obelisk of Theodosius, which
was erected during the A. D. 300's, depicts an organ with
bellows. In 757 Copronymos, a Byzantine emperor, sent
Pippin, the father of Charlemagne, an organ as a gift. In
England Bishop Aldhelm (ca. 640-709) described the powerful sound of the organ in his writings. Over 200 years
later Wulstan described a harsh sounding and loud organ,
which was built in Winchester, England, about 980. This
instrument required 70 men to keep the 26 bellows filled
with wind.

    Until the thirteenth century several ranks (complete
sets of pipes of the same type and quality) formed a large
mixture, and there had been no provision for separating
the individual ranks by the means of stops. In addition,
all of the pipes in one rank had the same width, which resulted in a somewhat rough sound in the lower, longer pipes
and progressed gradually to a milder sound in the upper,
shorter pipes. The familiar Ghent altar piece by Jan van

Eyck shows an angel playing a positive organ of this description.   During the thirteenth century keys controlling pallets under the pipes replaced slides, and the range of pitches encompassed three octaves.

The organ developed rapidly after 1300 when instruments grew in size and gained refinement in both sound and control.   Solo stops and softer stops were added to the medieval organ, which had contained only principals and mixtures.   The pedalboard was rather universally adopted in the Netherlands and Germany long before it became a standard part of the organs in other countries.   The organ in Halberstadt, Germany, built in 1361, had three manuals and an early form of the pedal clavier.   As an example of one of the larger instruments of that time, the organ in the Cathedral of Amiens contained 2500 pipes.   During this period two kinds of smaller organs were developed: the portative, a portable organ which was used in processions, and the positive, an organ of moderate size which was stationary.   Francesco Landini (1325-1397) was an expert performer on the organetto, as the portative organ was called in Italy.

The use of stops to render some ranks silent while others could be played probably began in Italy between 1400 and 1450.   An organ built in 1470 in the church of St. Petronio, Bologna, is the oldest organ which exists today to have stops.   By the end of the fifteenth century the organ in Germany had become an instrument similar to that of today in that it contained tonal resources for full chorus sounds, and solo registers of strongly contrasting timbres, all controlled from different keyboards.   Arnolt Schlick (before 1460-ca. 1521) described in detail the type of organ which existed early in the sixteenth century in his Spiegel der Orgelmacher und Organisten (1511).   The specification for a two manual and pedal organ found in Schlick's book is given below.   This specification indicated that independent voices were available on manuals and in the pedal, thus permitting polyphonic composition.

	Werk (F-a^2)	
Principaln 8'	Gemser hörner 4'	Rauss pfeiffen
(two ranks,	Gemser hörner 2'	or a
wide and	Hultze glechter	Schallmey
narrow)	Schweigeln	Zinck
Octaff 4'		Regal or
Doppelloctaff 2'		Super regall
Zymmell		
Hintersatz		

Positiff zü Ruck (F-a^2)
Principaln 4'   Gemsslein
Zymmelein
Hindersetzlein

Pedal (F-c^1)
Principaln 16'   Trommetten or
Principaln 8'   Bassaun
Octaff 4'
Hindersatz

The organs in England and Italy of this same period, however, contained stops having less variety of color and no pedal. The compositions written for this type of organ were homophonic in character. Another type of organ was the regal, a sixteenth-century Italian organ which utilized only reeds.

The beginnings of written keyboard music took place within about a century before the period known as the Renaissance. Renaissance is a French term which signifies "rebirth" and refers to the great interest in the arts and culture, especially of ancient Greece and Rome, for the pleasure and benefit of man. This general interest in the arts arose and flowered roughly between 1450 and 1600. During this period there was much interest in discovery and colonization of the New World by such powers as England, Spain, France, and Portugal. Two other historical events occurred during the Renaissance which had great significance to organ music: the invention of printing and the division of the Christian church into Roman Catholic and Protestant branches. Gutenberg's invention made it possible to obtain many copies of printed material of uniform quality, moderately priced, which could be disseminated over a wide area. After the break from the Roman Catholic Church, Martin Luther was interested in using music as a very important element of his form of congregational worship, and the rise of the Lutheran choral led to its utilization in various types of organ and choral music. The Roman Catholic Church continued to use the organ as a solo instrument and as an accompaniment for the choir.

During the Renaissance the musician's profession became raised to a higher level of importance from that of the Middle Ages (from the fall of the Roman Empire to the Renaissance). Both the church and courts, according to their wealth and musical inclinations, were the chief patrons

HISTORICAL BACKGROUND

ca. 1300-ca. 1370	French Ars nova
1305	Papacy moved to Avignon
1307	Dante The Divine Comedy
1337-1453	Hundred Years' War
1353	Boccaccio Decameron
1360	Machaut Messe de Notre Dame
1386	Chaucer The Canterbury Tales
1415	Battle of Agincourt
1426	van Eycks began Ghent altarpieces
1431	Jeanne d'Arc burned at the stake
1434-1494	Medici family held great authority in Italy
1454	Gutenberg invented printing from movable type
1455-1485	War of the Roses
1478	Botticelli La Primavera
1485-1603	Tudor dynasty ruled in England
1492	Columbus discovered America
1495	da Vinci The Last Supper
1498	Savonarola executed in Florence
1503	da Vinci Mona Lisa
1504	Michelangelo David
1511	Erasmus The Praise of Folly
1516	Raphael Sistine Madonna
1517	Luther posted theses at Wittenberg
1519	Magellan sailed around the world
1519-1556	Charles V ruled the Holy Roman Empire
1534	Parliament declared Henry VIII the head of the Catholic Church in England
1540	Society of Jesus founded
1545	Council of Trent convened; concluded 1563
1555	Peace of Augsburg
1558-1603	Reign of Elizabeth I in England
1562	Genevan Psalter
1588	War between England and Spain
1594	Shakespeare Romeo and Juliet
1597	Morley A Plaine and Easie Introduction to Practicall Music

of musicians.   More and more individual musicians gained
fame for their musical prowess.

It is important that some general characteristics of
Renaissance musical style should be kept in mind, even
though many medieval practices continued, and others, which
became much more highly developed during the Renaissance,
had been anticipated years earlier. During the later Middle
Ages musical texture had often been that of three lines of
quite different qualities of sound, and often each part entered separately. Renaissance compositions, however, often
began with all parts simultaneously, and the preferred tone
color was homogeneous. Harmonies of the Renaissance
generally employed triads and chords of the first inversion.
Tendencies toward the major-minor system had also begun.
Keyboard music was either systematically imitative or improvisatory in style. Sometimes chords alternated with
free melodies in conjunct motion, and sometimes rhythmic
patterns were employed. Instrumental forms no longer de-
pended upon texts to prove their worth, and new instrumental forms emerged which were complete and satisfying
in themselves. An international musical language was common to all countries until national musical idioms began to
make themselves known about the middle of the sixteenth
century.

During the Middle Ages solo voices sang polyphonic
music, and the clergy, cathedral chapters, or monastic
choruses sang plainchant in unison. About 1450 choruses
began to sing polyphonic sacred music. Sometimes instruments doubled the voice parts or substituted for voices to
an extent which is not known today. Instrumental arrangements of compositions which were originally vocal were
often performed with embellishments added by the performer,
but instrumental music was still closely related to vocal
music at the beginning of the sixteenth century.

The lack of any written keyboard music from pre-
Christian times and the first 1300 years of the Christian
era prevents our knowing much about such music. Before
1450 little instrumental music was permanently recorded
since most of the instrumental music performed was ap-
parently either improvised or played by memory. Prior
to 1600 keyboard notation in England, France, and Italy
was similar to the notation of today--notes written upon a
staff. The keyboard notation in Germany and Spain, however, was in tablature form. Tablature is the general

name applied to systems of instrumental notation to indicate
tones by means of letters, numbers, or other symbols,
sometimes in combination with a staff.

Most of the earliest keyboard music recorded in the
Middle Ages was written to be performed upon all keyboard
instruments, organs, clavichords, or harpsichords, not upon
only one type of keyboard instrument, because stylistic
traits for individual keyboard instruments had not been clearly
defined. Many sources of keyboard music from the fourteenth, fifteenth, sixteenth, and early seventeenth centuries
contained material which could be appropriately performed
on the organ. Four different types of literature were found
in these documents: intabulations (direct transcriptions of
polyphonic choral music such as motets and ballades),[1]
cantus firmus compositions (works based upon pre-existing
sacred or secular melodies), preambles (free preludes not
based on pre-existing melodies), and dances.[2]

The first document of keyboard music extant is the
Robertsbridge Codex, dated ca. 1325.[3] Although this manuscript is in the British Museum, certain notational practices
suggest that the codex might be French[4] or Italian[5] in origin.
Notes for the upper part are written on a staff of five lines;
pitches for the lower parts are indicated by letters written
under the notes. Three of the six compositions found in
the Robertsbridge Codex are intabulations. The three remaining compositions belong to a kind of medieval instrumental composition known as the estampie. The estampie,
which probably was a dance in origin, was the most important instrumental form of the thirteenth and fourteenth
centuries. It consisted of repeated sections called puncti.
Each punctus had two different endings, the first called
ouvert and the second, clos. The estampies from the
Robertsbridge Codex are written in two voices for the most
part: the lower part moves slowly, and the upper voice is
written in quicker time values. The archaic character of
these estampies, suggested by the use of parallel intervals
of fifths and octaves, is similar to polyphonic music of the
ninth century.[6]

The Reina manuscript[7] might be of Italian origin,
also. Two keyboard pieces are found among the French
and Italian secular compositions for polyphonic ensembles.
One of the pieces has been identified as an arrangement of
a ballata by Landini. The Faenza manuscript,[8] dated before 1520, is a significant source of keyboard music in

MAJOR ORGAN TABLATURES, MANUSCRIPTS, AND EARLIEST PRINTED ORGAN MUSIC

1300   1400   1500   1600

ca. 1325 Robertsbridge Codex
late 14th century Reina Manuscript
before 1420 Faenza Manuscript
1448 Ileborgh tablature
1452 Paumann Fundamentum organisandi
15th cent. Nikolaus Apel Codex
ca. 1470 Buxheimer Orgelbuch
1511 Schlick Spiegel der Orgelmacher und Organisten
1512 Schlick Tabulaturen etlicher Lobgesang
ca. 1510/24 tablatures by Buchner, Kotter, Sicher, Kleber
16th cent. Johannes de Lublin tablature
16th cent. Neresheim Orgelbuch von St. Ulrich und Afra
1531 Attaingnant tablatures
1571/75/83 Ammerbach tablatures
1577 B. Schmid the elder Zwey Bücher
1607 B. Schmid the younger Tabulatur Buch
1617 Johann Woltz Nova musices

Italy before 1500. This collection contains organ Mass sections and instrumental transcriptions of many Italian and French secular vocal compositions from the fourteenth and early fifteenth centuries. The upper part is decorated in a variety of ways, and the tenor of the original composition is given to the lower voice. Both parts are notated on staves of six lines each These pieces can be performed on stringed keyboard instruments as well as on the organ. The Mass sections of the Faenza manuscript assign the plainsong in long notes to the lower part. Only parts of the plainsong are used, which suggests that the pieces were planned for alternation between voices and organ in the Mass. These manuscripts, which contain Italian relationships, emphasize the major role Italy played in the early development of keyboard music.

The practice of alternation between liturgical organ music and Gregorian plainsong sung by a unison chorus developed as an outgrowth of at least two practices, responsorial singing of Psalmody (between soloists and choir) and alternation of polyphony and plainsong (between two choral bodies).   Only two examples of this second procedure, which was performed in the period from the twelfth through the sixteenth centuries, are the organa of the Notre Dame school and Tallis's Audivi vocem. Organ music in the alternation practice substituted for the polyphonic choir. Alternation between organ and plainsong sung in unison by the clergy or monastic bodies was practiced in performance of alternate verses of the Psalms, the Te Deum, and the Magnificat in one of the eight psalm tones, in alternate verses of Latin hymns such as the Salve Regina, and in the various sections of the Ordinary of the Mass (Kyrie, Gloria, Credo, Sanctus, and Agnus Dei).

The psalm tones were different melodic formulas which were used for the chanting of the complete book of the Psalms during the Roman Catholic Office. The basic melody of the first psalm tone is given in Example 1. This example shows the binary structure and the inflected monotone to which many of the syllables are sung.

Example 1.   Basic melody of the first psalm tone.

Example 2 shows how the psalm tone is applied to the first verse of the first Psalm.

Example 2.   First psalm tone applied to
the first verse of Psalm 1.

Example 3 shows how the same psalm tone is applied to the first two verses of the Magnificat, the canticle of Mary. [9] The organ settings were composed for either the odd verses or the even verses, and the alternate verses were sung.

Example 3.   First psalm tone applied to the
first two verses of the Magnificat.

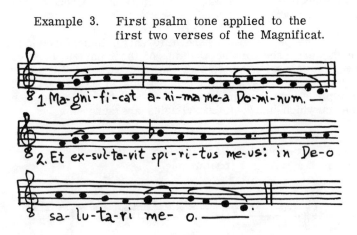

The most common alternation arrangement of a Mass Kyrie was: Kyrie (organ), Kyrie (plainsong sung by singers in unison), Kyrie (organ), Christe (plainsong), Christe (organ), Christe (plainsong), Kyrie (organ), Kyrie (plainsong), and Kyrie (organ).

Four smaller German sources of organ music are the Sagan Gloria fragment[10] (1433), two fragments from the Dominican monastery at Breslau[11] (1430 and ca. 1450), and another by Ludolf Wilkin of Winsem (Windesheim)[12] (1432). Most of the pieces found in these manuscripts are based on plainsong or are Mass movements. The Sagan fragment pieces are intended for alternation between singers and the organ. In all four of these manuscripts the lower part sustains long notes under an active upper part. Sometimes melodic and rhythmic patterns are treated sequentially in the upper part, and the melodic intervals generally move in a stepwise fashion. A few single notes are added from time to time to fill out the harmony.

The tablature of Adam Ileborgh[13] dated 1448 contains five short preambles (preludes), which were the first compositions written specifically for keyboard use. They are not based on pre-existing melodies. When there are two lower parts, they move in intervals of fifths and thirds and support the running upper part. The upper part covers a range which extends from a twelfth to two octaves. There are also a few chromatic alterations in the upper part, which usually progresses in conjunct intervals.[14]

The Fundamentum organisandi[15] (1452) by Conrad Paumann (ca. 1410-1473) is bound in a manuscript with the Lochamer Liederbuch. It was written primarily with the purpose of teaching how to write counterpoint for instruments.[16] Paumann's treatment of popular German songs as the basis of his composition is especially noteworthy. In Mit ganczem Willen much freedom is immediately noticed in that the melody is not always treated in long, equal notes in the lowest part. The melody enters at irregular intervals, sometimes on short note values, with other notes interpolated in the same voice. The number of voices also varies from two to five. The most common harmonic intervals between the two lower parts are fifths and thirds, although the texture is in two parts for about half the time. The uppermost voice contains much rhythmic variety but also utilizes rhythmic patterns.

From the Carthusian monastery at Buxheim in southern
Germany comes the very important Buxheimer Orgelbuch (ca.
1470). [17] This collection of compositions by many different
composers is in the "old" German tablature: the highest
part on a staff and the lower part(s) in letters beneath.   Although two-part and four-part writing is represented, the
majority of the writing is in three parts.   Over 250 different
compositions of various types, such as secular songs, German and Latin organ hymns, [18] Mass movements, and other
arranged vocal works, are found in this collection, with
titles in four different languages.   Twenty-seven pieces were
written for organ.   Paumann's name and a version of his
Fundamentum are found in the manuscript;   other composers
whose composition characteristics identify them have familiar
names, such as Binchois, Dufay, and Dunstable.   The intabulare and organisare techniques are used: the intabulare
technique takes an entire song and applies keyboard writing
techniques to all parts, especially the highest one;   the
organisare technique employs the melody of the original song
as cantus firmus, and adds an instrumental part to accompany it.   The Buxheim collection also contains settings of
Mass movements using the alternation practice.   A Kyrie
in four voice parts in chordal style is found in the book.
The Gloria[19] is an extensive movement having nine parts in
which, most of the time, the chant stands out in the lower
part in notes of equal value.   The free keyboard preambles
(preludes), which have no basis on pre-existing vocal compositions, are quite short.   Sometimes they have a free,
scalewise melody in the upper part without any harmonic
support;   this type of writing alternates with chordal sections.   Independence can also be observed in the lowest part,
no longer limited to equal length note values.

Paul Hofhaimer (1459-1537) was better known as a
performer and teacher than as a composer, but a few of his
compositions have survived through his pupils' efforts.   These
works demand considerable technical proficiency.   They contain the use of imitation, suspensions, and much florid decoration.   Excessive embellishment and the addition of cadenzas, passing tones, and runs has caused the name "colorists"
to be applied to the group of composers who utilized this
technique.   The group of pupils and composers who were
strongly influenced by Paul Hofhaimer were called "Paulo-
mimes."   This group included Buchner, Kotter, Sicher, and
Kleber.   These composers' works include both sacred and
secular compositions.   Sometimes keyboard decorations were
added or left to the performer to improvise, but both cus-

toms were common in the period.

Most of the 120 compositions which Hans Buchner (1483-1540) wrote for his Fundamentum[20] (ca. 1525) were composed in three or four parts. These pieces were Mass movements, introits, sequences, hymns, and responses, all based on sacred melodies. Some of the characteristics of Buchner's writing are a preference for duple rather than triple rhythm, imitation used freely, an altered cantus firmus, restriction to regular meter, and rather dense ornamentation in the upper voices at times.

Hans Kotter (1485-1541) used harmony in his tablature to establish form. He also fitted the melody and his musical ideas into a regular rhythmic unit. This differentiated his work from that of the Buxheimer Orgelbuch and the Ileborgh tablature. In chordal sections the sense of harmonic root movement by fifths is clearly shown; the melodic efforts are very short and are rigidly kept within the harmony. Diatonic lines flow at the interval of a tenth between the two lower parts and are balanced with the third voice, all within a clear sense of harmonic progression. The first application of the term fantasia to a keyboard composition and the earliest known dances in German tablatures are found in the Kotter book, four of which are settings of the Spagna[21] melody. The style of writing suggests that the settings might not be written for the organ but perhaps for some stringed keyboard instrument. [22]

Fridolin Sicher (1490-1546), a pupil of Hans Buchner, collected a large number of organ works in tablature,[23] most of which are intabulations, along with a few preludes and arrangements of cantus firmus vocal works. Long notes are often repeated, a fact which does not suggest an organ arrangement since there would be no difficulty in sustaining tones at the organ.

The tablature of Leonhard Kleber (1490-1556)[24] dated 1524 contains 112 numbers which show the strong influence of the Hofhaimer school, even though Kleber was not one of Hofhaimer's pupils. Most of these highly decorated pieces are transcriptions of vocal works. The influence of the Buxheimer Orgelbuch is noticeable in Kleber's 18 short preludes, which alternate chordal sections with improvisatory scale passages. [25]

Two Polish tablatures were written under German

influence. Johannes de Lublin assembled a very large collection[26] which contains a treatise on counterpoint and a
wide variety of intabulations of both sacred and secular works
by German, French, Italian, and Polish composers. The
brief preludes included in the tablature usually begin with
block chords, contain a contrapuntal section, and close with
a flourish. The second Polish tablature[27] (called the Cracow
tablature) is similar to the Lublin tablature. It contains a
wide variety of pieces such as preludes, Mass movements,
motets, Protestant hymns, canons, and secular songs from
several countries. [28]

In 1531 the printer Pierre Attaingnant issued the first
keyboard works published in France, which consisted of seven
books, four for secular purposes and three for use in the
church. The first of the three books for the church contained versets for the Cunctipotens and Fons bonitatis Kyries.
The versets were to be played in alternation with plainsong.
The second book contains two preludes, versets on the
Magnificat in eight tones, followed by versets on the Te
Deum. The third book consists of 13 motets by various
composers and one prelude arranged for organ. Attaingnant
probably wished to publish a collection for the organ which
would include works of divergent styles and conceptions. [29]
Even though Attaingnant called his works "tabulatures," he
used two staves of five lines each. Homophonic writing
(music in which one voice is predominant melodically; the
predominant voice is supported in an accompanimental way
by the other voices) prevails in the dances and in the chanson
settings, with decoration appearing most frequently in the
outer parts. In the motet arrangements the parts are elaborately decorated. The embellishment changes the melodic
lines into fantasies based on the original harmonies of the
vocal works. Three-part writing predominates in the organ
Mass movements.

A few collections introduced the French organ school.
The first collection to appear after Attaingnant's publications
was the Premier Livre de Tablature d'Espinette (1560), which
came from the printshop of Simon Gorlier. Charles Guillet
of Bruges issued Vingt-Quatre Fantasies à Quatre Parties,
Disposées Selon l'Ordre des Douze Modes in 1610 written as
much for strings as for the organ (tant pour les violes que
pour l'orgue). In this book there are many similarities to
Sweelinck's writing. [30] François Eustache Du Caurroy (1549-
1609) composed 42 contrapuntal Fantaisies in from three to
six voices. He often approached the variation form in these

works. Claudin Le Jeune (ca. 1530-1600), Valerien Gonet, and Guillaume Costeley (ca. 1531-1606) all wrote fantasies. Costeley's composition has the title of Fantazie sus Orgue ou Espinette.

Elias Nicolaus Ammerbach (1530-1597) wrote the first published German organ tablature (1571). Two other tablatures by him appeared in 1575 and 1583. The "new" German organ tablature in the first book uses only letters (no staves) with rhythmic signs. Both sacred and secular works are included in all three of Ammerbach's tablatures. Dances fill one section of the first tablature. Ammerbach's intabulations draw from famous choral composers such as Isaac, Senfl, Lassus, Clemens non Papa, and Josquin des Pres. The amount of coloration of the intabulations ranges from very little to extremely florid writing in every part. The number of parts extends from four to six, and there is a gradual widening of the vocal ranges.

In 1577 Bernhard Schmid the elder (1520-1590) published a keyboard tablature for musical amateurs, Zwey Bücher einer neuen künstlichen Tabulatur auff Orgeln und Instrumenten (Strassbourg: B. Jobin, 1577). Schmid pleaded for instrumental music in the church. The musical selections included in the book were Italian, French, and German secular songs, and a number of intabulated motets and dances. Most of the pieces are in five parts.

A volume for organists' use for all Sundays and festivals of the liturgical year was collected by Johann Rühling (1550-1615) and printed in 1583. Most of the 86 pieces (without the usual decorative instrumental writing) came from the Latin motets of Lassus and Clemens non Papa.

Jacob Paix (1556-after 1623) assembled two tablatures. The first, Ein Schön Nutz unnd Gebreulich Orgel Tabulaturbuch (1583), contains intabulated motets (principally by Palestrina and Lassus), fantasias, songs from France, Germany, and Italy, dances, and some of his own compositions. All were highly ornamented, especially the vocal works. Paix employed the thumb, and used parallel fifths and octaves, imitation, and spaces between measures to stand for bar lines. The second tablature, Thesaurus Motetarum (1589), contains 22 intabulated motets with no added coloration. [31]

The Dresden court organist August Nörminger (ca.

1560-1613) collected a large number of simple settings of
Protestant chorales, intabulated songs, and rather short
dances (pavans, galliards, passamezzi) with the coloration
at its most florid in the songs. The compilation was entitled Tabulaturbuch auff den Instrumente³² (1598).

A significant change in taste is shown in the younger
Bernhard Schmid's (1547-1625) preference for Italian works
in his published keyboard tablature, Tabulatur Buch ... auff
Orgeln und Instrumenten zu gebrauchen (1607). He included
ornamented motets, canzoni alla francese, Italian organ toccatas, intonations by Gabrieli, and dances.

In Johann Woltz's Nova Musices Organicae Tabulatura
(1617) the Italian influence is even greater. This book is a
large collection which contains 85 Latin motets, 53 sacred
German compositions, 50 canzoni alla francese, 20 fugae by
Simon Lohet, and seven miscellaneous compositions. The
coloration was to be added by the performer.

National schools or organ composition began to rise
about the middle of the sixteenth century. The earlier
stages of evolution of these different schools of organ composition will be studied in the next three chapters.

Notes

1. Sometimes original voice parts are omitted or are
    placed in a different range for ease of performance
    by the hands. Keyboard decoration and figuration are
    frequently added. Sometimes single notes or a new
    accompanying part is inserted for additional sonority.
2. The reader will find publication references to printed
    music, facsimiles, and some tablature transcriptions
    under the name of the composer or under the title
    of the more important manuscripts in Part II, the
    Biographical Catalog.
3. British Museum, Add. 28550.
4. Willi Apel, Geschichte der Orgel- und Klaviermusik
    bis 1700, Kassel, Germany: Bärenreiter Verlag, 1967;
    p. 21.
5. Archibald T. Davison and Willi Apel, Historical Anthol-
    ogy of Music, Cambridge, Mass.: Harvard University
    Press, 1946, 1949; p. 221-222.
6. Constant reference has been made to the definitive arti-
    cle by Clyde William Young, "Keyboard Music to 1600,"

Musica Disciplina, XVI (1962) and XVII (1963). This
excellent article also gives references to sources,
additional transcriptions, facsimiles, and the like.
Dr. Young has graciously given the author permission
to use material from this article, which makes further reference under individual topics unnecessary.

7. Bibliothèque Nationale, fr. nouv. acq. 6771.
8. Faenza, Biblioteca Communale 117.
9. The text of the Magnificat in Latin (Luke 1:46-55) follows: 1. Magnificat anima mea Dominum. 2. Et
exultavit spiritus meus: in Deo salutari meo.
3. Quia respexit humilitatem ancillae suae, ecce enim
ex hoc beatam dicent omnes generationes. 4. Quia
fecit mihi magna qui potens est: et sanctum nomen
ejus. 5. Et misericordia progenie in progenies
timentibus eum. 6. Fecit potentiam in brachio suo
dispersit superbos mente cordis sui. 7. Deposuit
potentes de sede, et exaltavit humiles. 8. Esurientes
implevit bonis, et divites dimisit inanes. 9. Suscepit Israel puerum suum: recordatus misericordiae
suae. 10. Sicut locutus est ad patres nostros,
Abraham et semini ejus in secula. GLORIA PATRI:
Gloria Patri, Filio, et Spiritui Sancto! Sicut erat in
principio, et nunc, et semper et in secula seculorum.
Amen.
10. Breslau [Wrocław], University Library, I. Qu 438.
11. Breslau [Wrocław], University Library, I. Qu 42 and
I. F. 687.
12. Berlin, Deutsche Staatsbibliothek, Theol. Lat. Quart.
290.
13. Curtis Institute of Music, Philadelphia.
14. Young suggests that the first indication of the use of
pedal might be in the Breslau manuscript, I. Qu 42
[note 11]. ("Keyboard Music to 1600," Musica Disciplina, XVI (1962), p. 119-120). Sumner suggests
that the first real evidences of the use of pedal are
found in the Ileborgh preludes (William Leslie Sumner,
The Organ 2nd ed., 1955, p. 71).
15. Berlin, Deutsche Staatsbibliothek, 40613.
16. The word fundamentum was the title chosen by several
composers for books which were designed to give instruction in writing counterpoint. Four of these books
were Conrad Paumann's Fundamentum organisandi, the
Buxheimer Orgelbuch, Buchner's Fundamentum, and
Johannes de Lublin's organ tablature.
17. Munich, Bayerische Staatsbibliothek, Cim. 352b, (olim
Mus. 3725).

18. The earliest organ settings of Latin hymns are found in Paumann's Fundamentum and in the Buxheimer Orgelbuch.
19. Folios 81v-82.
20. Zürich, Stadtbibliothek, Codex 284.
21. The Spagna (abbreviation of Il Re di Spagna) tune is a famous basse danse melody which was frequently used as the cantus firmus for polyphonic compositions during the fifteenth and sixteenth centuries. The basse danse was a dance which probably began with low [Fr., bas, low] gliding foot movements.
22. A manuscript similar to the Kotter tablature (Basle, Universitäts Bibliothek, F. IX. 58) contains two dances by Johann (or Hans) Weck, two Spagna settings, and five intabulations.
23. St. Gall, Stiftsbibliothek, 530.
24. Berlin, Deutsche Staatsbibliothek, 40026 (olim, Z 96).
25. An anonymous tablature from Trent (Biblioteca Civica, 1947) also shows influences from the Hofhaimer school.
26. Cracow, Academy of Sciences, Ms. 1716.
27. Warsaw, State Archives.
28. The small Munich Manuscript (Bayerische Staatsbibliothek, Ms. 2987) contains nine French chansons. The music is primarily chordal in character, and the coloration (decoration) does not interfere with the harmonic structure.
29. M. Alfred Bichsel, "The Attaingnant Organ Books," The Musical Heritage of the Lutheran Church, St. Louis: Concordia Pub. House, 1959; vol. V; p. 156-165.
30. Gotthold Frotscher, Geschichte des Orgelspiels und der Orgelkomposition, Berlin: Merseberger Verlag, 1959; vol. II; p. 667.
31. A number of other similar sources include the manuscript tablature (1585) of Christoph Löffelholtz (1572-1619) (Berlin, Deutsche Staatsbibliothek, Mus. Ms. 40 034), the Tabulatur-Buch Auff dem Instrument Hertzogk zu Sachsen (Dresden, Sächsische Landesbibliothek), a manuscript tablature (Berlin, Deutsche Staatsbibliothek, Mus. Ms. 40 115), the Künstlich Tabulatur-Buch (1594-1596) by Johann Fischer (sixteenth/seventeenth century) (Thorn, Ratsbibliothek), and a manuscript tablature ascribed to Cajus Schmidtlein (Danzig [Gdansk], Staatsarchiv).
32. Berlin, Deutsche Staatsbibliothek, Mus. Ms. 40 089.

Bibliography

Andersen, Poul-Gerhard. Organ Building and Design, trans-
lated into English by Joanne Curnutt. New York: Ox-
ford University Press, 1969; p. 140-142.
Apel, Willi. "Early German Keyboard Music," Musical
Quarterly, vol. XXIII (1937), p. 210-237.
_____. "Die Tabulatur des Adam Ileborgh, " Zeitschrift
für Musikwissenschaft, vol. XVI (1934), p. 193-212.
_____. "Du Nouveau sur la Musique Française pour
Orgue au XVIe Siècle," Revue Musicale, vol. XVIII
(1937), p. 96-108.
_____. Geschichte der Orgel- und Klaviermusik bis 1700.
Kassel, Germany: Bärenreiter Verlag, 1967; p. 100-
104.
Bedbrook, Gerald Stares, "The Buxheim Keyboard Manu-
script," Music Review, vol. XIV (1953), p. 288-295.
Benedictines of Solesmes, eds., Liber Usualis. Tournai,
Belgium: Desclée et Cie., 1950.
Bichsel, M. Alfred. "The Attaingnant Organ Books," The
Musical Heritage of the Lutheran Church. St. Louis:
Concordia Pub. House, 1959; vol. V, p. 156.
Bowles, Edmund A. "A Performance History of the Organ
in the Middle Ages," Diapason (January 1970), p. 13-
14.
Carapetyan, Armen. "The Codex Faenza, Biblioteca Com-
munale, 117," Musica Disciplina, vol. XIII (1959);
vol. XIV (1960); and vol. XV (1961).
Dart, Thurston. "A New Source of English Organ Music,"
Music and Letters, vol. XXXV (1954), p. 201-205.
Davison, Archibald, and Willi Apel. Historical Anthology
of Music. Cambridge, Mass.: Harvard University
Press, 1964; vol. I.
Frotscher, Gotthold. Geschichte des Orgelspiels und der
Orgelkomposition. Berlin: Merseberger Verlag, 1959;
vol. I: p. 1-175, 186, 221; vol. II: p. 717, 936.
Howell, Almonte C. "The French Organ Mass in the Six-
teenth and Seventeenth Centuries." Unpublished disser-
tation, University of North Carolina, 1953.
Jeppesen, Knud. Die italienische Orgelmusik am Anfang des
Cinquecento, 2 vols. Copenhagen: Munksgaard, 1943
(2nd ed., 1960).
Kendall, Raymond. "Notes on Arnold Schlick," Acta
Musicologia, vol. XI (1939), p. 136-143.
Kinkeldey, Otto. Orgel und Klavier in der Musik des 16.

Jahrhunderts. Leipzig: Breitkopf und Härtel, 1910.
Kinsky, Georg. "Kurze Oktaven auf besaitenen tasten-
    instrumente," Zeitschrift für Musikwissenschaft, vol.
    II (1919-1920), p. 65-82.
Lunelli, Renato. L'arte organaria del rinascimento in Roma
    e gli organi di S. Pietro in Vaticano dalle origini a
    tutto il periodo Frescobaldiana. Vol. X of Historiae
    musicae cultores biblioteca, Florence: 1958.
_____. Der Orgelbau in Italien in seinen Meisterwerken
    vom 14. Jahrhundert bis zur Gegenwart. Mainz,
    Germany: Rheingold, 1956.
Lowinsky, Edward E. "English Organ Music of the Renais-
    sance," Musical Quarterly, vol. XXXIX (1953), p. 373-
    395, 528-553.
Marrocco, W. Thomas, and Robert Huestis, "Some Specula-
    tions Concerning the Instrumental Music of the Faenza
    Codex 117," Diapason (May, 1972), p. 3.
Perrot, Jean. L'Orgue de Ses Origines Hellénistiques à
    la Fin du XIIIᵉ Siècle. Paris: Editions A. et J.
    Picard et Cie. , 1965 (English ed. , The Organ from
    Its Invention to the End of the Thirteenth Century,
    translated by Norma Deane, New York: Oxford Uni-
    versity Press, 1971).
Raugel, Félix. "The Ancient French Organ School," Musical
    Quarterly, vol. XI (1925), p. 560-571.
Rokseth, Yvonne. La Musique d'Orgue au XVᵉ Siècle et au
    Début du XVIᵉ. Paris: Librairie E. Droz, 1930.
Schering, Arnold. "Zur Alternatim-Orgelmesse," Zeitschrift
    für Musikwissenschaft, vol. XVII (1935), p. 19-32.
Schlick, Arnolt. Tabulaturen etlicher Lobgesang und Lidlein
    uff die Orgeln und Lauten. Klecken, [West] Germany:
    Gottlieb Harms, 1924.
Schnoor, Hans. "Das Buxheimer Orgelbuch," Zeitschrift
    für Musikwissenschaft, vol. IV (1921-1922), p. 1-10.
Schrade, Leo. "The Organ in the Mass of the 15th Century,"
    Musical Quarterly, vol. XXVIII (1942), p. 329-336,
    467-487.
Siebert, Frederick Mark. "Mass Sections in the Buxheim
    Organ Book: A Few Points," Musical Quarterly, vol.
    L (1964), p. 353-366.
_____. "Performance Problems in Fifteenth-Century
    Organ Music," Organ Institute Quarterly, vol. X, No.
    2 (1963), p. 5.
Stevens, Denis W. "Organ Mass," Grove's Dictionary of
    Music and Musicians, Eric Blom, ed. New York: St.
    Martin's Press, 1954; Vol. VI, p. 339-344.
Sumner, William Leslie. "The French Organ School," Sixth

Music Book. London: Hinrichsen Edition Ltd. , 1950; p. 281-294.

_____. The Organ: Its Evolution, Principles of Construction, and Use. London: Macdonald and Co. , 1952 (3rd ed. , 1962).

White, John R. "The Tablature of Johannes de Lublin," Musica Disciplina, vol. XVI (1963), p. 137-162.

Williams, Peter. The European Organ 1450-1850. London: Batsford, 1966.

Young, Clyde William. "Keyboard Music to 1600," Musica Disciplina, vol. XVI (1962), p. 115-150, and vol. XVII (1963), p. 163-193.

_____. "The Keyboard Tablatures of Bernhard Schmid, Father and Son." Unpublished dissertation, University of Illinois, 1957.

2. ITALY: 1350-1650

The organ in Italy was used for both secular and sacred purposes during the fifteenth, sixteenth, and seventeenth centuries. Varieties of organs for secular use included chamber organs, small reed organs called regals, portable organs, and outdoor organs. Organs were used in connection with opera, the "new" musical entertainment established by the Florentines, and with oratorio, another new seventeenth-century musical form. In churches organs were used with orchestral groups, and at Mass to accompany choirs or as a solo instrument at various prescribed places during the services. Costanzo Antegnati (ca. 1549-1624), who belonged to a famous family of organ builders, organ composers, theorists, and organists, wrote in his L'Arte Organica (Brescia, 1608) that the organ should be used only "to praise and magnify the Lord and not for other profane uses." The magnificent Cathedral of San Marco in Venice contained two organs and held difficult examinations for organists who wished to fill the coveted positions of first or second organist.

Two authors who wrote about matters related to the organ were Adriano Banchieri (1567-1634), whose Conclusioni nel suono dell'organo and Organo suonarino progressed through several editions, and Girolamo Diruta (1561-?), who wrote the first Italian organ method. Diruta's book, entitled Il Transilvano, was issued in two parts and was written in question and answer form. In addition to instruction in registration Diruta included organ pieces composed by himself and other composers. Luzzaschi, A. and G. Gabrieli, Merulo, and Diruta had works in Part I. Diruta, Luzzaschi, Fatorini, G. Gabrieli, Mortaro, and Banchieri were represented in Part II.

Before the sixteenth century, music composed for keyboard instruments consisted of dances, arrangements of vocal music, music for liturgical functions, and free preludes. A number of new keyboard forms developed in Italy during the sixteenth century. The close relationship of

HISTORICAL BACKGROUND

1492	Columbus' first voyage to America
1495	da Vinci Last Supper
1498	Petrucci received license to print music
1498	Savonarola burned at the stake
1503	da Vinci Mona Lisa
1504	Michelangelo David
1506	Michelangelo Sistine Chapel
1516	Raphael Sistine Madonna
1519	Charles V became Holy Roman Emperor
1527	Rome sacked by mercenaries
1538	Titian Venus of Urbino
1541	Michelangelo Last Judgment
1545	Council of Trent convened; concluded 1570
1576	Tintoretto Ascension of Christ
1582	Pope Gregory's calendar reform
1592	Tintoretto Last Supper
1597	Peri Dafne
1600	Peri Euridice; Caccini Euridice; Cavalieri La Rappresentazione
1602	Galileo discovered the law of gravity
1605	Monteverdi Fifth Book of Madrigals
1608	Frescobaldi became organist at St. Peter's
1615	G. Gabrieli Canzoni e sonate
1631	Galilei Dialogo dei due massimi ...
1642	Monteverdi L'Incoronazione di Poppea
1650	Carissimi Jephtha

---

instrumental music to vocal music is evident in two new forms which grew from vocal prototypes, the canzona and the ricercar. Italian organ music designed for use in the church were Mass movements, versets, and hymns. Free forms (completely original compositions, i. e. , compositions not based on preexisting material) such as toccatas, fantasias, and intonations probably emerged from improvisation, which was widely practiced during the Renaissance. Musical distinctions cannot always be made, however, between various titles such as canzonas, ricercars, and fantasias, in order to identify the form. Some characteristics which can be listed as primary identifying factors in determining nomenclature can be found in several different types of

ITALIAN ORGAN COMPOSERS: 1300-1650

| 1300 | 1400 | 1450 | 1500 | 1550 | 1600 |

1325 Landini 1397
Reina Manuscript

before 1420 Faenza Ms
          1468 Fogliano 1548
          1470/80 Antico (publisher)
    before 1490 Cavazzoni, M. after 1559
          1499 Segni, G. 1561

          1505 Buus 1564
          1510/20 Gabrieli, A. 1586
       ca. 1510 Tiburtino, G. 1569
          1517 Scandello 1580

       ca. 1520 Galilei, V. 1591
          1525 Cavazzoni, G. ?
          1525/26 Palestrina 1594
               Valente, Antonio
               Mortaro, Antonio 1595
          1527 Annibale 1575
               Bell'Haver, V. 1587

          1530/40 Rodio, R. 1615
          1532 Ponzio, P. 1595
          1533 Merulo, Claudio 1611
          1530/40 Guami, G. 1611

          1540 Vinci, P. 1584 (Sicilian)
       ca. 1540 Maschera 1584
          1545 Luzzaschi, L. 1607
          1547 Malvezzi, C. 1597
       ca. 1549 Antegnati, C. 1624
               Soderini, Agostino

        ca. 1550 de Macque 1614
        ca. 1555 Gabrieli, G. 1612
               Pasquini, E. 1608/20

        ca. 1560 Asola 1609
        ca. 1560 Belli, G. 1613
               Mayone, Ascanio 1627
               Pellegrini, V. 1631
               Cima, Andrea
          1561 Diruta, Girolamo
          1567 Banchieri, A. 1634

        ca. 1575 Trabaci, G. M. 1647

          1583 Frescobaldi, G. 1643
          1584 Cifra, A. 1627
       fl. 1580 Cantone, A. 1627
               Carradini, Nicolò

compositions. Loose terminology of the period does not permit limiting these forms to some exclusive features. As only one example, fantasia was sometimes used interchangeably with ricercar. Even though embellishment was frequently improvised in performance, the Italians often wrote out the ornamentation they wished. Northern Europeans used ornamentation symbols to indicate the embellishment they desired.

The first keyboard music printed in Italy was entitled Frottole intabulate da sonare organi, which was published by Andrea Antico in Rome (1517). Frottole were simple, secular songs for three or four parts which were primarily chordal in style; the melody in the upper part was predominant. This type of song flourished in northern Italian city-courts during the early part of the sixteenth century. Most of the pieces in the book published by Antico were four-part arrangements of frottole by Trombocino and Cara and were printed on two staves of five lines each. The unknown arranger changed the upper parts into flowing lines, but the lowest part was only slightly altered.

The canzona is important as one of the major keyboard forms which developed in Italy during the sixteenth century and the first half of the seventeenth century. Canzona is the Italian word for chanson, a short, strophic, vocal composition of the 1400 and 1500's of Franco-Flemish origin.[1] The text of the chanson was usually amorous. Many arrangements of the chanson for lute and keyboard were made during the sixteenth century in France, Spain, Germany, and Italy. Characteristics of the chanson were a lively tempo, themes of distinctive rhythmic character, sectional construction, with each section beginning with imitative counterpoint, and writing in both imitative and homophonic styles. The imitative counterpoint grew from the harmony. Although most of the sections were written in duple meter, some sections were composed in triple meter for variety. Many canzonas can be identified by the rhythm of the initial notes:

The first organ canzonas, which were probably keyboard transcriptions, were found in Recerchari motetti canzoni, Libro I (1523), by Marco Antonio Cavazzoni (fl. 1490-1559). The canzonas of Andrea Gabrieli (ca. 1515-1586) are

(cont. on p. 28)

ITALIAN ORGAN BOOKS: 1517–1616*

Pub. Date	Composer/Author	Title
1517	A. Antico (pub.)	Frottole intabulate da sonare organi
1523	M. A. Cavazzoni	Recerchari motetti canzoni, Libro I
1542	G. Cavazzoni	Intavolatura cioè ricercari, canzoni, himni, Magnificati
1543	G. Cavazzoni	Intabulatura d'Organo cioè Misse, Himni, Magnificat
1543	J. Buus	Il primo libro di Canzoni francese
1547/1549	J. Buus	Recercari ... da cantare et sonare d'organo et altri stromenti (two books)
1549	J. Buus	Intabolatura d'Organo di Recercari
1567	C. Merulo	Ricercari d'intavolatura d'organo
1568	C. Merulo	Messe d'intavolatura d'organo
1576/1580	A. Valente	Intavolatura de cimbalo; Secundo libro di Versi Spirituali
1584	F. Maschera	Primo libro di canzoni alla francese
1592	C. Merulo	Canzoni d'intavolatura d'organo
1593	G. Diruta	Il Transilvano, Part I (editions 1597, 1612, 1625)
1593	A. Gabrieli	Intonationi d'organo ... et Giovanni suo nepote
1595	A. Gabrieli	Ricercari ... composti & tabulati per ogni sorte di stromenti da tasti

1596	A. Gabrieli	Terzo libro de Ricercari
1598/1604	C. Merulo	Toccate d'Intavolatura d'organo (two books)
1599	V. Pellegrini	Primo libro delle Canzoni de intavolatura d'organo...
1603/1609	A. Mayone	Diversi capricci (two books)
1603	G. M. Trabaci	Ricercate, Canzone francese, Capricci...
1604	Annibale Padovano	Primo libro di Toccate ed Ricercari d'organo
1605	A. Banchieri	L'organo suonarino (other editions 1611, 1628, 1638)
1605	A. Gabrieli	Canzoni alla francese... (two books)
1606	C. Merulo	Canzoni d'intavolatura d'organo
1607/1608	C. Merulo	Ricercari d'intavolatura d'organo (books 2 and 3)
1608	A. Soderini	Libro delle canzoni
1608	C. Antegnati	Intavolatura de Ricercari d'organo
1609	G. Diruta	Il Transilvano, Part II (second edition: 1622)
1609	A. Banchieri	Conclusioni del suono dell' organo (later edition: 1626)
1611	C. Merulo	Canzoni d'intavolatura d'organo
1615	G. M. Trabaci	Il secundo libro de Ricercate...
1616	G. M. Trabaci	Ricercari per l'organo

*A similar table of the published compositions of Frescobaldi is provided later in this chapter.

also mostly arrangements of vocal chansons. The first effort to write original canzonas instead of arrangements of chansons was taken by Girolamo Cavazzoni (1525-?), the son of Marco Antonio. Girolamo used thematic material from the chanson Il est bel et bon in one canzona and Josquin's chanson Faulte d'argent in his Canzone sopra Falt d'argent, but he altered the elaboration of the themes. The canzonas written "in the French style" were called canzoni alla francese.

The canzonas of Claudio Merulo (1533-1604) were published in three books (1592, 1606, 1611). Five of Merulo's 23 canzonas were arrangements; the 18 remaining canzonas were original, but they might have been intended for instrumental performance. A large number of Italian composers wrote original organ canzonas toward the end of the sixteenth century and deep into the seventeenth century. Important composers of the canzona form during this period were Vincenzo Pellegrini (?-1631), Ascanio Mayone (fl. late 1500's to early 1600's), Andrea Cima (second half, 1500's), Giovanni Maria Trabaci (ca. 1575-1647), Agostino Soderini (second half, 1500's), and Girolamo Frescobaldi (1583-1643). Canzonas of Trabaci were the earliest canzonas which are known to have followed the practice of using rhythmic and melodic variants of the same theme as themes for the various sections of the canzona. This type of canzona has been called the variation canzona. Frescobaldi used the variation principle in many of his canzonas; several of Frescobaldi's compositions in canzona form used phrases from popular songs which he adopted for development and imitative treatment.

The keyboard canzona contributed its lively character and the marked rhythmic nature of its themes to the fugue; the contrasting sections of the instrumental canzona led to the seventeenth-century sonata.

The ricercar was another prominent form in Italian organ literature of the sixteenth and seventeenth centuries. The word ricercar comes from an Italian verb which means "to look for, " "to search, " or "to attempt. "[2] The first use of the term ricercar was applied to lute music in which the pieces resembled preludes. The development of the organ ricercar began with two ricercars found in Marco Antonio Cavazzoni's Recerchari motetti canzoni (1523). The ricercars in Cavazzoni's book precede two motets in the same keys and might have been intended to function as preludes

to the motets. These long ricercars are similar to preludes, because the ricercars are continuous and improvisational, and they contain alternations of chordal and scale
passages. The ricercars of Jacopo Fogliano (1468-1548)
contain a greater use of imitation than those of Cavazzoni
and thus point to the imitative ricercar.

The earliest ricercars in a more contrapuntal style
were four ricercars composed by Girolamo Cavazzoni (1525-
?) in his Intavolatura per organo cioè recercari canzoni
himni magnificati (1542). In the younger Cavazzoni's ricercars the number of themes is smaller, and the themes are
usually slow and lack rhythmic or melodic individuality.
These ricercars contain from five to nine rather lengthy
sections, and each section has its individual theme method-
ically treated in imitation. Free, non-imitative passages
are sometimes found between sections.

Andrea Gabrieli wrote at least 17 imitative ricercars
in which he tightened the form by reducing the number of
sections and themes. About one-third of Gabrieli's ricercars
are monothematic (i. e. , employ only one theme); several
have only two or three themes. The countersubject of the
fugue was foreshadowed by Gabrieli's use of the same melodic material each time a new entry of the principal theme
occurred. Gabrieli also incorporated into his ricercars the
contrapuntal devices of diminution, augmentation, inversion,
and stretto.

Ricercars were also composed by the italianized
Netherlander Jacques (Giaches) Buus (1505-1564) and Anni-
bale Padovano (1527-1575). Both of these composers wrote
instrumental ensemble ricercars and keyboard ricercars.
Claudio Merulo's (1533-1604) ricercars contain many sections
and themes, although at least one ricercar is monothematic.
Other Italian composers who contributed to ricercar literature were Ascanio Mayone, Costanzo Antegnati, and Trabaci. [3]

The word toccata comes from the Italian infinitive
toccare (to touch). The toccata in the hands of early Italian
keyboard composers was an improvisatory, free form which
employed full chords and running scale passages. The toccatas of Andrea Gabrieli were written in this style. Claudio
Merulo, a major contributor to the form, enlarged and varied
the materials used in the toccata by alternating sections of
chordal and imitative writing and by balancing the activity
between the different voice parts. Later the larger toccatas

of Frescobaldi were written in short sections and in different moods. Frescobaldi also wrote short pieces which are now called liturgical toccatas in a slow, dignified style. These stately toccatas were rather chromatic and were performed at designated places in the Mass such as before the Mass (Toccata avanti la Messa delli Apostoli) and for the elevation (Toccata per l'elevatione). Trabaci and Mayone preceded Frescobaldi in writing this type of toccata.

Capriccios were imitative contrapuntal works written for organ by such composers as Mayone, de Macque, Trabaci, and Frescobaldi. As the word caprice suggests, a capriccio was a free, lighthearted composition written with a variety of musical material in no standardized form or order, and often connected with one special musical feature, such as the cuckoo motif, dance melodies, or a tune constructed from tones of the hexachord. [4]

The sixteenth-century organ prelude in Italy was called an intonatione (intonazione). Andrea Gabrieli and his nephew Giovanni wrote intonationi for their publication Intonationi d'organo di Andrea Gabrieli, et di Gio. suo nepote (1593). These rather short intonations, which were written for liturgical use, were composed in the church modes and were similar to the earliest toccatas in which full chords were interlaced by running scale passages.

Organ Masses of the sixteenth-century Italian school often included all five parts of the Mass Ordinary (Kyrie, Gloria, Credo, Sanctus, and Agnus Dei) and were written to be performed at the organ in alternation with Gregorian chant portions which were sung. Sometimes the Credo was omitted as an organ composition. Mass movements composed by Buus have been found in a manuscript from Castell' Arquato dated ca. 1540. Three plainsong Masses composed according to the alternation principle were written by both Girolamo Cavazzoni and Claudio Merulo. The organ Masses by these two composers were named Missa Domenicalis, Missa Apostolorum, and Missa Beata Virgine. Frescobaldi also wrote three organ Masses by similar titles in his Fiori Musicali (1635). Frescobaldi provided organ pieces, however, for only the Kyrie of the Ordinary of the Mass. The remainder of his Mass compositions were free compositions intended for other places in the Mass, such as before the Mass (Toccata avanti la Messa), after the epistle (Canzona dopo l'Epistola), after the Credo (Ricercare dopo il Credo), for the elevation (Toccata per l'elevatione), and after the post-communion prayer (Canzona dopo il Post Comune).

Organ settings of Latin hymn melodies also appeared
in sixteenth-century Italian organ literature.   Girolamo
Cavazzoni included 12 organ hymns in his Intavolatura cioè
ricercari canzoni himni magnificati (1542).   Cavazzoni wrote
the plainsong melody in notes of uniform value.   Two of the
plainsong hymn melodies most frequently arranged by Italian
composers of this period for organ were Pange lingua and
Veni creator spiritus.

Girolamo Frescobaldi was Italy's most important
organ composer.   He was an outstanding performer and
teacher, and his influence was great.   For this reason it
is appropriate to study his works in detail.

It is difficult to differentiate between Frescobaldi's
imitative contrapuntal forms such as the canzonas, ricercari,
fantasias, and capriccios. [5]   Since Frescobaldi did not allow
established ideas to inhibit his great creative powers, there
are always exceptions to general statements about his treatment of forms.   The ricercari are not based on pre-existing
tunes.   They are dignified, monothematic, and are composed
in a more strictly contrapuntal, academic fashion than the
other three imitative forms.   The ricercari are consistent
in character and never change from the common meter with
which they begin.   The other three forms are more sectional.
They are light and cheerful in character and employ contrasting materials of harmony, figurations, and other free,
virtuoso elements.   Four ricercari and three capriccios are
based on themes built from tones representing hexachord
syllables.

The canzoni alla francese of Frescobaldi were based
on popular secular melodies from which melodic fragments
were treated contrapuntally.   The canzoni alla francese
utilized variation techniques in which the initial theme received both rhythmic and melodic alteration;   this practice
is called thematic metamorphosis.   The canzonas (not canzoni alla francese) also used the distinctive identifying rhythm
at the beginning in each voice but were not based upon pre-
existing melodies.   Both the canzonas and the canzoni alla
francese have at least three sections, of which one section
(usually a middle one) is in triple meter. [6]

The fantasias printed in 1608 usually fall into three
sections which are indicated by the meter changes.   Of 12

ORGAN PUBLICATIONS OF FRESCOBALDI 1608-1645

Type of works	Date	Title (and vol. no. in Pidoux ed.)	Publisher (and place)
• 12 fantasies	1608	Il Primo Libro Delle Fantasie...(I)	Tini and Lomazzo (Milan)
• 10 ricercari	1615	Il Primo Libro di Capricci...et Arie...	Zannetti (Rome)
{ 5 canzonas and	1624	Il Primo Libro di Capricci, Canzon	Soldi (Rome)
11 capriccios, arias	1626	Francese e Recercari...et Arie (II) (pub. without Capriccio sopra l'aria: Or che noi rimena; added Capriccio sopra un soggetto. Both are included in Pidoux ed.)	Vincenti (Venice)
• combined into:	1642	repub. without change	
• toccatas, kyries, canzonas, ricercari	1635	Fiori Musicali (V)	Vincenti (Venice)
• 12 toccatas, variations on dances, arias	1637	Toccate d'Intavolatora... Partite di Diversi Arie et Corrente, Balletti, Ciaccone, Passachagli... Libro Primo (III)	Borbone (Rome)
• 11 toccatas, 6 canzonas, 3 hymns, 3 Magnificat verses, variations on dances	1637	Il Secondo Libro di Toccate, Canzone, Verse d'Hinni, Magnificat, Gagliarde, Correnti et Altre Partite d'Intavolatura ...(IV)	Borbone (Rome)
• 11 canzonas (published posthumously)	1645	Canzoni alla Francese in Partitura ...(I)	Vincenti (Venice)

fantasias, three each are based on one subject (sopra un soggetto), two subjects, three, and four subjects. The full texture is four-part. The imitative entries often change the melodic intervals while maintaining the same rhythm of the initial subject.

Frescobaldi used a number of different sources for his capriccio themes: melodies constructed from the hexachord, popular tunes, aria melodies, musical materials such as durezze (dissonances) and ligature (suspensions), martial or trumpet motifs, and pastoral themes. The theme occurs against many different kinds of counterpoint and in different meters. One capriccio (Capriccio di obligo di cantare, 1626) has an unusual technique, that of using a solo voice without text in combination with the organ; the voice part is an integral part of the composition. Frescobaldi followed this same technique in the ricercar before the elevation toccata in the third Mass of the Fiori Musicali, the Messa della Madonna.

In general, the toccatas are florid. They maintain the same meter and virtuoso character throughout, with partly imitative, partly figurative components. Frescobaldi's liturgical toccatas in Fiori Musicali, however, are brief, simple, slow, and meditative compositions. Brief melodic imitation between the parts is found, but there is no change from four-part texture. There are two toccatas "alla levatione" found in the Secondo Libro, (1637) which are much longer. Chromaticism is used in the slower toccatas for color. Less interesting works are the variations (partite) on popular tunes and dances.

Frescobaldi's attitude toward his compositions, their performance, and their use as didactic works is revealed in the prefaces to his publications. [7]

The compositions of Frescobaldi have a number of striking characteristics, some of which are listed here: frequent changes of meter, chord root movement of seconds and thirds, shifting harmonies, unusual resolutions of dissonances, chord functions in unusual relationships, and rhythmic and melodic alterations of themes.

The sound of Italian organs of the Renaissance was vocal, sweet, silvery, light, quick, and sensitive. Although Italian organs of the sixteenth century usually had only one manual, the richness of principal and flute sonorities avail-

FIORI MUSICALI (1635)

Forms	Messa della Domenica Kyries: (Orbis factor)	Messa delli Apostoli (Cunctipotens genitor Deus)	Messa della Madonna (Cum jubilo)
liturg. toccata cantus firmus settings of the sections of plainsong Kyries	Toccata Kyrie: 2 Kyries; 4 Christes; 6 Kyries	Toccata Kyrie: 3 Kyries; 2 Christes; 3 Kyries	Toccata Kyrie: 2 Kyries; 2 Christes; 2 Kyries
canzonas	Epistle: Canzon dopo la Pistola (Canzona after the Epistle)	Epistle: Canzon dopo la Pistola	Epistle: Canzon dopo la Pistola
ricercari	Credo: Recercar dopo il Credo (Ricercar after the Credo)	Credo: Toccata avanti il Recercar (Toccata before the ricercar); Recercar Cromaticho post il Credo (Chromatic ricercar after the Credo); Altro recercar (another ricercar)	Credo: Recercar dopo il Credo; Toccata avanti il Recercar; Ricercer con obligo di cantare la quinta parte senza toccarla (Ricercar with the fifth part sung and not played)
liturgical toccatas	Elevation: Toccata Cromaticha per le levatione (Chromatic toccata for the Elevation)	Elevation: Toccata per le levatione Recercar con obligo del Basso come appare (Ricercar with obligatory bass, as is evident)	Elevation: Toccata per le levatione
canzonas	Communion: Canzon post il Comune (Canzona after the Communion)	Communion: Canzon Quarti Toni dopo il Post-Comune (Canzona in the fourth mode after the Post-Communion [Prayer])	Bergamasca; Capriccio sopra la Girolmeta

able provided a wide variety of possibilities for the music of
the period. The tonal design of these organs was based upon
the ensemble concept and had become somewhat standardized
by 1500. Italian organ builders were faithful to this concept
for three and a half centuries. The ripieno (organum plenum)
was constructed of individual ranks of flutes and principals at
various pitches (16', 8', 4', 2 2/3', 2', 1 1/3', 1', 2/3',
1/2', 1/3', 1/4').[8]

Pedals of early Italian organs have been called "pull
downs," because the pedals were attached to the lower keys
of the manual and, when played by the toes, pulled down the
key desired. The pedal compass was no more than two octaves, and the lower octave was what is called a short octave;[9] the upper octave was chromatically complete. One
of the earliest Italian organs which had pedals was one built
by Fra Domenico di Lorenzo in 1379 for the Annunziata
church in Florence; the organ in this church had 12 pedals
of a primitive type.

The specification given below is found in Costanzo
Antegnati's book as an example of a model organ specification. An organ of this specification was built by a member
of the Antegnati family in Brescia.

Brescia, Italy: Old Cathedral, built by
G. G. Antegnati in 1536

50 notes

Principale	16
Principale	16
Ottava	8
Decimaquinta	4
Decimanona	2 2/3
Vigesimaseconda	2
Vigesimasesta	1 1/3
Vigesimanona	1
Trigesima terza	2/3
Flauto in ottava	8
Flauto in decimaquinta	4
Vigesima seconda	2

Pedal: C-c
Lower octave of the second
   Principale 16

The books of Antegnati, Banchieri, and Diruta gave instruction about registrations which should be used for different types of music, different modes, and for different parts of the Mass.[10] In general, Italian registration practices for some of the different forms are as follows: ricercars should use principals of only unison pitches (8', 4', 2'); toccatas and intonations use the full sound of the ripieno; canzonas employ flutes or lighter combinations of flutes and principals; soft toccatas for the elevation should utilize the delicate sound of the Voce Umana. The Voce Umana (sometimes called Fiffaro), however, is not the same as the German Vox Humana or the French Voix Humaine, both of which are regals, but a principal stop found only in the upper part of the manual. The Voce Umana was usually tuned sharp so that it would have a gentle undulation when it was combined with the Principal 8'.

In summary, the Italian imitative forms, especially the canzona and the ricercar, contributed elements such as marked rhythmic character and learnedness to the development of the fugue, which led to the fugues of J. S. Bach. Many German organ composers, who were deeply influenced by Frescobaldi, drew upon his works for inspiration and developed certain characteristics into larger forms, such as the capriccios of Froberger. The influence of Frescobaldi can be observed to a great extent in the South German school and to a lesser degree in the Middle German school, both of which will be studied in subsequent chapters.

Notes

1. Josquin, Janequin, Crecquillon, Sermisy, Lassus, and Jacob were the principal composers of the French chanson.
2. Apel suggests that "study" might be a general translation of the word ricercar.
3. Italian composers of the second half of the 1600's who contributed to ricercar literature were Giovanni Salvatore (early 1600's-ca. 1688), Bernardo Storace (second half, 1600's), Fabrizio Fontana (?-1695), and Bernardo Pasquini (1637-1710).
4. The hexachord originated from the initial syllables of six successive lines of a hymn to St. John the Baptist. The syllables were used by Guido d'Arezzo as an aid to memorizing pitches. The pitches were arranged in the order of ut (do), re, mi, fa, sol, la (c, d, e, f, g, a). Composers such as Frescobaldi, Sweelinck, and

English virginalists selected tones represented by syllables from the hexachord to construct simple themes
which were used as bases for compositions.

5. Charlene Polivka Dorsey, "The Fantasie and Ricercari
of Girolamo Frescobaldi," American Guild of Organists
Quarterly, vol. XII, no. 3 (July 1967), p. 101-105,
122.

6. This type of sectional composition in different meters
gave rise to the sectional capriccio or canzona of
Frescobaldi's pupil Froberger.

7. The reader is encouraged to study the preface to the
Fiori Musicali in the Pidoux translation and the other
prefaces to books written by Frescobaldi and provided
by Pidoux for information on performance practice.

8. The Regal (Cornamusa or Zampogna) reed stop was
added later, perhaps in the seventeenth century. Cantus firmus compositions in which the melody stood out
in sharp relief from the other voices by means of a
reed stop were composed in northern Europe and
France but not in Italy during this period.

9. The short octave was so called because it was incomplete
and contained fewer keys than a complete chromatic octave. The E key sounded low C, the F-sharp key D,
and the G-sharp key E.

10. Peter Williams, The European Organ 1450-1850, London:
Batsford, 1966; p. 214. Also Luigi Ferdinando Tag-
liavini, "The Old Italian Organ and Its Music," Diapason
(February 1966), p. 14-16.

Bibliography

Apel, Willi. "The Early Development of the Organ Ricercare," Musica Disciplina, vol. III (1949), p. 139-150.
_____. "Neopolitan Links between Cabezón and Fresco-
baldi," Musical Quarterly, vol. XXIV (1938), p. 419-
437.

Dart, Thurston. "Cavazzoni and Cabezón," Music and Letters, vol. XXXVI (1955), p. 2-6.

Dorsey, Charlene Polivka. "The Fantasie and Ricercari
of Girolamo Frescobaldi," American Guild of Organists
Quarterly, vol. XII, No. 3 (July 1967), p. 101.

Frotscher, Gotthold. Geschichte des Orgelspiels und der
Orgelkomposition. Berlin: Merseberger Verlag, 1959;
vol. I, p. 175-243, 360-377.

Jeppesen, Knud. Die italienische Orgelmusik am Anfang des
Cinquecento, 2 vols. Copenhagen: Munksgaard, 1943

(2nd ed. , 1960).

Kratzenstein, Marilou. "A Survey of Organ Literature and
   Editions: Italy," Diapason (February 1972), p. 22-24.

Pidoux, Pierre, ed. Girolamo Frescobaldi Orgel- und
   Klavier Werke. Kassel, Germany: Bärenreiter Verlag,
   1959; vol. V, preface.

Redlich, Hans Ferdinand. "Girolamo Frescobaldi," Music
   Review, vol. XIV (1953), p. 262-274.

Schrade, Leo. "Ein Beitrag zur Geschichte der Tokkata,"
   Zeitschrift für Musikwissenschaft, vol. VIII (1925-1926),
   p. 610-635.

Shannon, John R. "A Short Summary of the Free Organ
   Forms in Italy, 1450-1650," American Guild of Organists Quarterly, vol. VI, no. 3 (July 1961), p. 75.

Sutherland, Gordon. "The Ricercari of Jacques Buus,"
   Musical Quarterly, vol. XXXI (1945), p. 448-463.

Tagliavini, Luigi F. "The Old Italian Organ and Its Music,"
   Diapason (February 1966), p. 14-16.

Tusler, Robert L. The Organ Music of Jan Pieterzoon
   Sweelinck, 2 vols. No. 1 of Utrechtse Bijdragen tot
   de Muziekwetenschap, Bilthoven, The Netherlands,
   1958.

Vennum, Thomas, Jr. "The Registration of Frescobaldi's
   Organ Music," Organ Institute Quarterly, vol. II,
   No. 2 (Summer 1964).

3. ENGLAND AND THE NETHERLANDS: 1475-1650

England

Early English keyboard music was designed for organs or virginals, a general term applied to all kinds of
harpsichords in England toward the end of the sixteenth century. English church musicians were more interested in
choral music than instrumental music and therefore very
small organs satisfied their needs in the church. Many
English organs of the sixteenth century had only one manual,
no pedal, and about six stops. An extract from an indenture
made on July 29, 1519, shows that "Antony Duddyngton,
Citizen of London, Organ-Maker," agreed to build for All
Hallows Church, Barking, "an organ of one stop, called
Pryncipale except for its bass, called Diapason, having
double pipes, inner and outer, with natural keys only."[1]

From the time of the separation of the English Church
from the Roman Catholic Church the organ in churches often
symbolized popery. Puritanism gradually increased within
the English Church during the sixteenth century to the extent
that Royal Visitors were commissioned to inspect churches'
worship practices in order to make recommendations and
corrections, which would make the services conform to the
will of the high church officials. The Royal Visitors also
sometimes abolished use of certain types of music or organist positions. Some high officials in the English church, who
were influenced by Calvinist thought, wished to abolish singing and organ playing entirely. The general discouragement
of using the organ at services led to the complete disposal
of the organ Mass in England toward the middle of the sixteenth century. Although there were brief periods of interest
in organs and organists during the reign of Mary and of
James I, so many organs were neglected or destroyed that
the need for liturgical music for organ was greatly reduced.
One of the few churches which was able to continue using an
organ in worship was the Chapel Royal, where two organists
were often appointed to share the duties. The Chapel Royal
was exempt from the jurisdiction of a bishop and was under

HISTORICAL BACKGROUND

1485	Tudor dynasty established
1509-1547	Reign of Henry VIII
1516	Sir Thomas More Utopia
1534	Separation of English Church from Roman Catholic Church
1536	Dissolution of the monasteries
1544	Cranmer, Archbishop of Canterbury, translated and arranged the Litany in English
1549	The Book of Common Prayer
1547-1553	Reign of Edward VI
1553-1558	Reign of Mary Tudor
1558-1603	Reign of Elizabeth I
1562	Sternhold and Hopkins One and Fiftie Psalmes
1564-1616	Shakespeare
1577	Sir Francis Drake began voyage around the world
1588	War between Spain and England; English defeat of the Spanish Armada
1588	Marlowe Doctor Faustus
1590	Edmund Spenser The Faerie Queen
1594	Shakespeare Romeo and Juliet
1601	Shakespeare Hamlet
1603-1625	Reign of James I
1609	Henry Hudson explored Hudson River
1611	King James version of The Bible
1620	Pilgrims arrived at Cape Cod
1625-1649	Reign of Charles I
1630	Puritans established Boston
1649	Commonwealth established; concluded 1660

the direct supervision of the sovereign.

An unnamed piece, which has been attributed to John Dunstable (ca. 1385-1453), and a Felix namque seem to be the total of all presently known English organ composition of the fifteenth century. The unauthenticated Dunstable piece is usually in three-part texture and contains a considerable amount of rhythmic variety and syncopation, especially in the lively upper part. Open fifths and octaves occur frequently between parts, and there is no use of imitation.

The melody of the plainsong offertory Felix namque
was frequently used as a cantus firmus for organ pieces of
the sixteenth and seventeenth century in England.

Example 4.   Felix namque es (Offertory)

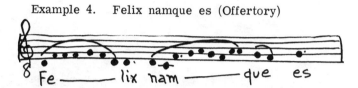

Composers who wrote polyphonic elaborations on this theme
included John Redford (ca. 1485-1547), Thomas Tallis (ca.
1505-1585), William Blitheman (ca. 1510-1591), Thomas
Preston (ca. 1564-?), and Thomas Tomkins (1572-1656).

Thomas Taverner (ca. 1490-1545) used a plainsong
antiphon as the basic melody for his Mass Gloria tibi Trinitas. In the Benedictus of Taverner's Mass this same melody
appeared with the text in nomine and subsequently became
known as the "in nomine" melody and the inspiration for
most of the pieces for organ or viols by that title rather
than by its proper title Gloria tibi Trinitas. [2]   In nomine and
Felix namque compositions were written by English composers only.

Example 5.   Gloria tibi Trinitas (antiphon
             for Vespers, Trinity)

The one extant example of an English organ setting
of the Ordinary of the Mass was written by Philip ap Rhys
(sixteenth century). A setting of the Credo is not included
in this Mass. The Mass is found in a composite manuscript. [3] Thomas Preston wrote a setting of Mass propers
based on Gregorian melodies which follows the alternation
principle.

Arrangements of Latin hymns, antiphons, and offer-

ENGLISH ORGAN COMPOSITION: 1300-1650

1300   1350   1400   1450   1500   1550   1600   1650

ca. 1325 Robertsbridge Codex
      ca. 1385 Dunstable 1453

147? Burton, A. 154?
ca. 1485 Redford, J. 1547
ca. 1490 Taverner, J. 1545
   1497 Tye, Christopher 1572
      ca. 1505 Tallis, T. 1585
         ca. 1510 Blitheman, Wm. 1591
            Thorne, J. 1573
            ap Rhys, Philip; Coxsun, Robert
         ca. 1530 White, R. 1574
               Woodson; Kyrton; Shepherd, John
               Wynslate, Richard 1572
         ca. 1543 Byrd, William 1623
               ca. 1550 Allwood, Richard
                  ca. 1560 Mulliner Book
                     1560 Philips, Peter 1628
                  ca. 1563 Bull, John 1628
                  ca. 1564 Preston, Thomas
                        Strogers, Nicholas
                           1572 Tomkins, Thomas 1656
                           1579 Amner, John 1641
                        ca. 1572 Ferrabocso, A. 1628
                           1583 Gibbons, O. 1625
                              Carleton, Nicolas
                              Fitzwilliam Virginal Book
                           1592 Jenkins, John 1678
                              1602 Lawes, William 1645
                              1605 Philips, Arthur 1695
                                 Hingeston, John 1683

tories were common cantus firmus compositions in this period.   Some plainsong fantasias were quite long and were
actually a series of variations, because the cantus firmus
was repeated with different types and styles of accompaniment.   The longer fantasias were probably not designed for
the liturgical service, but the shorter, easier plainsong fantasias were so designed.   One of the earlier English composers, John Redford, used the technique of substituting a
melody derived from the original plainsong at the interval of
the lower sixth or octave.   Redford then used the arranged
melody as the cantus firmus for his setting rather than the
original plainsong melody.   An example of this technique is
Redford's O lux on the faburden.   At least four of Redford's
titles end: "... with a meane" which might refer to the
middle part of his three-voice polyphonic composition.   The
significance of this term is vague, as are the three whole
note chords with fermatas at the end of Glorificamus.   The
middle chord is a discord which seems to have little relation to what has preceded or to what follows. [4]   These unusual chords suggest that a keyboard convention might have
existed which has not yet been deciphered.

Composers, such as Allwood, Preston, Thorne, and
Coxsun, wrote similar compositions based upon Gregorian
melodies.   Three-part texture seems to have been preferred,
and the rhythms frequently change, even as often as from
measure to measure, a technique which promotes a restless
feeling in the music.

One of the largest sources of sixteenth-century organ
literature is called the Mulliner Book (ca. 1560), [5] which
was named for its compiler Thomas Mulliner.   Redford,
Tallis, Allwood, Taverner, and Tye are represented in the
collection, of which over half of the pieces are based on
sacred melodies.   The book contains 120 compositions for
organ or virginal (harpsichord) and eleven pieces written in
lute tablature.   The Mulliner Book also contains dances and
two pieces of the prelude type called voluntaries.   The
voluntary is free and rather improvisatory.   In the Mulliner
Book the voluntaries are short and written in imitative
counterpoint.   Some other short pieces which are based on
one subject and which are treated imitatively are called
points.   Voluntaries, points, and verses were appropriate
for liturgical use.

The long life of Thomas Tallis spanned the reign of
Henry VIII and a major portion of the reign of Elizabeth I.

Most of his keyboard music had a religious character and
was intended for the organ, although it was also playable on
the stringed keyboard instruments. Most of the pieces by
Tallis are short settings of plainsong melodies and usually
have the melody in the tenor. The even numbered verses of
Ecce tempus idoneum were written by Tallis as organ settings to be played in alternation with verses one, three, and
five to be sung in unison. Two compositions by Tallis which
are entitled Felix namque are long pieces; these compositions contain characteristics which denote virginal writing
such as passages of notes of small denomination, scales in
parallel thirds or sixths, and figures built on broken chords.

     Late sixteenth- and early seventeenth-century key-
board music in England was centered in virginal books. Organ music in the early part of the 1500's had been principally of religious character, but later in that century all
keyboard music underwent a gradual secularization. The
principal virginal collection is the Fitzwilliam Virginal Book,
which contains 297 works by a large number of composers
and exhibits a wide variety of types of compositions. Although some of these compositions might have been performed on the organ and some show characteristics of organ-
istic writing, the general purpose of the Fitzwilliam Virginal
Book is for performance on stringed keyboard instruments
and not for liturgical use. Several compositions by Jan
Pieterszoon Sweelinck appear in this collection, a fact which
testifies to the close musical relationship between England
and the Netherlands.

     Thomas Tomkins, organist of Worcester Cathedral
from ca. 1596-1646, wrote more than 30 pieces for keyboard
between 1646 and 1654. About half of these pieces are
dances. The fancies, voluntaries, or verses are contrapuntal pieces which generally begin with imitative entries,
usually are written in four parts, and are liberally ornamented with dashes (/) and double-dashes (//) which indicate slides and double mordents or trills. Some of these
pieces are short and others long and sectional. Many tran-
sient modulations or cadential patterns to near-related keys
are employed. These pieces show the transition between
vocally written organ works of the sixteenth century and the
compositions which employ rhythmic figures and scale passages for a keyboard instrument and a skillful keyboard
performer. [6]

     The disposition of the organ Tomkins played in

Worcester after 1613 is given below (numbers are probable pipe lengths).

Worcester, England, Cathedral. Built
Thomas Dallam, 1613.

Great Organ		Chaire Organ[7]	
Two open diapasons	8	Principal	4?
Two principals	4	Diapason	8
Two fifteenths	2	Flute	8
Twelfth	2 2/3	Fifteenth	2
Recorder	8	Two-and-Twentieth	1

Orlando Gibbons (1583-1625) was the outstanding English composer-performer at the turn of the seventeenth century.   His works are found in several virginal books of the period and follow the same general style as those of Tomkins.   The lines are vocal, usually moving in step-wise motion with few leaps greater than a fourth. [8]

The Netherlands

The Lowlands ("nether lands") covered a wide area in the sixteenth and seventeenth centuries, from what is now northern France, through Belgium and Holland to Denmark. By the marriage of Mary of Brabant to Maximilian the Lowlands became a part of the Holy Roman Empire.   In 1555 the Lowlands passed from Emperor Charles V to his son Philip II of Spain, against whom the Netherlands fought for their independence.   Toward the latter part of the sixteenth century the Calvinistic northern section of the divided country achieved independence, but the southern part was unable to wrest itself from Spanish rule and stayed within the Catholic fold.

Dutch Protestant clergymen objected to having "popish" organs in the churches, but their objections were to little avail because of the power of the burgomasters, the cities' secular authorities.   The city magistrates had the organs built as objects of great municipal pride and in rivalry with other communities, whether church authorities approved or not.   Sometimes, in the larger churches, organ recitals were held daily, either before or after the church services. The tradition of organ recitals in Haarlem probably dates from early in the sixteenth century. [9]

HISTORICAL BACKGROUND

After the Norman conquest of England in 1066 the Low Countries were connected ecclesiastically and politically with France and Germany, economically and culturally with England.

1405	Duchy of Brabant established
1425-1432	University of Louvain founded
	Rise of independent cities; leading merchants formed town councils to govern autonomous cities
1464	Estates-General (representative assemblies) established
1482	Maximilian I, Holy Roman Emperor, became regent of the Netherlands
1511	Erasmus The Praise of Folly
1515-1555	Reign of Charles V, Holy Roman Emperor
1555	Netherlands passed to Philip II of Spain
1566	Brueghel the Elder The Wedding Dance
1567-1573	Duke of Alba, Spanish governor of the Netherlands, sent to enforce the Inquisition and taxation
1568-1648	Eighty Years' War: revolt of Netherlands against Spain organized by William the Silent, founder of the House of Orange
1579	Union of Utrecht joined seven northern provinces
1581	Independence of the Netherlands declared; northern provinces gained independence, southern provinces remained under Spanish rule
1585	Elizabeth of England sent Earl of Leicester to aid the Netherlands
1588	English defeat of the Spanish Armada
1591	Peter Philips' works began to be published in Antwerp
1599-1641	Van Dyck
1602	Dutch East India Company founded
1609-1620	English Pilgrims found refuge in Leiden
1613	John Bull settled in Antwerp
1624	Franz Hals The Laughing Cavalier
1626	Peter Minuit bought Manhattan
1631	Rembrandt The Anatomy Lesson
1632-1675	Jan Vermeer

1642	Rembrandt The Night Watch
1648	Treaty of Westphalia concluded Eighty Years' War with Spain
1664	New Amsterdam became New York
1689	William III of Orange became King of England

The use of the organ in services became more important when singing and chanting were discontinued about the last quarter of the sixteenth century. The organ was used for a new and quite different purpose--accompanying congregational singing on the metrical psalms--by 1649. [10]

The compositions of sixteenth- and seventeenth-century Dutch organ composers included organ hymns, fantasias, fugues, canzonas, ricercars, toccatas, variations on sacred and secular melodies, and dances. The earliest printed Dutch keyboard music was written by Henderick Joostszoon Speuy (ca. 1575-1625). In 1610 Charles Guillet (?-1654) published Vingt Quatre Fantaisies à Quatre Parties Disposées Selon l'Ordre des Douze Modes. The Tabulatur-Boeck by Anthoni van Noordt (?-1675), the organist of the Nieuwe Kerk, Amsterdam, contains fantasies and psalm settings in variations. Abraham van den Kerckhoven (1627-1702) wrote short organ hymns and organ verses in various modes. These short pieces were written in four-part texture, often in imitation.

Jan Pieterszoon Sweelinck (1562-1621) was the most outstanding organist, composer, and teacher in northern Europe during this period. Many organists travelled to Amsterdam to hear him play and to study with him. Since many of his pupils came from Germany, Sweelinck gained the reputation of being a deutscher Organistenmacher, a "maker of German organists." As a composer his works are transitional from the Renaissance to the early Baroque period because he knew the techniques of the sixteenth century and was able to anticipate some of the changes to come in the approaching musical period. His pupils carried on these developments which led to the works of J. S. Bach. His composition style combined figurations and variation techniques of virginal writing with strong contrapuntal writing.

The forms used by Sweelinck were fantasies, toccatas, variations on chorale, secular, and dance melodies, preludes, and ricercars. In his variations the basic melody remains in approximately the same form, but the counterpoint changes from variation to variation or even within the same variation. [11] Rhythmic patterns provide much vitality and interest and often progress

ORGAN COMPOSERS OF THE NETHERLANDS: 1550-1900

1550	1600	1650	1700	1750	1800	1850	1900

Busnois 1492
ca. 1550 Dalem 1601
ca. 1557 Luython 1620
1562 Cornet, P. 1626
1562 Sweelinck 1621
ca. 1563 Bull, John 1628 (English)
1560/61 Philips, P. 1628 (English)
1575 Speuy 1625
Pool, Philippus 1734
Guillet, C. 1654
van Noordt, A. 1675
1627 van den Kerckhoven 1702
1657 Erlebach, Philipp 1714
1664 Milleville 1675
1725 Boutmy, J. B. J. 1782+
1811 deLange, Samuel, Sr. 1884
1822 Litzau, J. B. 1893
1823 Eyken, J. A. 1868
1838 Tours, Berthold 1897
1840 deLange, Samuel, Jr. 1911

to more active patterns in each successive variation. Sweelinck
used chromaticism for added color and maintained a strong tonal
center (Ricercar brevis and Fantasia chromatica). He and some
of his English contemporaries wrote pieces based upon themes
built on various arrangements of the hexachord syllable tones
(Fantasia Ut, re, mi, fa, sol, la). Points of imitation are used
at the beginning of pieces and at the beginnings of sections. The
fantasias and toccatas are Sweelinck's most extended works. In
them his writing sometimes resembles works of his English vir-
ginalist contemporaries. The echo fantasias utilize dramatic
contrasts of volume and quality, which are easily attained at the
organ by alternating louder and softer combinations on two manuals. The texture usually encompasses no more than four voices
with frequent reduction of the texture to two or three parts. The
pedal part of Sweelinck's compositions is never very active because the pedal division of Dutch organs at that time was quite
limited.

Sweelinck wrote many variations and allowed the color of
various organ stop combinations to add interest to his writing.
His variations, like those of Cabezón, do not present the theme
in simple form at the beginning, but start immediately with the
first variation. The variations on the secular melody Mein
junges Leben hat ein' End' are especially interesting.

The specifications are given below of the famous Amsterdam organ which was played by both Sweelinck's father and later
by Sweelinck.

Amsterdam, The Netherlands, Oude Kerk.
Built by Hendrik and Herman Niehoff,
and Hans Suys von Köln, 1539-1542

Hoofdwerk (50 notes)	Bovenwerk (41 notes)	Rugwerk (38 notes)
Prestant 16	Prestant 8	Prestant 8
Octaaf 8 (and 4 ?)	Holpijp 8	Octaaf 4
Mixtuur	Openfluit 4	Mixtuur
Scherp	Quintadeen 8(4 ?)	Scherp
	Gemshoorn 2	(Quintadeen 8 ?)
	Sifflet 1 (1 1/3 ?)	Holpijp 4
	Terscimbel	Kromhoorn 8
	Trompet 8	(Regal 8 ?)
	Zink	Baarpijp 8
	(Nazard 2 2/3 ?)	Schalmei 4
		(Siffluit ?)

Pedaal

could be coupled to the Hoofdwerk for notes F to d[1].
Nachthoorn 2
Trompet 8

Couplers: Hoofdwerk to Rugwerk
Bovenwerk to Rugwerk
Tremulant

Sweelinck's pupils took home to Germany, Warsaw, and
Danzig their strong impressions of this instrument. In the last
half of the seventeenth century, Dutch organs such as those in
central Holland and in the A-Kerk, Groningen, increased the
size of the pedal division to accommodate new organ music demands. Churches even commissioned new instruments or had
their instruments rebuilt to adapt to the new organ music and
newer uses of the instrument in church services.

Arp Schnitger was the famous Hamburg builder who
brought the design of the northwest German organ to Holland.
Schnitger's sons built organs of great importance in Zwolle and
Alkmaar. The Pedal and Great divisions of the Alkmaar organ
were built in the German tradition of no duplication of ranks and
full compass of pitches from 32' to 2', in addition to both solo
and chorus stops. [12]

During Sweelinck's lifetime some English composers
crossed the English Channel for political, religious, or other
reasons. John Bull, one of these English composers, became
a good friend of Sweelinck. Reference has already been made to
the fact that compositions by Sweelinck are found in the Fitzwilliam Virginal Book, which indicates that close musical communication existed between England and the Netherlands. Sweelinck also wrote Pavana Philippi, a set of variations on a pavane
melody by Peter Philips, another English composer who had left
his native land.

Dr. Bull wrote most of his music for the virginal. His
Prelude and Carol on the Dutch melody Laet ons met herten
reijne contains explicit organ registration markings, probably
the first such exact registration indications, which are found in
red ink in the original manuscript. [13]

Notes

1. Margaret Glyn, ed. , Early English Organ Music, Lon-

don: Plainsong and Medieval Music Society, 1939; preface.
2. The Allwood In nomine is not based on this melody.
3. British Museum [B. M.] Add. 29 996.
4. Taverner also has three whole note chords with fermatas at the end of an In nomine.
5. B. M. add. Ms. 30513.
6. Willi Apel, Geschichte der Orgel- und Klaviermusik bis 1700, Kassel, Germany: Bärenreiter Verlag, 1967; p. 309-314.
7. The English term Chaire organ might come from the fact that this division, which was attached to the gallery rail, furnished a sitting place for the organist while he played the larger (Great) division. See John Fesperman, The Organ as Musical Medium, New York: Coleman-Ross, 1962; p. 55. Sumner traces the meaning of the old word chair as a "helper," one who "takes a turn" and proposes this as one explanation of the English term Chair Organ, as one which was "turned to" or one that "took a turn. " See William Leslie Sumner, The Organ: Its Evolution, Principles of Construction and Use, 2nd ed. , London: Macdonald, 1955; p. 156.
8. Willi Apel, Geschichte der Orgel- und Klaviermusik bis 1700, Kassel, Germany: Bärenreiter Verlag, 1967; p. 314-318.
9. Peter Williams, The European Organ 1450-1850, London: Batsford, 1966; p. 27.
10. Ibid. , p. 37-38.
11. Research has proved that many of the 24 cycles of chorale variations which Seiffert included in the 1943 edition of Sweelinck's works were written by composers other than Sweelinck such as Heinrich Scheidemann, Henderick Speuy, and possibly Jacob Praetorius. Although some of the cycles may be incomplete, at least 13 can be considered authentic. See Sweelinck Opera Omnia: The Instrumental Works, Amsterdam: Vereniging voor Nederlandse Muziekgeschiedenis, 1968; vol. I, fasc. II, Introduction.
12. Peter Williams, The European Organ 1450-1850, London: Batsford, 1966; p. 41.
13. John Klein, First Four Centuries of Organ Music, New York: Assoc. Music Pub. 1948; vol. I, p. 148.

Bibliography

ENGLAND

Apel, Willi. Geschichte der Orgel- und Klaviermusik bis
    1700, Kassel, Germany: Bärenreiter Verlag, 1967;
    p. 21-24, 298-306, 319-337.
_____. Masters of the Keyboard. Cambridge, Mass. :
    Harvard University Press, 1947; p. 56-59.
Benedictines of Solesmes, eds. Liber Usualis. Tournai,
    Belgium: Desclée and Co. , 1950.
Caldwell, John. "Keyboard Plainsong Settings in England,
    1500-1660," Musica Disciplina, vol. XIX (1965), p. 129-53.
_____. "The Pitch of Early Tudor Organ Music," Music
    and Letters, vol. 51, no. 2 (April 1970), p. 156.
Dart, Thurston. "John Bull, 1563-1628," Musical Times,
    no. 1442, vol. 104 (April 1963), p. 252
_____ et al. "Early English Organ Pedals," Musical
    Times, no. 1416, vol. 102 (February 1961), p. 107-9.
Foster, Donald H. "The Organ Music of Thomas Tomkins,"
    Diapason (July 1970), p. 23-25.
Frotscher, Gotthold. Geschichte des Orgelspiels und der
    Orgelkomposition. Berlin: Merseberger Verlag, 1959;
    vol. I, pp. 263-300.
Glyn, Margaret Henrietta. Early English Organ Music.
    London: The Plainsong and Medieval Music Society,
    1939; preface.
le Huray, Peter. Music and the Reformation in England.
    London: Jenkins, 1967.
Lowinsky, Edward E. "English Organ Music of the Renais-
    sance," Musical Quarterly, vol. XXXIX (1953), p. 373-
    395, 528-553.
Marigold, W. G. "An Episode in the Early Development
    of the Organ Pedal," Musical Opinion, no. 1109, vol.
    93 (February 1970), p. 261-263.
Maslen, Benjamin J. "The Earliest English Organ Pedals,"
    Musical Times, no. 1411, vol. 101 (September 1960),
    p. 578.
Mellers, Wilfrid. "John Bull and English Keyboard Music,"
    Musical Quarterly, vol. XL (1954), p. 364-383, 548-71.
Miller, Hugh W. "John Bull's Organ Works," Music and
    Letters, vol. XXVIII (1947), p. 25-35.
_____. "Sixteenth Century English Faburden Compositions
    for Keyboard," Musical Quarterly, vol. XXVI (1940), p. 50.
Pfatteicher, Carl. John Redford, Organist and Almoner of
    St. Paul's Cathedral in the Time of Henry VIII: With
    Especial Reference to His Organ Composition. Leip-
    zig: C. G. Röder, 1934.

Stevens, Denis, ed. Early Tudor Organ Music, II: Music
for the Mass, Early English Church Music, vol. 10.
London: Stainer & Bell, 1969.
_____. "The Keyboard Music of Thomas Tallis," Musical
Times, (July 1952), p. 303-307.
_____. The Mulliner Book: A Commentary. London:
Stainer and Bell, 1952.
_____. "Organists and Organ Music of Tudor Times,"
American Guild of Organists Quarterly, vol. V, no. 2
(April 1960), p. 43-47.
_____. "Pre-Reformation Organ Music in England,"
Proceedings of the Royal Musical Association, vol.
LXXVII (1952), p. 1-10.
_____. "Thomas Preston's Organ Mass," Music and
Letters, vol. XXXIX (1958), p. 29-34.
_____. Thomas Tomkins. New York: St. Martin's
Press, 1957.
_____. Tudor Church Music. New York: Merlin Press,
1955.
_____. "A Unique Tudor Organ Mass," Musica Disciplina,
vol. VI (1952), p. 167-175.
West, John E. "Old English Organ Music," Proceedings of
the Musical Association, vol. XXXVII (1911), p. 1-16.
Young, Clyde William. "Keyboard Music to 1600," Musica
Disciplina, vol. XVII (1963), p. 185-187.
(Also see the following articles in the Harvard Dictionary of
Music: "Felix namque," "In nomine," "Virginal
Book," Organ hymn section in "Organ Chorale," and
"Meane."

THE NETHERLANDS

Curtis, Alan. Sweelinck's Keyboard Music: A Study of
English Elements in Seventeenth-Century Dutch Com-
position. New York: Oxford University Press, 1969.
Tusler, Robert L. The Organ Music of Jan Pieterzoon
Sweelinck, 2 vols. No. I of Utrecht Bijdragen tot de
Muziekwetenschap. Bilthoven, The Netherlands:
Creyghton, 1958.
_____. "Style Differences in the Organ and Clavicembalo
Works of Jan Pieterszoon Sweelinck," Tydschrift voor
Musikwetenshap, vol. XVII (1959), p. 149-166.
Williams, Peter. "Sweelinck and the Dutch School," Musical
Times, no. 1522, vol. 110 (December 1969), p. 1286-
1288.

4. SPAIN AND PORTUGAL: 1500-1600

At the turn of the sixteenth century small positive organs existed in Spain. The disposition of a positive sometimes used in processions is given below.

> León, Spain, Cathedral. Positive organ,
> <u>ca. 1550?, divided, with no pedal.</u>

Left Hand stops	Right Hand stops
Flautado 8	Flautado 8
Octava 4	Octava 4
Lleno	Lleno
	Corneta

An important sixteenth-century organ was the so-called Emperor's Organ in the Cathedral of Toledo. The instrument was designed along conservative lines which resembled the organs planned according to the Blockwerk principle about 1450 and offered little variety in sound quality. The chorus ranks, moreover, were not separated as in Italian organs, which made the Spanish organ much less versatile. The Toledo organ, which was begun by Gonzalo Hernandéz de Córdoba and finished by Juan Gaytan between 1543 and 1549, had two chests and possibly two manuals. The Main chest supported the Blockwerk (Principal 16', Flautado 8', partial stopped 8' rank, Octave, and eight or nine other ranks) plus another mixture, which contained from eight to 28 ranks. The second chest supported a Principal 8' and a mixture. The pedal consisted of 13 keys which played the lowest chromatic octave of the Principal 16'.[1]

The strong influence of Italian musicians was felt throughout Europe during the sixteenth century. The leading musicians from Germany, the Lowlands, and the Iberian peninsula were willing to endure the hardships of travel to

HISTORICAL BACKGROUND

1491-1556	Ignatius de Loyola
1492	Unification of Spain; Ferdinand and Isabella
1492	First voyage of Columbus to America
1497	Vasco da Gama sailed to India
ca. 1509-1586	Morales
1513	Balboa discovered the Pacific Ocean
1515-1582	St. Teresa
1518	Cortes' conquest of Mexico
1519	Magellan sailed around the world
1519-1555	Charles V ruled as Holy Roman Emperor
1540	Society of Jesus founded by Loyola
ca. 1541-1614	El Greco
1541	de Soto discovered the Mississippi River
1545	Council of Trent convened; concluded 1563
1555-1598	Reign of Philip II
1568	Revolt of the Netherlands began
1571	Naval battle of Lepanto
1588	War between Spain and England
1588	Defeat of the Spanish Armada
1605	Cervantes Don Quixote, Part I
1605	Thomas Luis da Victoria Requiem

gain inspiration and instruction from musicians in Italy. Naples belonged to the Spanish crown from 1503 until 1707, and Spanish musicians traveled in other European countries in the retinue of their royal patrons. It was natural, therefore, that there should be close relationships between Italian and Spanish music of the period.

In addition to dances and intabulations of chansons and motets the musical forms and types used by keyboard composers of the Iberian peninsula were tientos (the Spanish counterpart of the Italian ricercar; Portuguese, tento), organ hymns, psalm and Magnificat versets, variations, and Mass movements, forms which were employed at the same time by composers in Italy. Keyboard music was written for both harpsichords and organs.

The Spanish composer F. de la Torre (ca. 1500-?) wrote a basse danse called Alta in which the two lower parts

move slowly under a quickly moving soprano part. The
tenor is the basic melody part around which the other parts
are built. [2]

Most of our knowledge about Spanish musical practices of the sixteenth century is drawn from texts written by
two theorists, Juan Bermudo (fl. 1500's) and Fray [Brother]
Tomás de Santa [Sancta] Maria (?-1570). Bermudo's work
is entitled Declaración de instrumentos musicales (Osuna,
1549, 1555). Musical compositions in the work included
settings of liturgical melodies and hymn arrangements.

Tomás de Santa Maria's work Libro llamado Arte de
taner fantasia assí para tecla como para vihuela (Valladolid,
1565) is similar in theoretical content. His compositions
are no longer than 40 or 50 measures and illustrate the
technique of writing in two, three, and four parts. These
pieces employ strict imitation and are simple, direct, and
dignified. Tomás principally used notes of larger denomination. The imitative entries always appear after discreet
intervals, and the four parts establish strong cadences.
After cadences thinner textures present more imitation which
grows naturally from the preceding material.

The first of two printed collections of Spanish keyboard music is the Libro de cifra nueva para tecla, harpa
y vihuela (Alcalá de Henares, 1557) compiled by Luys Venegas de Henestrosa. It contains Spanish pieces, intabulations
of both French and Spanish composers' vocal writings, and
some Italian instrumental music. The Spanish composers
represented are Francisco Perez Palero, Pedro de Soto,
Pedro [Pere] Vila (1517-1582), and Antonio, who was probably Cabezón (1510-1566). The Italian composer represented
was Giulio Segni (1498-1561). Some of the tientos consisted
of polyphonic writing throughout. Other tientos only begin
with imitative entries and continue without using any particular polyphonic devices. Latin hymn settings are included
which contain several different styles of writing such as
scale passages, imitative sections, decoration going from
part to part, and the melody part played above an active
lower part or between two other voices. Mass movements
and versos (psalm or Magnificat versets) were written in
these same ways. Venegas de Henestrosa rearranged the
music; this is especially noticeable in the transcriptions of
vihuela (stringed instrument) and lute music. The Christmas
carol from this collection employs double canon as its primary unifying element.

SPANISH AND PORTUGUESE ORGAN COMPOSERS: 1500-1600

1500   1550   1600

ca. 1500 de Soto, Francisco ------------------------ 1563
ca. 1500 de la Torre, F.
ca. 1500 Morales, Cristóbal de ---------------- 1553
1502 Paiva, Heliodoro de ------------- 1552
1510 Cabezón, Antonio de -------- 1566
ca. 1510 Bermudo, Juan
1510/20 Santa María, Tomás de ----- 1570
1517 Vila, Pedro Alberto ------------------- 1582
before 1520 Mudarra, Alonso -------------------- 1580
Yepes (Portuguese)
ca. 1525 Carreira, Antonio ----------- 1587/97 (Portuguese)
ca. 1549 Victoria, Tomás Luis de -----------------------1611
Daça, Estevan
Macedo, António de
Ximenez
ca. 1550 Paléro, Francisco Fernandez
1557 Libro de Cifra Nueva para tecla, harpa y vihuela
ca. 1560 Lacerna, Estacio ------------- after 1626
ca. 1560 Peraza, Sotomayor Jeronimo ----- 1617
1560/70 Aguiléra de Herédia, Sebastián after 1620
1564 Peraza, Francisco ----------- 1598

The music by Antonio Cabezón is generally somber
and reserved. Twelve years after his death Antonio's son,
Hernando, published <u>Obras de Música para tecla, arpa y
vihuela</u> (Madrid, 1578). This collection contains compositions
principally by Antonio, but there are a few by Hernando and
one selection by Antonio's brother Juan.

In addition to tientos Cabezón wrote variations
(<u>diferencias</u>) on popular secular tunes, harmonized settings
(<u>versillos</u>) of all eight psalm tones, Magnificat settings
in eight tones (<u>fabordone y glosas</u>), some plainsong hymn
settings, and decorated intabulations of pre-existing chansons or motets. In Spain these were called <u>glosas</u>.
Cabezón wrote several sets of variations. Different polyphonic settings on the same theme presented in different
voices provided an opportunity to demonstrate his great
contrapuntal ability. The themes for the variations
were so well known that the composition begins, not
with the theme, but with the first variation. Examples
of this practice are the diferencias on <u>El Canto llano
del Caballero</u>, on <u>La Pavana Italiana</u>, and on <u>Guardáme las
vacas</u>. In the <u>Caballero</u> piece there are five variations:
in variation one the melody is stated simply in the soprano
voice; variation two offers the melody in the soprano part
slightly decorated; variation three has the unembellished
melody in the tenor; variation four has the melody in the
alto; variation five is in three-part texture with the melody
in the lowest part. <u>La Pavana Italiana</u> progresses smoothly
from variation to variation, but keeps the melody in the
uppermost part and sometimes decorated. Another series
of variations following this type with decorated melody remaining in the soprano is <u>Diferencias sobre la Gallarda
Milanesa</u>. Other characteristics of Cabezón's variations
are that they flow continuously from one to the other, they
fluctuate between modal and tonal harmonies, and, although
the writing is always contrapuntal, little imitation is employed.

Cabezón freely glossed such pieces as Josquin des
Pres' motet <u>Ave Maria</u> and Philippe Verdelot's <u>Ultimi mei
suspiri</u> and <u>Ardenti mei suspiri</u>. Here his imagination encouraged him to add much decorative material to the instrumental transcription, extending the length beyond that of
the original.

The liturgical compositions of "the Spanish Bach" fall
into two general categories, hymns and the versos (<u>versillos</u>).

The hymns are short, with some independence of the three
or four parts permitted. Cabezón wrote four settings for
each psalm tone. In each instance he first wrote a setting
with the melody in the soprano. The second setting has the
melody in the alto, the third in the tenor, and the fourth in
the bass. He has similarly arranged the Magnificat verses
with at least six settings on each tone, frequently employing
points of imitation.

Less significant composers used the prevailing forms
for their keyboard works. Alonso Mudarra (1506-1580) was
a contemporary of Cabezón. In one 16-measure tiento by
Mudarra imitation is not used. Its principal interest lies
in the harmony and might have been more appropriately
played on the harp. Pere Alberch Vila (1517-1582) wrote a
tiento which is highly unified. Vila's tiento uses imitative
devices and is in motet style.

A Tiento de sexto tono by Pedro de Soto (fl. 1500's)
alternates between two-part and four-part texture, and the
counterpoint grows from the harmonic background. A similar composition is one by Francisco Fernandez Palera[o]
(fl. 1500's) entitled Versillo de octavo tono. The Medio
registro alto de primer tono by Francisco Peraza (1564-
1598) offers the opportunity to use a different quality of
sound in the right hand solo part from the left hand accompaniment. This was possible on Spanish and Italian instruments in which certain stops were available for the upper
register of one manual, and different stops were available
for the lower register on the same manual. Sebastián
Aguiléra de Herédia (1570-?) is represented by a work of
large dimension and great variety of mood in his Obra de
octavo tono alto.

A work which contains contrasting musical ideas is
the Tiento de cuarto tono por E la mi a modo de Canción
by Francisco Correa de Arauxo (1576?-1663). Three sections begin with imitative entries, but an interlude and the
final section have quite different rhythmic and melodic character from that of the standard tiento.

The Portuguese Yepes (fl. 1500's) glossed one of
Thomas Crequillon's chansons, Je Prens en Gre. Ornamentation is added where long notes are sustained by the voices
in the original.

In addition to versets Jiminez (fl. 1500's) wrote a

Batalla de sexto tono.   Battle pieces were popular program
pieces of the sixteenth and seventeenth centuries, which suggested the drama of war by imitating the cries of the
wounded, the general confusion, trumpet fanfares, drum
rolls, and the exchange of gunfire.   Repeated notes on one
pitch, answering back and forth between voices on extremely
simple, primary harmonies, and sections of changing meters
were musical characteristics of these battle pieces.

Notes

1.   Peter Williams, The European Organ 1450-1850, London:
       Batsford, 1966;   p. 236-237.
2.   Archibald T. Davison and Willi Apel, eds. , Historical
       Anthology of Music, Cambridge, Mass. :   Harvard
       University Press, 1946;   vol. I, p. 227.

Bibliography

Anderson, Poul-Gerhard.   Organ Building and Design, trans-
       lated into English by Joanne Curnutt.   New York: Ox-
       ford University Press, 1969;   p. 156-159.
Apel, Willi.   "Early Spanish Music for Lute and Keyboard
       Instruments," Musical Quarterly, vol. XX (1934), p.
       289-301.
_____.   "Spanish Organ Music of the Early 17th Century,"
       Journal of the American Musicological Society, vol. XV
       (1962), p. 174-181.
Dart, Thurston.   "Cavazzoni and Cabezón," Music and Let-
       ters, vol. XXXVI (1955), p. 2-6.
Frotscher, Gotthold.   Geschichte des Orgelspiels und der
       Orgelkomposition.   Berlin: Merseberger Verlag, 1959;
       vol. I, p. 243-263.
Howell, Almonte C.   "Cabezón: An Essay in Structural
       Analysis," Musical Quarterly, L (1964), p. 18-30.
Kastner, Santiago.   Cravistas Portuguezes, 2 vols.   Mainz,
       Germany: B. Schotts Söhne, 1935-1950.
Kratzenstein, Marilou.   "A Survey of Organ Literature and
       Editions: Spain and Portugal," Diapason (October 1971),
       p. 22-24.
Sharp, G. B.   "Antonio de Cabezón," Musical Times, no.
       1485, vol. 107 (November 1966), p. 955; and no. 1486,
       vol. 107 (December 1966), p. 1053.
Speer, Klaus.   "The Organ Verso in Iberian Music up to
       1700," Journal of the American Musicological Society,
       vol. XI (1958), p. 189-199.

Stevenson, Robert Murrell. <u>Juan Bermudo</u>. The Hague:
Nijhoff, 1960.
Williams, Peter. <u>The European Organ 1450-1850</u>. London:
B. T. Batsford, 1966; p. 235-244.
Young, Clyde William. "Keyboard Music to 1600," <u>Musica
Disciplina</u>, vol. XVII (1963), p. 179, 182-189.

5. NORTH GERMAN SCHOOL: 1600-1725

Chorale-Based Works

It is astounding to observe how prolific the German composers of the first half of the seventeenth century were and to discover the high quality of their compositions when one remembers that the bulk of these composers' work was done in the midst of the ravages of the Thirty Years' War (1618-1648).   The initiator of the North German School of organ literature was the Dutchman Sweelinck, whose most famous pupils were Jacob Praetorius (1586-1651) and Heinrich Scheidemann (ca. 1596-1663) in Hamburg, Melchior Schildt (1592/93-1667) in Hannover, Paul Siefert (1586-1666) in Danzig, Anders (Andreas) Düben II (ca. 1590-1662), who settled in Stockholm, and the illustrious Samuel Scheidt (1587-1654) of Halle.   Two other students of Sweelinck were Peter Hasse the Elder (ca. 1585-1640) and Gottfried Scheidt (1593-1661).   Most of these composers wrote with simplicity of style and seriousness of purpose.

Chorale literature is the body of German hymnody of the Lutheran Church.   Sources of chorale melodies were plainsong, secular songs, pre-Reformation sacred songs, and newly composed melodies.   Authors of texts for chorales include Martin Luther (1483-1546), Leonhard Lechner (ca. 1550-1606), composer-poet Philipp Nicolai (1556-1608), Martin Rinkart (1586-1649), Paul Gerhardt (1607-1676), Johann Rist (1607-1667), and Joachim Neander (1650-1680).

The congregation of Lutheran churches first sang the chorale in unison and unaccompanied.   Toward the end of the sixteenth century the choir led the congregation in the singing of the chorales.   About 1650 the organ began to accompany the congregational singing.   When choir, congregation, and organ combined forces on the chorales, the alternation between organ and congregation on different stanzas of the chorale fell into disuse, although the alternation practice is encouraged in some churches today. [1]

HISTORICAL BACKGROUND

1546	Death of Martin Luther
ca. 1550-1606	Leonhard Lechner
1556-1608	Philipp Nicolai, chorale composer-author
1585-1672	Heinrich Schütz
1586-1649	Martin Rinkart, author of chorale texts
1605	M. Praetorius Musae Sionae
1607-1676	Paul Gerhardt, author of chorale texts
1607-1667	Johann Rist, author of chorale texts
1617	Schein Banchetto musicale
1618-1677	Johann Franck
1618-1648	Thirty Years' War, Catholics vs. Protestants
1619	Praetorius Syntagma musicum
1623	Schütz Historia der ... Auferstehung
1624	Scheidt Tabulatura Nova
1629	Schütz Symphoniae Sacrae I
1637-1657	Reign of Ferdinand III, Holy Roman Emperor
1640	Frederick William became Elector of Brandenburg
1645	Hammerschmidt Dialogues; Schütz Seven Last Words
1646-1716	Gottfried Leibnitz, philosopher
1647	Johann Crüger Praxis pietatis melica
1650-1680	Joachim Neander, hymnwriter
1650	Scheidt Görlitzer Tabulatur-Buch
1664	Schütz Christmas Oratorio
1685-1750	Bach
1685-1759	Handel
1689	Kuhnau Clavier sonatas
1700-1746	Reign of Philip V of Spain
1701	Frederick I of Prussia crowned
1704	Telemann founded Collegium musicum(Leipzig)
1711-1740	Reign of Charles VI, Holy Roman Emperor
1722	Zinzendorf reestablished Moravian Brotherhood
1724-1804	Immanuel Kant
1725	Fux Gradus ad Parnassum
1731	Treaty of Vienna
1740-1786	Reign of Frederick the Great of Prussia
1742-1745	Reign of Charles VII, Holy Roman Emperor
1745	Stamitz went to Mannheim
1748	War of Austrian Succession ended
1749-1832	Goethe
1750	Quantz Flute concertos
1755	Graun Der Tod Jesu
1759-1805	Schiller
1759	Haydn First Symphony
1770-1827	Beethoven
1791	Mozart Requiem
1798	Haydn Creation

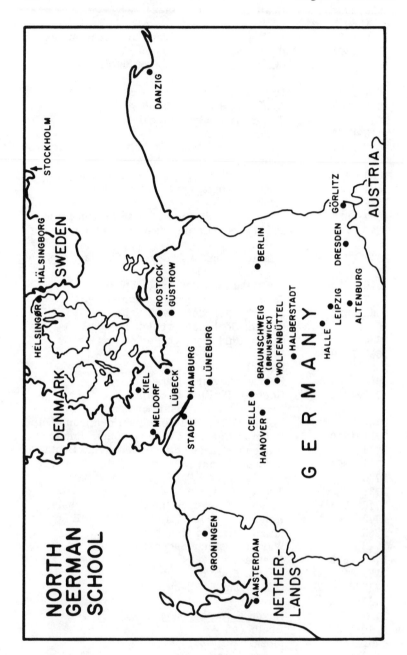

The use of chorale melodies as <u>cantus firmi</u> of organ compositions developed into three general types of chorale settings: a series of variations (chorale partita), an extended treatment of each phrase of the chorale melody continuously in a variety of ways (chorale fantasia), and shorter pieces with the melody of one stanza of the chorale rather clearly emphasized (chorale prelude or organ chorale).   The chorale prelude was played as an introduction to the congregational singing of the chorale, but later all organ arrangements based upon chorale melodies were called chorale preludes, whether they were played before the congregation sang the chorale or in some other function.

Most of Sweelinck's chorale-based works were variations on chorale melodies and usually included several of the following types of treatment in various combinations: a simple four-part setting of the tune, with the melody in the soprano part; a two-part setting with the chorale melody as one of the parts (<u>bicinium</u>) or trio setting (hands on two manuals, with or without pedal), which employed rhythmic figures, both eighth-note and 16th-note scale passages, and repeated rhythmic patterns outlining the harmony; use of parallel thirds, sixths, or tenths, which were often varied by being changed into stereotyped, virginalistic figures of broken thirds, which were carried into numerous and sometimes monotonous sequences; and free contrapuntal treatment of the voices with the melody in any voice.

Sweelinck's most famous pupil was Samuel Scheidt, and many of Scheidt's compositional techniques can be traced directly to Sweelinck's influence.   Scheidt spent most of his life in the small university town and cultural center of Halle where, although his principal responsibility was to the ducal court, he served churches as well.   The works of Scheidt display great clarity, even though they are not oversimplified, and include use of imitation, chromatic alteration, and, in chorale or Latin hymn settings, the <u>cantus firmus</u> is always clear and distinct from the other parts.   Unlike many liturgically oriented organ books the chorale and hymn settings of Scheidt are not arranged in order according to the church year.

Scheidt's very important <u>Tabulatura nova</u> appeared in 1624 in three parts.   In this work he employed the Italian method of writing for the keyboard, called <u>partitura</u>, which placed each voice line on a separate staff.   At the end of the third part of <u>Tabulatura nova</u> a number of interesting

NORTH GERMAN SCHOOL OF ORGAN COMPOSITION: 1600-1725

1550	1600	1650	1700	1750	1800

(1562 Sweelinck--1621)
ca.1585 Hasse, P. the elder 1640
1586 Siefert, Paul------------1666
1586 Praetorius, Jacob-----1651
1587 Scheidt, Samuel------------1654
ca.1590 Düben, Anders II-----1662
1592/93 Schildt, M. ------1667
1593 Scheidt, Gottfried ----1661
ca.1596 Scheidemann, H. ------1663
1596 Decker, Johann ------1668
? Abel, David 1639
? Meyer, D.   ?
1601 Strungk, Delphin-------1694
? Olter, Marcus   ?
1613/14 Karges, Wilhelm   1699
1614 Tunder, Franz 1667
1621 Weckmann, M. 1674
1623 Reincken, Johann Adam------1722
1626 Flor, Christian 1697
1629 Capricornus (Bockshorn), S. 1665
1637 Buxtehude, Dietrich 1707
1649 Kneller, Andreas-------1724
Middle seventeenth century Lüneburg Tablatures
? Hasse, Peter, the younger ?
1654 Lübeck, Vincent-----------1740
1661 Böhm, Georg----------1733
1664 Leyding, G.   1710
1665 Bruhns, N.   1697
1665 Hanff, Johann   1711/12
ca.1670 Brunckhorst, A. --1720
1681 Telemann, Georg P. --------------1767

instructions on registration and playing are given for the
organist. Scheidt stated that these pieces were written for
an organ with two manuals and pedal, and he emphasized
that the melody must be brought out on a strong stop in
order to be understood clearly ["... auff den Rückposetif mit
einer scharffen Stimme (den Choral desto deutlicher zu
vernehmen) spielen ... den Bass mit dem Pedal"], the bass
part played in the pedal. He indicated different methods of
playing the pieces, what to avoid when assigning both the
tenor and bass to the feet, and registration suggestions.

Scheidt's Instructions
from <u>Tabulatura nova</u>,

Part III

To the Organists.

These Magnificats and hymns as well as several
Psalms to be found in the first and second parts of my
<u>Tabulatura nova</u> can be played on any organ with two
manuals and pedal, the melody being in the soprano or
tenor particularly on the Rückpositiv with a sharp stop
so that one hears the chorale melody even more clearly.
If it is a bicinium and if the chorale melody is in the
soprano, one plays the melody with the right hand on
the upper manual or the Great manual and the second
part with the left hand on the Rückpositiv. If the melody is in the highest of four parts, one plays the melody on the Rückpositiv with the right hand, the alto and
tenor on the upper manual or on the Great with the left
hand, and the bass with the pedal. If the melody is in
the tenor, one plays it on the Rückpositiv with the left
hand and the other parts on the upper manual or on the
Great with the right hand, and the bass in the pedal.
Within four parts the alto can also be played on
the Rückpositiv but one should take the soprano on the
upper manual with the right hand, and play the tenor
and bass on the pedal, the two voices simultaneously.
But in addition it must be arranged that the tenor is
not higher than c^1 because one seldom finds the d^1 on
the pedal and the two voices cannot be set too far apart
for the octave, fifth or third, otherwise they cannot be
reached with the feet.

N. B.

However, the most beautiful and easiest arrangement is to play the alto in the pedal;   there is also an
advantage for the hands as far as the stops of the organ are concerned because one can distinguish between
4' and 8' tone.   The 8' tone must always be on the
Positiv and 4' tone in the pedal ... Various registrations or stop combinations to pull if one wishes to play
a chorale on two manuals in a manner so that it can
be heard distinctly:
On the Great: Grob Gedact 8', Klein Gedact 4',
these two together, or Principal 8' alone, and other
stops or combinations according to one's taste.
On the Positiv: a sharp stop to bring out the
chorale clearly.   Quinta dehn or Gedact 8', Klein Gedact or Principal 4', Mixtur or Zimmel or Superoctaf,
these stops together or other combinations according
to one's taste.
In the Pedal to bring out the chorale distinctly:
Untersatz 16', Posaunen Bass 8' or 16', Dulcian Bass
8' or 16', Schalmei, Trommete, Bauer Flöte, Cornet
and other stops which are often found in small and
large organs.   All this I have put down for the sake
of those who do not yet know such a way of performance and yet want to make use of it, also for the
sake of other noble and knowledgeable organists who,
however, may make use of it at their discretion.
Vale.

Luther's associate Justus Jonas might have prepared
the Kirchenordnung (Church-Ordinance) for Halle, of which
only a fragment exists today.   The instructions given in the
Kirchenordnung apply more to the singing of the choir than
to the singing of the congregation.   The use of Latin in
Lutheran churches was quite common for more than a century after Luther's death, although the practice was gradually
being discarded.   Choirs often sang Latin hymns which had
no German translations at that time.   German was used much
more after the end of the Thirty Years' War, but the Halle
city council did not completely discard the use of Latin in
Lutheran services until 1702. [2]   Thus, the Magnificat was
sung in Latin, as were a number of other portions of the
service.   Inasmuch as St. Moritz, the church in which Scheidt
was organist, was the youngest and least favored place of worship in the city when special music was called for at festivals,

Samuel Scheidt: Tabulatura Nova (1624)

PART I

4 variation cycles on chorale melodies (Nos. 1, 3, 5, 12)
3 fantasias: continuous pieces but sectional according to changing rhythms (Nos. 2, 4, 13)
3 dances: variations on a passamezzo (No. 6); two courantes (Nos. 8, 9)
3 variation cycles on secular melodies (Nos. 7, 10, 11)
12 canons on chorale melodies, a hexachord melody, psalm tones, Latin hymn melodies (No. 14)

PART II

2 fugues (Nos. 1, 3)
2 echo pieces (No. 2)
3 variation cycles on chorale melodies (Nos. 4, 5, 9)
2 fantasias (one listed as a toccata) (Nos. 6, 12)
1 variation cycle on a secular melody (No. 8)
2 variation cycles on dances: allemands (Nos. 10, 11)
1 variation cycle on a Latin hymn melody (No. 7)

PART III

1 set of alternation verses on Kyrie and Gloria (No. 1)
9 sets of six versets on reciting tones of Magnificat; the ninth is on the Tonus peregrinus (Nos. 2-10)
6 variation cycles on Latin hymn melodies (Nos. 11-16)
1 setting of the Credo (Wir glauben) with the melody in only the bass part (No. 17)
1 variation cycle on a chorale melody (No. 18)
2 pieces for full organ (organo pleno) (Nos. 19, 20)
Instructions on how to play and how to register the organ pieces

the organ often had to substitute for a less musically
able choir. This might explain why there were a number of
Scheidt settings of the Magnificat.

Toward the end of Scheidt's life the publishing of his
Tabulatur-Buch was subsidized by the town council of Görlitz
in 1650. This volume contains the harmonizations of 100
chorales, which Scheidt believed to be the most widely used
in Germany at that time. Scheidt's Tabulatur-Buch was similar to many cantionals published about this time by such
composers as Raselius, Calvisius, Hassler, and Eccard.
In cantionals the chorale melody was placed in the uppermost
voice part and was harmonized in simple, homophonic settings. The Tabulatur-Buch can hardly have served as a
Choralbuch, since a congregation would find it difficult to
sing to these harmonizations,[3] and it differs a great deal
from other chorale books of the time. However, it contains
four-part organ settings of chorale melodies which could well
have been used in alternation with congregational singing,
with the organ playing every other stanza. The Mecklenburg
Kirchenordnung (1650) says: "Where organs are available,
there should the organist play every other stanza." The organ solo verses were played in a variety of styles: iso-
metric or rhythmic, highly decorated or plain, or in different harmonizations.[4]

Other North German pupils of Sweelinck such as
Düben, Scheidemann, and J. Praetorius incorporated imitative entries developed from the initial chorale phrase melody
in the lower three parts. When the final voice enters (usually the fourth voice), the melody is very simply stated in
notes of long value or occasionally, as in some of Praetorius' writing, the melody becomes highly ornamented. In
some of Heinrich Scheidemann's chorale settings the melody
is frequently presented in long notes in the pedal. Scheidemann also sometimes indicated manual changes for echo effects, one of Sweelinck's most characteristic idioms. Andreas Kneller (1649-1724) and Vincent Lübeck (1654-1740)
also wrote chorale works in a series of variations similar
to examples of the Sweelinck school. Nikolaus Bruhns
(1665-1697) contributed a long, sectional chorale fantasia on
Nun komm der Heiden Heiland ("Now Comes the Gentiles'
Saviour") which contains a wealth of musical ideas.

Franz Tunder (1614-1667), organist of the Marienkirche, Lübeck, showed how the florid, virtuoso writing of
the North German School was incorporated into chorale-

based works. Some of his musical characteristics are
flourishes of rapid 16th-notes at the beginning of his chorale
settings (a technique also found in compositions of his son-
in-law, Dietrich Buxtehude), use of double pedal, echo passages, brief imitative sections drawn from inner phrases of
the chorale melody, and a wide variety of compositional devices applied to the chorale phrases throughout the piece.
Tunder contributed considerably to the development of the
chorale fantasia; an excellent example is his lengthy work
on Komm, Heiliger Geist, Herre Gott ("Come, Holy Ghost,
Lord God").

        Dietrich Buxtehude (1637-1707) wrote most of his
chorale settings for two manuals and pedal   The format is
usually limited to a short, concentrated setting of only one
stanza (the shortest one is only 21 measures long).   Three
present the melody with little or no decoration.   Coloratura
(highly embellished) treatments are the most frequent, in
which ornaments, pauses, and rests in the middle of phrases
heighten the interest and make Buxtehude's style personal.
Tiny interludes separate the various phrases. With the
melody in the right hand the accompanying parts make use
of Vorimitation[5] and develop simply and naturally the accompanying style already begun.   The chorale settings by Buxtehude are subjective, warmly expressive, and full of flights
of imagination inspired by the melody itself and a word or
phrase of the chorale text.   His sound-painting employs
chromaticism to depict words such as "pain, " "death, " or
"sin. "

        Buxtehude's chorale variations sometimes have the
melody clearly delineated, sometimes decorated.   The variations on Auf meinen lieben Gott ("In My Beloved God") form
a small suite, with the melody treated in different dance
styles (sarabande, courante, and gigue).   The chorale fantasias were probably used to conclude the church services.
One extended fantasia presents the melody in richly varied
forms and styles including sections in imitative counterpoint,
florid 16th-note scale passages, flowing or broken thirds,
sixths or tenths, independent pedal parts, triplet or gigue
sections, [6] echo effects, and sections which change meter or
were like ricercars.

        The specifications of the Lübeck organ, which both
Tunder and Buxtehude played, are given on the following
page.

Lübeck, Germany, Marienkirche "Totentanz"
sacristy Chapel organ.

Brustwerk	Hauptwerk
built by Henning Kröger, 1621-1622	partially built by J. Stephani, 1475-1477

Gedackt 8'
Quintadena 4'
Hohlflöte 2'
Quint 1 1/3'
Scharff IV
Krummhorn 8'
Schalmey 4'

Quintadena 16'
Prinzipal 8'
Oktave 4'
Mixture VIII-X
Quintade 16'
Spitzflöte 8'
Nasat 2 2/3'
Rauschpfeife II
Trompete 8'

Rückpositiv built by Jacob Scherer, 1557-1558	Pedal 1475-1477, 1621-1622

Prinzipal 8'
Oktave 4'
Scharff VI-VIII
Quintatön 8'
Rohrflöte 8'
Rohrflöte 4'
Sesquialtera II
Sifflöte 1 1/3'
Dulzian 16'
Trechterregal 8'

Principal 16'
Oktave 8'
Oktave 4'
Oktave 2'
Mixture IV
Zimbel II
Subbass 16'
Gedackt 8'
Quintaton 4'
(Nachthorn 1' ?)
Posaune 16'
(Dulzian 16' ?)
Trompet 8'
Schalmey 4'
Kornett 2'

Coupler: Rückpositiv/Hauptwerk
Tremulant

The strong influence of Buxtehude is suggested in the chorale compositions of Johann Nicolaus Hanff (1665-1711/12) by the coloratura settings of only one stanza, imitative entries on the melodies of successive chorale phrases, and other characteristics, such as the florid codetta at the end of Wär Gott nicht mit uns diese Zeit ("If God Be for Us").

Nine out of 14 chorale-based works by Georg Böhm (1661-1733) are in the form of variations. Each variation is called a partita, a versus, or a variatio. Some of the variations suggest performance on stringed keyboard instruments rather than on organs, for they can be performed without pedal (manualiter, i. e. , on manuals alone) and resemble Böhm's suites for stringed keyboard instruments.

The final important North German composer of the organ chorale considered here is the Hamburg organist Georg Philipp Telemann (1681-1767). His collection of chorale settings is entitled 24 fugierende und veränderte Choräle[7] and contains both a bicinium and a three-part arrangement of 23 different chorale melodies plus one additional bicinium and three-part treatment (i. e. , four in all on one melody) of Herr Jesu Christ, dich zu uns wend ("Lord Jesus Christ, Turn Thou to Us"), all of which make 48 different settings. The style is extremely simple and occasionally includes ostinato (continuously repeated) figures. Most of the arrangements have the melody in the upper voice, which could be taken by a 4' stop in the pedal. These settings could have been used between stanzas sung by the congregation.

Free Organ Works

Free compositions of the North German School were usually cast in the forms of a präambulum (prelude), toccata, fantasia, a rare capriccio, and later, fugue, even though no clearly defined structure had been established for these types of compositions by the middle of the seventeenth century. Two streams of musical influence upon composers of the North German School came from Sweelinck and Frescobaldi. Composers such as Marcus Olter (fl. 1600's), Wilhelm Karges (1613/14-1699), and Tunder show the influence of Frescobaldi. Karges also wrote in the slow, harmonic style of North German contemporaries such as David Åbel (?-1639) and Peter Hasse the elder (ca. 1585-1640).

In addition to works whose composers can be readily identified, the Lüneburg organ tablatures are a collection of free compositions, chorale variations, chorale preludes, and dances dating from seventeenth century which are of uncertain provenance. Some works have been identified as compositions by Sweelinck, Weckmann, Scheidemann, Schildt, and Capricornus, but the remaining pieces in these tablatures are anonymous. The large majority of the free works are preludes of from six to 128 measures in length, with the titles

in the singular form spelled in a number of different ways
(praeambulum, praeludium, praelude, preludium, praeam).
Most of the preludes are basically homophonic and have
rhythmic imitation as well as melodic imitation at times.
Their harmonic rhythm is rather slow with an exchange of
notes between parts in the prevailing harmony over a sustained pedal part.   Some of the shorter preludes closely
resemble intonations.   Other free works include fantasias,
fugues, toccatas, and one cantzoem. [8]

   Preludes had been single, short pieces such as those
found in the fifteenth- and early sixteenth-century präambeln
in Kleber's tablature (1524), those by Melchior Schildt, and
those found in the Lüneburg tablatures.   Some of Schildt's
preludes have less than ten measures.   During the second
quarter of the seventeenth century the prelude evolved into
a piece in two sections, the first slow and harmonic, the
second more contrapuntal and lively in character, developing
material in a fugal style.   Works of this type were written
by Jacob Praetorius, Decker, and Tunder.   As composers
enlarged their contrapuntal material, the second section began to stand alone as a longer piece, and this practice
eventually led to the distinctly separated larger preludes
and fugues of J. S. Bach.

   The first section of the early seventeenth-century
präludium contained chords which moved slowly in root position and in first inversions.   The harmonies were decorated
in simple ways, perhaps with no more than passing tones or
a few decorated resolutions of suspensions.   The piece never
strayed far from the original key, usually only enough to
suggest another closely related key.   There was little, if
any, ornamentation indicated.   Perhaps Jacob Praetorius
showed real daring by putting a flourish of 16th-notes or
32d-notes at the end of the sections in his preludes.   Two
preludes of Christian Flor (1626-1697) are more florid and
active than most earlier seventeenth-century preludes.

   The works of Franz Tunder in the prelude genre exhibit more inventive writing than the free works of his contemporaries.   Tunder's preludes were divided into two parts,
a slower part followed by a fugal one;   there is no complete
break between the two sections.   The fugal section actually
sounds the entry of the first voice while the final chord of
the slower section is being held.

   The style of Matthias Weckmann (1621-1674) strongly

strongly suggests the influence of the Frescobaldi school by metamorphosis of the same melodic subject (Fantasia in D Minor).   Weckmann's fugal subjects frequently employ a repeated note at their beginnings.   Weckmann's canzonas and toccatas were designed to be played on manuals alone.

The sectional structure of Frescobaldi's canzonas might have had an effect upon Johann Adam Reincken (1623-1722), whose Toccata in G is divided into five contrasting sections.   The form of Reincken's toccata is similar to the toccatas of Froberger and Muffat of the South German School.

The large number of imaginative free organ works of Dietrich Buxtehude (1637-1707) can be divided into preludes, toccatas, fugues, canzonas, canzonettas, and the variation forms of chaconne and passacaglia.

The preludes (or toccatas) and fugues of Buxtehude seem to be a group of loosely related sections.   If there are five, there might be as many as three different fugue expositions, sometimes ending with or separated by dignified harmonic interludes or brief, improvisatory sections.   In the fugues Buxtehude assigned the pedal part as much importance as any other individual voice part.   The rather loosely woven works entitled "toccata" contain a wide variety of compositional devices with just a sampling of each.   The Toccata in F, for example, reveals a fugue as well developed as in the compositions named prelude (or toccata) and fugue.   Profuse ornamentation was not indicated by Buxtehude.   Trills and a few mordants were the chief ornaments used.   He sometimes chose to write out the ornamentation rather than to use embellishment symbols.   Furthermore, Buxtehude incorporated a wider range of keys than his predecessors and contemporaries did: E major and F-sharp minor are two examples of keys which were unusual at that time.   One example of the vigor in Buxtehude's writing is exhibited by the recurrence of the gigue rhythm.   Repeated notes, too, occur frequently in his themes of fugue subjects, as in the D major fugue, which begins with six A's.   One of the fugues in A minor has a subject which contains four eighth-note E's followed by four eighth-note D's;   the ostinato of the famous C Major Chaconne begins with four C's in the pedal.   In summary, Buxtehude's writing has exuberance, variety, and vitality.   His compositions are fresh and interesting.

Although few in number and not long in duration,

Georg Böhm's free organ compositions exhibit fine craftsmanship in unifying and developing his material. His Prelude and Fugue in C Major contains a stirring pedal cadenza
at the beginning of the prelude, a feature usually connected
with the North German School.

Vincent Lübeck wrote six preludes and fugues. The
structure of these pieces is similar to that of some compositions by Buxtehude because they generally alternate toccata sections with fugal ones. Active pedal passages, rapid
scale figures for the manuals, voice lines outlining chords,
and series of repeated notes and chords are characteristics
of Lübeck's free organ works.

Notes

1. Albert Schweitzer, J. S. Bach, New York: Macmillan,
    1947 [reprint]; vol. I, p. 31-37.
2. Walter E. Buszin, "The Life and Work of Samuel
    Scheidt," The Musical Heritage of the Lutheran Church,
    St. Louis: Concordia Pub. House, 1959; vol. V,
    p. 55.
3. Ibid., p. 63. Schweitzer wrote that the Scheidt Tabulatur-
    Buch was intended for accompaniment of congregational
    singing. See Albert Schweitzer, op. cit., p. 35.
4. Walter E. Buszin, op. cit., p. 63-64.
5. Vorimitation ("anticipatory imitation") is a contrapuntal
    device often used in settings of chorale melodies for
    organ in which the melody of the chorale phrase (in
    long notes or in a decorated form) is anticipated by
    several voices sounding the same tune, usually in
    diminution, sometimes in inversion. Another similar
    term, Zwischenimitation ("inner imitation"), refers to
    the same anticipatory imitation of inner phrase melo-
    dies used as each new chorale phrase is forthcoming.
6. The strong, markedly accented rhythms usually asso-
    ciated with the gigue are either

    or rhythms derived from these basic patterns.
7. Sometimes printed 24 fugirte und verändernde Choräle.
8. John Shannon, ed., Free Organ Compositions from the

Lüneburg Tablatures, 2 vols., St. Louis: Concordia
Pub. House, 1958; preface.

Bibliography

Bradshaw, Murray C., "Pre-Bach Organ Toccatas: Form,
    Style, and Registration," Diapason (March, 1972),
    p. 26-28.
Buszin, Walter E.   "Buxtehude: On the Tercentenary of His
    Birth," Musical Quarterly, vol. XXIII (1937), p. 465-
    490.
_____. "The Life and Work of Samuel Scheidt," The
    Musical Heritage of the Lutheran Church.   St. Louis:
    Concordia Pub. House, 1959; vol. V, p. 43.
Fosse, Richard C.   "Nicolaus Bruhns," The Musical Heri-
    tage of the Lutheran Church.   St. Louis: Concordia
    Pub. House, 1959; vol. V, p. 92.
Frotscher, Gotthold.   Geschichte des Orgelspiels und der
    Orgelkomposition.   Berlin: Merseberger Verlag,
    1959; vol. I, p. 377-470.
Hedar, Joseph.   Dietrich Buxtehudes Orgelwerke.   Stock-
    holm: Wilhelm Hansen, 1951.
Pauly, H. J.   Die Fuge in den Orgelwerken Dietrich Buxte-
    hudes.   Regensburg, Germany: G. Bosse, 1964.
Powell, Kenneth G.   "An Analysis of the North German
    Organ Toccatas," Diapason (April 1971), p. 27-29.
Schuneman, Robert A.   "The Organ Chorales of Georg Böhm,"
    Diapason (March 1970), p. 12-14.
Schweitzer, Albert, J. S. Bach, 2 vols., New York: Mac-
    millan, 1947 [reprint].
Shannon, John, ed.   Free Organ Compositions from the
    Lüneburg Tablatures, 2 vols.   St. Louis: Concordia
    Pub. House, 1958.
_____. "North-German Organ Music: A Short Study of
    a Style," Music/The A. G. O. -R. C. C. O. Magazine,
    vol. III, no. 9 (September 1969), p. 22.
Sharp, G. B.   "Franz Tunder: 1614-1667," Musical Times,
    no. 1497, vol. 108 (November 1967), p. 997.
_____. "Nicolaus Bruhns," Musical Times, no. 1482,
    vol. 107 (August 1966), p. 677.
Spiess, Lincoln B.   "Michael Praetorius Creuzburgensis:
    Church Musician and Scholar," The Musical Heritage
    of the Lutheran Church.   St. Louis: Concordia Pub.
    House, 1959; vol. V.

6. SOUTH GERMAN SCHOOL: 1600-1775

[The Historical Background chart found at the beginning of
Chapter 5 is also appropriate for this chapter.]

Chorale-Based Works

There were few compositions based on chorale melodies in the South German School because there were few
Protestant composers in southern Germany and Catholic organists in their services had no use for pieces based on
Lutheran melodies. Composers in Catholic cities seemed
to write little for the church but were more interested in
the secular suite and contrapuntal forms. The organ Mass
had virtually vanished. Published organ music was designed
for either liturgical use or for teaching.

The chorale-based works composed by this school of
organ composers were written by Ulrich Steigleder (1593-
1635), Johann Pachelbel (1653-1706) and his son Wilhelm
Hieronymus Pachelbel (1686-1746), Johann Erasmus Kindermann (1616-1655), Johann Kaspar Ferdinand Fischer (ca.
1667-1746), Johann Philipp Förtsch (1652-1732), and Johann
Krieger (1652-1735). W. H. Pachelbel composed a Fantasia
on Meine Seele, lass es gehen, which incorporates broken
chords and other stringed keyboard instrument figures. Johann Philipp Förtsch wrote 32 canons in from two to eight
voices on Christ der du bist der helle Tag ("O Christ, who
art both day and light"). Fischer included four chorale settings and five short ricercars on Ave Maria klare at the end
of his Ariadne Musica Neo-Organoedum (1702, 1710, 1715).

The most productive composer of chorale-based works
was the Nürnberg master Johann Pachelbel. Pachelbel's
compositions are characterized by their simplicity of conception, natural flow, and uncontrived sound. The cantus
firmus is always clearly heard. The principal characteristic
of his chorale-based works is the frequent use of Vorimitation.
Although this technique was adopted by many other composers

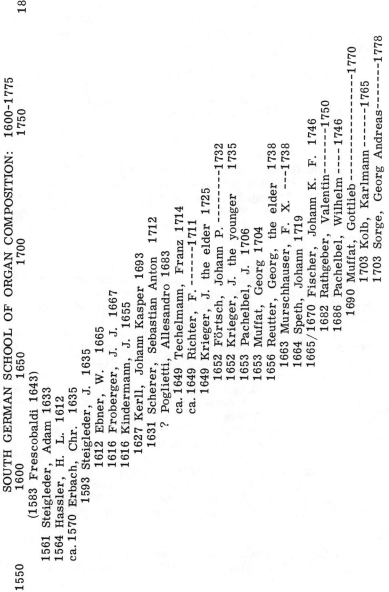

SOUTH GERMAN SCHOOL OF ORGAN COMPOSITION: 1600-1775

1550   1600   1650   1700   1750   1800

(1583 Frescobaldi 1643)

1561 Steigleder, Adam 1633
1564 Hassler, H. L. 1612
ca.1570 Erbach, Chr. 1635
        1593 Steigleder, J. 1635
            1612 Ebner, W. 1665
            1616 Froberger, J. J. 1667
            1616 Kindermann, J. 1655
                1627 Kerll, Johann Kasper 1693
                    1631 Scherer, Sebastian Anton 1712
                    ? Poglietti, Allesandro 1683
                        ca.1649 Techelmann, Franz 1714
                        ca.1649 Richter, F. ----1711
                            1649 Krieger, J. the elder 1725
                                1652 Förtsch, Johann P. -------1732
                                1652 Krieger, J. the younger 1735
                                1653 Pachelbel, J. 1706
                                1653 Muffat, Georg 1704
                                    1656 Reutter, Georg, the elder 1738
                                    1663 Murschhauser, F. X. ---1738
                                        1664 Speth, Johann 1719
                                    1665/1670 Fischer, Johann K. F. 1746
                                        1682 Rathgeber, Valentin-----1750
                                            1686 Pachelbel, Wilhelm ----1746
                                                1690 Muffat, Gottlieb----------------1770
                                                    1703 Kolb, Karlmann -----1765
                                                    1703 Sorge, Georg Andreas-----1778

of chorale settings, it is especially connected with Pachelbel's name.   Pachelbel frequently used a combination form which links an introductory prelude on the first phrase melody (sometimes called a prelude-fugue) to a setting of one stanza of the chorale with the cantus firmus in the pedal in long notes.   In the latter part the left hand often doubles the cantus, while the soprano and alto parts are written in flowing 16th-notes.   The famous Vom Himmel hoch pastorale-trio is followed by this type of setting.

Pachelbel also wrote three-part chorale settings with one of the parts playing the melody in long notes.   His chorale variations frequently contain settings which seem to be written for cembalo (harpsichord) and not for organ.

Free Compositions

The Italian forms adopted by the Catholic South German school were the non-liturgical toccata, canzona, ricercar, capriccio, fantasia, and fugue.   The pedal division of the organs in that area was much less developed than the pedal divisions in northern Germany.   The music written, therefore, required little, if any, pedal work.   A toccata primi toni by Adam Steigleder (1561-1633) is found in the Woltz tablature (1617), in which there is simple elaboration (usually 16th-note scale passages) of unsurprising harmonic progressions;   this toccata closely resembles an intonation. It was obviously written for the organ and no other medium.

The South German School made several contributions to the development of the fugue.   Kindermann placed two different kinds of fugues in his Harmonia organica (1645): some were the type we would now expect to find under the title and the others were based on chorale melodies.   Pachelbel's fugue subjects were broken into figurative motifs and developed separately.   These various elements from several different composers point to the rise of the fugue form and the decline of the canzona and ricercar.

Hans Leo Hassler (1564-1612) employed the organ forms of his teacher, Andrea Gabrieli: the ricercar, canzona, and toccata.   Christian Erbach (ca. 1570-1635) used these same forms and also wrote versets for the alternation practice.

One of the outstanding composers in this school was Johann Jacob Froberger (1616-1667), who was sent by

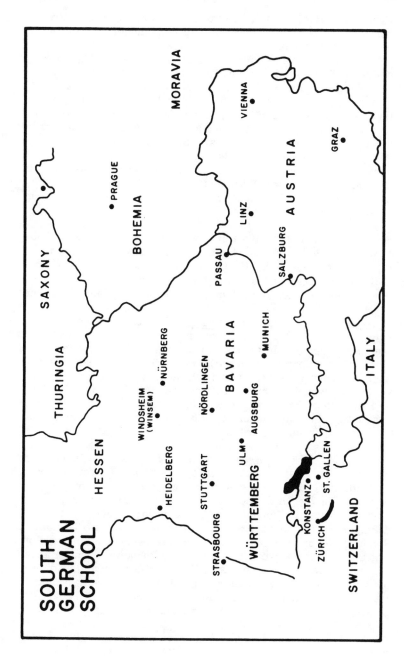

Ferdinand III of Austria to study with Frescobaldi. Froberger assimilated much from his Italian teacher and adopted
many of his techniques. The toccata in the hands of Froberger was a composite form, a miniature suite. The form was
sectional and had meter changes for each section. Free,
recitative sections often began and closed his toccatas. A
typical order of the sections in a Froberger toccata is: a
fantasia-recitative section, a short fughetta, a strongly rhythmic section, and a final free, fantasia section. Even though
his toccatas were sectional, all parts seem to belong to one
entity and progress smoothly from one to another. Froberger's composition was formed from techniques absorbed from
Italian, German, and French sources. His influence was
particularly strong on the Viennese and south German group
of composers.

     The Modulatio organica of Johann Kasper Kerll (1627-
1693) contains seven short Magnificat versets for each of the
eight chant tones. Kerll and Johann Erasmus Kindermann
(1616-1655) continued to write canzonas and ricercars, although their canzonas no longer used the traditional canzona
rhythm at the beginning. Kerll made use of pedal point
throughout the Toccata per li Pedali. Kerll's lengthy Passacaglia in D Minor is a virtuoso number built on a descending
four-note theme. It is easy to understand why a talented
composer-performer of Kerll's reputation attracted pupils
such as Johann Pachelbel and Franz Murschhauser. Kerll
wrote at least two capriccios, one on the "cuckoo" theme
and the other Der steyrische Hirt. Both pieces employ keyboard figures which sound better on a stringed keyboard instrument than on the organ.

     The works of Sebastian Anton Scherer are in two
books. The first book is entitled Intonationes breves per
octo tonos (1664) and the second Partitura in cymbalo et
organo. In the first book are found four intonations for
each of the eight chant tones. One pedal note is sustained
during several measures while the manual writing is florid.
Some of the intonations do not use the pedal. Some employ
imitation, flowing parallel thirds in 16th-notes, and balanced
movement between the parts. The Partitura contains eight
toccatas which change meter without altering the pace and
lessen the sectionality found in earlier toccatas. Pedal
points are sustained under much parallel writing.

     Alessandro de Poglietti (?-1683) was an Italian who
lived in Vienna. He is known for his ricercari. Franz

Mathias Techelmann (ca.1649-1714) and Ferdinand Tobias
Richter (ca.1649-1711) were in the same Viennese circle.
Johann Philipp Krieger the Elder (1649-1725) wrote a simple
Toccata in A Minor.   The accompanying fugue exhibits neat
cadences and transitional contrapuntal material, which help
to clarify the form.   Johann Philipp's brother, Johann Krieger (1651-1735), composed much more music in the standard
Italian forms, including a very long Ciacona[1] with many variations and a Passacaglia. [1]   Most of these pieces use the
pedal sparingly and many do not use the pedal at all.

The chief work for which Georg Muffat (1653-1704) is
known is the Apparatus musico-organisticus (1690), which
contains 12 sectional toccatas, one ciacona, and one passacaglia.   Some of the sections are short, but the tempo
changes are striking, as from grave to allegro.   The pieces
are improvisatory in nature and are liberally graced with
embellishments.   Again, little pedal is needed.   The 11th
toccata from the Apparatus suggests a suite because of its
series of related, but contrasting, short pieces.   This toccata begins with a slow, homophonic alla breve section followed by a faster, fugal, four-part movement.   A lyric,
dignified Adagio in $\frac{3}{2}$ meter then precedes a $\frac{3}{4}$ Allegro.   After
a tiny Adagio interlude the toccata concludes with a dancing
$\frac{6}{8}$ movement.   Syncopation, some chromaticism, and sequences are tastefully employed.

Johann Pachelbel, Froberger, and J. K. F. Fischer
are the three outstanding composers of the South German
School.   Pachelbel spent the last part of his life in southern
Germany.   Pachelbel's free works include preludes, toccatas,
fugues, ricercars, and a few chaconnes and fantasies.   Pachelbel's writing, while not profound, is direct and interesting.
The voice leading is always clear and flowing within simple
but strong harmonic progressions.   Pachelbel used chordal
figurations and sequences to excellent effect.   The pedal is
used principally to support the basic harmonies by holding
sustained tones.   Additional characteristics are echo effects,
off-beat repeated or separated 16th-notes against a legato
line in the other hand, brilliant passages of scale passages
in 16th-notes, preference for two-part and three-part writing,
and practically no ornamentation.   The Pachelbel toccatas
are not broken into obvious sections and are medium length,
unified pieces of from 30 to 50 measures.

Pachelbel chose to write many double fugues: two
subjects developed independently and then combined.   This

technique is observed in some of his fugues and ricercars
which were inspired by the Magnificat.   Pachelbel wrote 94
of these fugues for use in the Lutheran vesper service.
These short compositions were used in alternation with the
singing of Magnificat verses or as introductions to the Magnificat, but only a few of these fugues are actually based on
the chant tones.

Pachelbel's free compositions were generally conceived as ensemble works and not for melodies with accompaniment.   Pachelbel spent the last 11 years of his life in
his native Nuremberg as organist of the Sebalduskirche.   The
specifications of the organ there, which are given below, re-
veal that there were few mutations, mixtures, and only one
reed, and that the organ contained a small pedal division.
The simple design of the instrument is closely related to the
unaffected, natural flow of Pachelbel's contrapuntal lines.

Nuremberg, Germany: Sebalduskirche.
Built by Heinrich Traxdorf, 1444;
rebuilt by Sigmund Layser, 1691

Hauptwerk	Pedal
Principal 8	Principal 16
Octava 4	Octav 8
Quinta Cymbel II	Quint 3
Super Octava und Decima	Sub Bass 16
2 and 1 1/2	Violon Bass 8

Rückpositiv

Principal 4
Grob Gedackt 8
Quinta cum Octava 3 and 2
Super Octava 2 and 1
Quintaton 8
Cymbel II
Dulcian 8

Georg Reutter the Elder (1656-1738) wrote in the
forms of toccata, capriccio, fugue, and canzona.   Among
other works a short toccata in G major by one of Johann
Pachelbel's sons, Wilhelm Hieronymus, gives evidence of
a style similar to that of his father.   Another son, Karl
Theodore Pachelbel, became influential in early American
musical circles.

Johann Kaspar Ferdinand Fischer (1665/1670-1746) wrote 20 short preludes and fugues in 19 different keys with five short ricercari on chorale melodies which form the Ariadne Musica. All of these pieces are brief; the shortest prelude contains only seven measures and the longest, 25. Ariadne foreshadowed Bach's Wohltemperirte Clavier of 48 preludes and fugues.

In Fischer's Blumen Strauss each of eight preludes composed in a different church tone is followed by six brief "fugues" and a finale, which usually is closely related to the prelude. Franz Xaver Anton Murschhauser (1663-1738), a pupil of Kerll, wrote the Octi-tonium novum organicum (1696) along the same pattern as Fischer's Blumen Strauss, with an extra cycle written for the Quinti toni irregularis. His other major work was the Prototypen longo-breve organicum (1703, 1707).

The toccatas of Johann Speth (1664-1719), found in his Ars magna consoni et dissoni (1693) resemble those of Froberger in length and structure, with a few similar to Pachelbel's nonsectional toccata. His Magnificats are simpler than those found in Kerll's Modulatio.

In 1743 the Musicalischer Zeit-Vertreib of Valentin Rathgeber (1682-1750) was published. This work contains 60 two-part and three-part song and dance pieces in the style galant. [2] The last ten pieces are Christmas pastorales.

Another volume of short works arranged in cycles is the 72 Versetl samt 12 Toccaten (1726) by Gottlieb Muffat (1690-1770), the son of Georg Muffat. Twelve short toccatas are written in 12 keys. Each toccata is followed by six brief fugues (versetl). None of these miniature pieces uses the pedal. Another major work by Gottlieb Muffat was the Componimenti musicali (1739). The Toccata I and Fugue was composed along the same general lines as those of his contemporary, Bach--two separate and well-developed pieces.

The Certamen aonium (1733) of Karlmann Kolb (1703-1765) is similar to the cyclic works of Muffat and Fischer. A praeludium is followed by three verses and a cadentia for each one of the eight church modes. These pieces frequently adopt cembalo figures. Georg Andreas Sorge (1703-1778), who was strongly influenced by Italian music, wrote a Toccata per ogni Modi.

BOOKS PUBLISHED BY LEADING COMPOSERS IN THE SOUTH GERMAN SCHOOL

Date	Composer-Author	Title
1645	Kindermann	Harmonia Organica
1664	Scherer	Intonationes Breves per octo octo tones
1664	Scherer	Operum musicorum secundum
1683	Pachelbel, J.	Musicalischen Sterbens-Gedancken
1686	Kerll	Modulatio organica
1690	Muffat, Georg	Apparatus musico-organisticus
1693	Pachelbel, J	Erster Theil etlicher Choräle
1693	Speth	Ars magna consoni et dissoni
1696	Murschhauser	Octi-Tonium novum Organicum
1699	Pachelbel, J.	Hexachordum Apollinis
1702	Fischer	Ariadne Musica Neo-Organoedum
n.d.	Fischer	Blumen Strauss
1703	Murschhauser	Prototypen longo-breve organicum
1726	Muffat, Gottlieb	72 Versetl samt 12 Toccaten
1733	Kolb	Certamen Aonium
1739	Muffat, Gottlieb	Componimente Musicali
1743	Rathgeber	Musicalischer Zeit-Vertreib

Many composers of this school wrote pieces which
were conceived for either harpsichord or organ.   Instruction
books, which included music for these instruments, came
under the strong and debilitating influence of operatic, secular, orchestral, concert, and dance music.   This weakened
the integrity and strong tradition of fine organ music and its
influence during the eighteenth and nineteenth centuries.

Notes

1.   The chaconne (ciacona) and passacaglia are two closely
     related, baroque, variation forms.   The terms were
     rather indiscriminately interchanged because, in addi-
     tion to their being variation forms, both forms are con-
     tinuous and are usually found in triple meter.   In gen-
     eral the passacaglia is based on an ostinato (repeated
     melody) which usually occurs in the bass, and the cha-
     conne is a continuous series of variations based upon
     recurring harmonies.
2.   Style galant is a term applied to the light, homophonic
     (accompanied melody) music of the rococo period in
     the eighteenth century which contrasts with the serious
     polyphonic music of the baroque period.   The emphasis
     changed from the purposeful to the amusing and en-
     couraged a general deterioration of musical quality.

Bibliography

Buszin, Walter E.   "Johann Pachelbel's Contribution to Pre-
     Bach Organ Literature," The Musical Heritage of the
     Lutheran Church.   St. Louis: Concordia Pub. House,
     1959; vol. V, p. 140.
Frotscher, Gotthold.   Geschichte des Orgelspiels und der
     Orgelkomposition.   Berlin: Merseberger Verlag,
     1959; vol. I, p. 470-559.
Kratzenstein, Marilou, "A Survey of Organ Literature and
     Editions: South Germany," Diapason (March 1972),
     p. 18-21.
Nolte, Ewald.   "The Magnificat Fugues of Johann Pachelbel:
     Alternation or Intonation," Journal of the American
     Musicological Society, vol. IX (1956), p. 19-24.
Sharp, G. B.   "J. J. Froberger: 1614-1667, a Link Be-
     tween the Renaissance and the Baroque," Musical
     Times, no. 1498, vol. 108 (December 1967), p. 1093.

7. MIDDLE GERMAN SCHOOL: 1600-1750

[The Historical Background chart found at the beginning of Chapter 5 is also appropriate for this chapter.]

Thuringia and Saxony lie in the heartland of Germany. Into this middle section of Germany flowed organ compositional features of style and form from both the North and South German Schools.

Generations of the Bach family lived in and around Thuringia. Religion and music were probably the two most important factors in the lives of this family, and several of the earlier branches of the Bach family tree who contributed to organ literature used the chorale melody as the basis of their compositions.

Both Johann Michael Bach (1648-1694) and Johann Bernhard Bach (1675-1749) wrote variations on chorale melodies. The Choraele, welche bey wärenden Gottes Dienst zum Praeambuliren by Johann Christoph Bach (1642-1703) contains 44 chorale settings. Johann Heinrich Bach (1615-1692) was probably the earliest member of the family whose organ compositions have come down to us. Both Friedrich Wilhelm Zachau (Zachow) (1663-1712), Handel's teacher in Halle, and Johann Gottfried Walther (1684-1748), a cousin of J. S. Bach, composed chorale variation cycles on Jesu, meine Freude ("Jesus, Joy and Treasure").

Organ chorales were frequently written for manuals alone (manualiter) in either two or three parts and had the melody in long notes in the uppermost part or in the pedal. Imitative settings might offer the chorale melodies of each phrase treated as points of imitation (chorale motet), as a chorale fughetta, or more extensively as a chorale fantasia.

One of the leading composers of the Middle German School was Michael Praetorius (1571-1621), a versatile musician whose life was founded in the Reformation movement and also one who was alert to new styles in music. Praetorius

MIDDLE GERMAN SCHOOL: 1600-1750

1600   1650   1700   1750

(1587 Scheidt, Samuel 1654)
1571 Praetorius, M. 1621
     1615 Bach, Johann Heinrich 1692
     1625 Ahle, Johann Rudolf 1673
          1640 Strungk, N. A. ----1700
          1642 Bach, J. Christoph 1703
          1645 Werckmeister, A. 1706
          1645/1650 Ritter, Christian ca. 1725
          1647 Alberti, J. F. -----1710
          1648 Bach, J. M. 1694
               1660 Kuhnau, Johann-----1722
               1663 Zachau, Friedrich 1712
               1666 Buttstett, Johann----1727
               1666 Vetter, Nicolaus-----1734
                    1675 Bach, Johann Bernhard----------1749
                    1678 Volckmar, Tobias--------------1754
                    ? Heuschkel, Johann ?
                    1679 Armsdorff, A. 1699
                    1679 Kauffmann, G. F. 1735
                    1684 Walther, Johann Gottfried 1748
                         1685 Bach, Johann Sebastian   1750

is famous for his treatise in three volumes on music, the
Syntagma musicum (1619). Volume One deals with a history
of church music, and Volume Two, De Organographia, is a
significant survey of instruments, with special emphasis on
organ building and information about organs existing at that
time. [1] Volume Three is concerned with the subject of music theory. Praetorius' compositions for organ include nine
organ hymns, one set of variations on Nun lob mein Seel den
Herren ("Now Praise the Lord, my Soul") (1609), and a collection of bicinia and tricinia (1610), which were based on
chorale melodies. The bicinia were written for two singers
or to be played on two manuals. In the tricinia the organist
plays the middle part with the two outer parts which are
sung, an unusual type of sacred music. Six of the organ
hymns are Latin (dating perhaps as early as 1607), and
three are German chorale settings (1609). The chorale fantasias on Ein' feste Burg ("A Mighty Fortress") and Wir
glauben all in einen Gott ("We All Believe in One True God")
treat all the chorale phrases as a point of imitation. It
was the publishing practice of the time of Praetorius to
print each of the voice lines separately in part books for
both choral and organ music. Each individual organist then
had to transcribe and arrange the parts for his own instrument and into the type of notation which suited him best.
The organ hymns of Praetorius were written some 15 years
before Scheidt's Tabulatura nova appeared in 1624. The set
of variations uses mechanical figurations similar to those of
the English virginalists. [2]

     Several styles of counterpoint were used by different
composers of the Middle German School in setting chorale
melodies. The counterpoint of Johann Friedrich Alberti
(1647-1710) was harmonically oriented. Ach Herr, mich
armen Sünder ("O Lord, My Grievous Sins") by Johann
Kuhnau (1660-1722) is another expressive example of the
same kind of counterpoint. Zachau's treatment of Komm,
heiliger Geist, Herre Gott ("Come, Holy Ghost, Lord God")
returned to the style of a ricercar. Georg Friedrich Kauffmann (1679-1735) introduced the use of solo instruments such
as the oboe, which played the unadorned chorale melody
while decorative and supporting contrapuntal lines (usually
in three parts) were played by the organist. Kauffmann's
large collection is entitled Harmonische Seelenlust (1733).

     Johann Gottfried Walther (1684-1748) was the author
of the first musical dictionary, the Musikalisches Lexicon
(1732). He composed at least 290 extant pieces for the

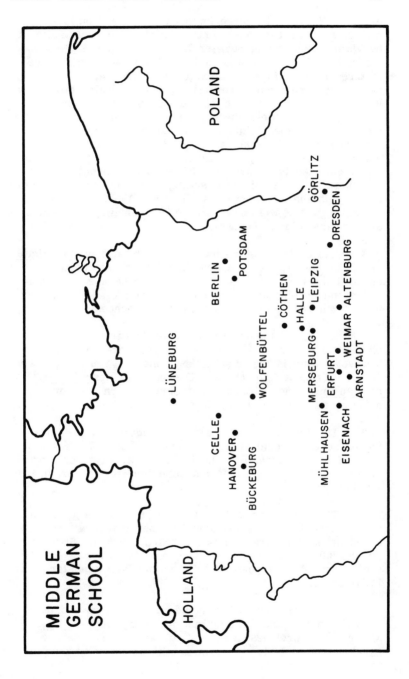

MIDDLE
GERMAN
SCHOOL

HOLLAND

POLAND

GÖRLITZ
DRESDEN

POTSDAM
BERLIN

CÖTHEN
HALLE
LEIPZIG
ALTENBURG

LÜNEBURG

WOLFENBÜTTEL
MERSEBURG
WEIMAR
ERFURT
ARNSTADT

CELLE
HANOVER
BÜCKEBURG
MÜHLHAUSEN
EISENACH

organ. Of these the large majority are based on chorale
melodies. The two most common types of chorale settings
by Walther are the manualiter three-part motet style with
the melody in the soprano part and the pedal chorale type
in three-part or four-part texture with the melody in the
pedal. The next most frequent types of chorale settings by
Walther are the four-part manualiter and canonic treatment
of the melody between the soprano and pedal parts. Walther
also employed the bicinium technique, pedaliter (an organ
composition which employs the pedal) motet, and a few
coloratura and melody chorale arrangements. All of these
last mentioned types are usually settings of one stanza of
the chorale. Most of these settings were intended for alternation with the congregation's singing. A small portion of
the settings was written to precede the singing of the chorale,
as a means of introducing the chorale to the congregation.

Walther's counterpoint included the use of Vorimitation
and Zwischenimitation devices, and free counterpoint which
outlined the harmony. He made a generous use of ornamentation and chromaticism for color. Walther also added notes
to final chords in order to strengthen cadences.

Not all of the 14 Walther chorale partitas were first
planned to be played in a series. Five were so planned,
however. One is the famous Jesu, meine Freude ("Jesus,
Joy and Treasure") partita. [3] One partita, Herr Jesu Christ,
dich zu uns wend, ("Lord Jesus Christ, Turn Thou to Us"),
contains as many as 13 settings of the tune.

The free works of Walther include a few preludes,
fugues, one concerto of five movements, and 14 transcriptions of violin concerti. [4] J. S. Bach may have received
inspiration for his concerto transcriptions for the organ from
Walther.

There are only a few free works by other composers
of this school which have survived other than those composed by Johann Sebastian Bach. Nicolaus Adam Strungk
(1640-1700) used the double-fugue form in rather lengthy
works, and the compositions of Andreas Werckmeister (1645-
1706) are canzonas.

Kuhnau's free works include two preludes and fugues
in B-flat major and G major and a lengthy Toccata in A
Major. The preludes are dignified, and the chords are
filled out irregularly, sometimes with as many as eight

chord tones sounding.   The fugues are plain and uneventful; they continued the same style which was set forth in the pre- ludes.   The toccata, however, is rich in variety of subject matter and contains an active pedal part in the north German manner.   The toccata is composed of many short sections of widely diversified character marked by strongly contrasting tempos.   The sections include an opening fantasia, a dotted- note figure which introduce a repeated chord section, a short chromatic interlude, a lengthy fugue in triple meter, and an Adagio recitative-fantasy.   The form of this work suggests the toccatas of Froberger.

Three free works by Zachau were called fugues. The first fugue is in two sections; the second part was constructed from a diminutive form of the same subject. The second "fugue" contains a Grave chordal section of 15 measures before the fugue actually begins.   The third fugue, which resembles the sectional works of Frescobaldi, con- tains themes which evolved from the same subject.

The next chapter covers the works of J. S. Bach, the giant of organ literature, who is the outstanding organ composer of the Middle German School.

Notes

1.   Praetorius wrote about performance practices as well. Other theorists who wrote about registration practices of the late baroque period were Werckmeister, Mat- theson, Adlung, and Marpurg.
2.   Lincoln B. Spiess, "Michael Praetorius Creuzburgensis: Church Musician and Scholar," The Musical Heritage of the Lutheran Church, St. Louis: Concordia Pub. House, 1959; vol. V, p. 69-72.
3.   Richard A. Carlson, "Walther's Life; Walther's Works," Organ Institute Quarterly, vol. V, no. 4 (Autumn 1955), p. 38.
4.   The composers whose concerti Walther transcribed for organ were Albinoni, Blamr, Corelli, Torelli, Gregori, Mangia, Meck, and Telemann.

Bibliography

Carlson, Richard A.   "Walther's Life; Walther's Works," Organ Institute Quarterly, vol. V, no. 4 (Autumn 1955), p. 29-39.

Frotscher, Gotthold. Geschichte des Orgelspiels und der
    Orgelkomposition. Berlin: Merseberger Verlag,
    1959; vol. I, p. 559-661.
Praetorius, Michael. Phantasy on the Chorale A Mighty
    Fortress Is Our God, Heinrich Fleischer, ed. Intro-
    duction. St. Louis: Concordia Pub. House, 1954.
Spiess, Lincoln B. "Michael Praetorius Creuzburgensis:
    Church Musician and Scholar," The Musical Heritage
    of the Lutheran Church. St. Louis: Concordia Pub.
    House, 1959; vol. V, p. 69-71.
Johann Gottfried Walther Orgelchoräle, Hermann Poppen, ed.
    Kassel, Germany: Bärenreiter Verlag, 1956; preface.

8. BACH: 1685-1750

The artistic contributions to organ literature made by J. S. Bach (1685-1750) are so great that the work of this musical genius seems to be the vortex of organ study. For convenience the works of Bach are usually grouped in three large periods: the earlier years and Weimar period (1695-1717), 22 years in all, during which a large portion of the organ works were written; the middle, Cöthen period (1717-1723), six years principally concerned with orchestral composition; and the third, Leipzig period of 27 years (1723-1750) spent in composition of choral works such as the cantatas and the passions, and also the mature organ works. In order to cover this large body of material easily and thoroughly the first major period will be divided into three parts with a brief study of the chorale-based works and the free compositions in each part. [1]

A brief summary of major contributions to types of chorale settings before Bach is appropriate at this point. Many of the technical possibilities and artistic foundations of the chorale prelude were established by Samuel Scheidt as early as 1624, for he indicated that the melody of the chorale could be placed in any voice part and that even double pedaling could be accomplished at the organ. Pachelbel contributed the chorale fugue, fugal treatment of phrases of the chorale melody. Böhm expressed the chorale melody in luxuriant coloratura settings. The chorale preludes of Buxtehude treat the chorale melody in both easy and complex ways: sometimes the melody is stated very simply with only slight ornamentation, and sometimes he expressed the chorale melody rhapsodically in fantasias. The mature Bach, inspired by the texts of the chorales, took the methods of treatment worked out by earlier masters and infused greater imagination and color into them, thus raising those same forms to even greater heights.

Dates	Chronology	Music Composed	Age
1685	born, March 21, Eisenach		
1694	mother died		
	Earlier Years and Weimar Period:		
1695	father died; lived with brother in Ohrdruf 5 years		10
1700-1702	singer, St. Michael's school, Lüneburg	Organ: chorale settings, partitas	15
1703	chamber orchestra musician to Duke Johann Ernst, Weimar, April to August		18
1703-1707	organist, New Church, Arnstadt; trip to hear Buxtehude, Lübeck, Oct. 1705 to Jan. 1706	Organ: chorale settings, small free works	18
1707	married Maria Barbara Bach		22
1707-1708	organist, St. Blasii, Mühlhausen, 1 year		22
1708-1717	court musician, organist for Duke Wilhelm Ernst, Weimar, 10 years	Organ music: larger free works; chorale settings; 6 concerti	23
1717		Orgelbüchlein	
	Cöthen Period:		
1717-1723	Kapellmeister to court of Prince Leopold, Cöthen, 6 years	Instrumental music	32
1721	married Anna Magdalena		36
1721	Wülcken		
	Leipzig Period:		
1723-1750	Cantor, St. Thomas and St. Nicholas Churches, Leipzig (27 years)	cantatas; passions; organ music: 6 trio sonatas; larger preludes, fugues	38
1739		Clavierübung, Part III pub.	54
1746-1747		Six Chorales (Schübler) pub.	60
1746-1747		Canonic Variations on Vom Himmel hoch pub.	60
1750	died, July 28, Leipzig		65

I. EARLIER YEARS AND WEIMAR PERIOD (1696-1717)

Ohrdruf, Lüneburg, Weimar (1696-1703)

This period of about nine years is represented by chorale-based works with one possible exception, the Pedal exercitum. In addition there are about 22 chorale settings which might have been written in this early period, although their authenticity is doubtful. One of these is the little trio on In dulci jubilo ("In Sweetest Joy") (BWV 751). Most of the chorale partitas were written in this period. Some of the variations might have been composed a few years later, however. The variations are for manuals alone; Keller suggests, therefore, that these were, for the most part, intended for the clavichord or Positiv in the home rather than for performance on a large organ in church. [2]

Arnstadt, Mühlhausen (1703-1708)

Bach composed his first free organ works while he was working in Arnstadt and Mühlhausen. In addition to two sets of chorale variations, there are ten chorale settings, including the A major fantasy on In dulci jubilo (BWV 729) and the trio setting of Nun freut euch ("Lift Up Your Hearts, Ye Christians All") (BWV 734), which assigns the cantus firmus to the pedal part.

The little Prelude and Fugue in C Minor (BWV 549) and Fugue in C Minor (BWV 575) show that they are early works because they contain such a diversity of material and lack unity. The Pastorale (BWV 590) exhibits more coherence in each one of its four sections. The virile "Gigue" Fugue in G Major (BWV 577) resembles the Buxtehude Fugue in C Major and contains similar rhythmic intensity. Three tempo indications in French (très vitement, grave, lentement) mark the three divisions of the Fantasia in G Major (BWV 572). The long alla breve middle section separates two toccata sections. These early free works omit use of the pedal for complete sections, or the pedal sustains long pedal points.

Weimar (1708-1717)

Most of the chorale settings found in the Kirnberger collection[3] suggest that they were written in the earlier part of the Weimar period, as does Bach's one setting of Ein' feste Burg ("A Mighty Fortress"). Five variations from the Sei gegrüsset ("Be Thou Welcome") partita might have been written during this period.

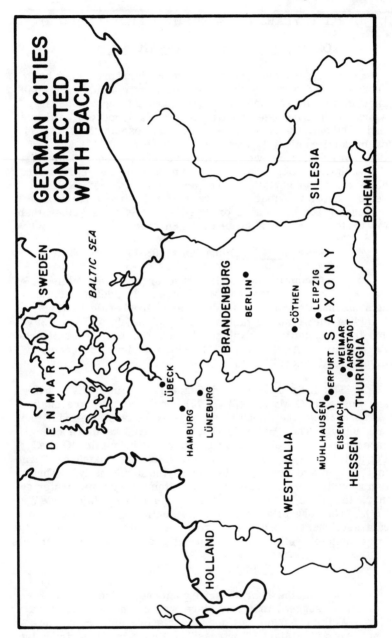

By far the most important chorale treatments at the end of the Weimar period are those found in the Orgelbüchlein (Little Organ Book). Bach knew chorales intimately and used them constantly. It is possible that the collection might have been planned for Wilhelm Friedemann Bach's instruction.

A LITTLE BOOK FOR THE ORGAN
wherein the beginning organist
may learn to perform chorales of every sort
and also acquire facility in the use of the pedal
which, in the chorales found herein, is
handled entirely obbligato.
To the most high God alone be praise,
For what herein is written for man's instruction.
Composed by
Johann Sebast. Bach,
pro tempore Capellmeister
to His Serene Highness the Prince
of Anhalt-Cöthen

Bach planned this book at Weimar. The design had been to include 164 settings of 161 melodies on 92 sheets of paper. The task was not completed, however, because he accepted, against the will of the Duke of Weimar, the court musician's office for Prince Leopold of Anhalt-Cöthen. It is quite possible that most of the Little Organ Book was written while Bach was detained by the Duke of Weimar and perhaps a few more chorales were added in Cöthen. Since his duties in Cöthen did not call for this type of music, he never finished the book. The order of these splendid miniatures was that found in the hymnbook of the Grand Duchy of Weimar authorized for use in 1713. The contents fall into two parts: chorales arranged according to the Christian year and chorales of faith and different aspects of the Christian life. Part one was to contain 60 settings, of which Bach finished 36; part two was to have 104 settings of which only 10 were completed. These 46 pieces are examples of the Orgelchoral, a setting of one stanza of the chorale, without interludes, incorporating rich harmonizations and colorful decoration; two settings of the same chorale, Liebster Jesu, wir sind hier ("Blessed Jesus, We Are Here") are included. Most of these pieces are of four-part texture with the melody in the soprano. Three are coloratura settings: Das alte Jahr ("The Old Year Now Has Passed Away"), O Mensch, bewein dein Sünde gross ("O Man, Bewail Thy Grievous Sin"), and Wenn wir in höchsten Nöthen sein ("When We Are Found in Greatest Need").

Bach repeatedly used certain motives which could be
named or associated with different words. The theory of
affections was manifested in choice of key, figuration types,
textures used, and harmonic progressions. Words such as
"joy," "weeping," "arising," and "sorrow" stimulated his
imagination. [4] As examples, many Christmas chorales have
descending motives symbolizing Christ's coming down from
heaven to earth, the incarnation. Herr Christ, der ein'ge
Gottes Sohn ("Lord Christ, Thou Only Son of God") (BWV
601) uses a trumpet or fanfare motive, which suggests Christ,
the King; in Durch Adams Fall ist ganz verderbt ("Through
Adam's Fall Was All Destroyed") (BWV 637) the fall is pic-
tured musically by a jagged, angular leap downward of a
diminished seventh. These individual motives were used to
unify the composition and to offer one central idea or concept for one particular setting.

At Weimar Bach was able to study many scores by
Italian composers such as Legrenzi, Corelli, Vivaldi, and
Frescobaldi. It was here in 1714 that he copied Frescobaldi's Fiori musicali, which probably inspired Bach's Canzona in D Minor (BWV 583). The Fugue in C Minor (BWV
574) adopts a theme by Legrenzi, and the Fugue in B Minor
(BWV 579) uses a melody by Corelli as a subject. In Weimar Bach also transcribed six concerti for organ: the first
and fourth on concertos by Prince Johann Ernst; the second,
third, and fifth by Vivaldi; the sixth has long been listed as
of doubtful authenticity, and has now been proved to be a
concerto by Vivaldi. The stirring first movement of the
second concerto in A minor and the beautiful siciliano of the
Concerto in D Minor are especially appealing.

The Allabreve in D Major (BWV 589) might also have
grown from Italian prototypes. Bach's interest in older composers' works and in established forms rather than in the
more commonplace music of his day led some contemporaries to consider him out-of-date. His music was the outgrowth of a fusion of several types of organ writing, Italian,
German, French, of forms new and old, derived from many
influences, and yet uniquely fashioned.

Keller suggests, with many good reasons, that the
Eight Little Preludes and Fugues (BWV 553-560), known to
most organ students at an early stage of development, could
have been written by Bach's favorite pupil, Johann Ludwig
Krebs. [5] This does not suggest that they are not worthy of
use as instruction pieces.

Several elements of the dual, combination form of prelude (fantasia or toccata) and fugue can be pointed out which recur to different degrees in the principal periods of Bach's organ composition. One element used frequently in the Weimar period is the virtuoso style drawn from the North German school and expressed in brilliant toccata passages for manuals, in the long, ornate pedal solos, in many different kinds of figuration, massive chords, dramatic pedal points, and in improvisational and recitative sections. Another element of prominence was drawn from Italian instrumental works, the concertato (orchestral) style, in which there is marked contrast between smaller and larger choruses or between solo (or thin) texture and chorus. Many of Bach's themes built on broken chords suggest the Italian violinistic style of Vivaldi and Corelli.

The "Cathedral" Prelude and Fugue in E Minor (BWV 533) is of small dimension but of serious and moving quality. The "Little" Fugue in G Minor (BWV 578), the subject of which is similar to a folksong, is another work of moderate length but one of great beauty and contrapuntal craftsmanship. The careful organization and flowing counterpoint of the fugue make it a delight to perform and to hear.

The Prelude and Fugue in D Major (BWV 532) is a combination of two virtuoso pieces of great vitality. An ascending D major scale in the pedal opens the prelude. After nine measures of fanfare a passage in F-sharp minor continues in French overture style and closes by employing tremolando in both hands. A 32d note flourish up the D major scale ends the first of three sections of the prelude. The Allabreve middle part contains 80 measures, which are composed of many sequences and possibilities for echo effects between manuals. A free-recitative Adagio, which incorporates double pedaling and rich harmonic progressions in five-part texture, closes the prelude. The head of the fugue subject is based on a germ-motive composed of the repetition of three notes, D, E, and F-sharp, in 16th-notes. The fugue concludes with a stunning solo pedal passage built upon the initial motive arranged sequentially.

The combination of a prelude stemming from the earlier part of the Weimar period (ca. 1709) and a fugue from the Leipzig period or reworking of earlier composed works is the Prelude and Fugue in A Minor (BWV 543). A variety of rhapsodic ideas make up the prelude. The fugue, however, is highly unified, with the architecture of the work

easily delineated by the performer if he changes to a lighter
registration for secondary sections unaccompanied by pedal
and then returns to the Great manual for the principal parts
of the fugue.   This work closes with a brilliant pedal cadenza
and virtuoso manual display, both characteristics which are
identified with the North German school.

The popular Toccata and Fugue in D Minor (BWV
565) contains a large number of opportunities for echo effects (a prominent characteristic of Baroque organ music)
in both the toccata and the fugue.   Pyramids of tone arising
from broken chords and striking tempo changes are some of
the easily noticed factors in the toccata.   The violinistic
fugue subject moves in 16th-notes stepwise downward from
A to D and returns upward while repeating the note A between each successive scale step.   After a striking deceptive
cadence in D minor, the final section of the fugue contains
a fiery recitative-fantasy which leads to a dignified close in
a short Adagio section.

The great Toccata, Adagio, and Fugue in C Major
(BWV 564) is a magnificent composition of imposing grandeur
and balanced construction.   The toccata offers opportunities
for echo effects in both the manual and pedal parts.   A long
pedal cadenza follows the brilliant, virtuoso first section on
the manuals.   After the introductory section comes a closely
unified section of much rhythmic vitality.   One can change
manuals to underline the three figurational thematic ideas,
although this treatment might sound complex and confusing
to the listener;   to play the entire section on one manual
lends a sense of unity to the whole.   The Adagio in A minor
is a highly embellished aria, which is accompanied by piz-
zicato pedal and neutral harmonic background.   A brief
interlude of rich harmonies and seven-part texture, which
resembles the old Italian toccata di durezze e ligature, mod-
ulates from A minor to C major for the stunning fugue.   The
fugue subject is in four segments, which are separated by
rests.   The first three segments are constructed from approximately the same terse, rhythmic, violinistic motive,
but the second and third segments are placed on successively
higher tonal levels.   The sequence leads to a 16th-note
figure built upon a stepwise melody which rises and falls
from a repeated D.   The return to the principal manual for
the closing section brings a sharp and startling finish on a
brief eighth-note chord.   The concertato style is especially
noticeable in this Toccata, Adagio and Fugue.

The last of the larger preludes and fugues of the
Weimar period is the Prelude and Fugue in A Major (BWV
536).   The prelude is a short, light, sparkling piece, and
the fugue is sober and contains thematic material of a more
pastoral nature than that found in the prelude.

The exuberant toccata and the restrained alla breve
fugue in F major (BWV 540) make a strongly contrasting
combination.   Although the canonic writing over a pedal
point might suggest the use of two manuals at the beginning
of the toccata, the addition of a third voice soon afterwards
nullifies that type of treatment.   Brilliant pedal cadenzas
follow the two canonic sections.   The second pedal solo section ascends to f^1 on the pedal board, a pedal note not found
on many pedal divisions of that era.   The balance of the
438-measure long toccata is based on a new theme drawn
from an ascending arpeggiated figure on a triad which is
followed by chords on the second and third beats.   Neapolitan
sixth chords bring a surprise element to the harmony several
times.   The fugue in ricercar style is dignified, and Bach's
contrapuntal mastery is constantly exhibited in the double
fugue.

Keller places the great C minor Prelude and Fugue
(BWV 546) in the Leipzig period,[6] although for the fugue
Schmieder suggests the late Weimar period and Leipzig for
the prelude. [7]   The prelude has a number of different components: the double-chorus, the "sighing motive," triplets
along the scale line, and a regular use of the Neapolitan
sixth chord, all organized into a grand whole.   Although the
fugue might seem to suggest that it is a double-fugue, it
does not actually become one.

A theme which was extracted from a suite by Raison
is raised to much greater heights than in its original form
by the artistry of Bach in the Passacaglia in C Minor (BWV
582).   The theme is eight measures long and is followed by
20 variations and the Thema fugatum, which has two counter-
subjects.   Even though the theme is at times broken into
two voice parts (or even one), and taken from the pedal and
put into other voices, it is always present.   Although some
manuscripts indicate that this work was composed for "cembalo ossia organo," the Passacaglia could not possibly reach
such a wonderful variety of expression on a harpsichord as
on the organ.   Toward the end of the fugue there is a dramatic use of the Neapolitan sixth chord before the fugue is
closed.

It is interesting to study the stop list of the organ
Bach had at his disposal while he worked in Weimar.

Weimar, Germany, Schlosskirche.
Built by Ludwig Compenius, 1658;
rebuilt by Heinrich Nicolaus Trebs, 1719-1720.

Hauptwerk	Positiv	Pedal
Quintatön 16'	Prinzipal 8'	Gros untersatz 32'
Prinzipal 8'	Viola di gamba 8'	Sub-bass 16'
Gemshorn 8'	Gedackt 8'	Violon bass 16'
Gedackt 8'	Kleingedackt 4'	Prinzipal bass 8'
Octave 4'	Octave 4'	Posaune bass 16'
Quintatön 4'	Waldflöte 2'	Trompeten 8'
Mixtur VI	Sesquialtera II	Cornetten bass 4'
Cymbel III	Trompeta 8'	
Glockenspiel	Tremulant	
Tremulant		

Hauptwerk / Pedal coupler; Positiv / Hauptwerk coupler;
(upper manual)   (lower manual)
Cymbelstern

Many twentieth-century organs have been built in imitation of the art of Baroque organ builders, which reached
its zenith about the turn of the eighteenth century. The
Baroque organ is known for its brilliance and clarity, its
homogeneous ensemble, and facilities for emphasizing one
voice and accompanying with less aggressive sounds. The
two outstanding organ builders of the Baroque period were
Arp Schnitger (1648-1720), working in northern Germany and
the Netherlands, and Gottfried Silbermann (1683-1753), who
built organs in eastern France and central Germany.

II. CÖTHEN (1717-1723)

One of the most celebrated works of Bach, the Fantasia and Fugue in G Minor, is associated with Bach's audi-
tion for the organist's position at St. Jakobi Church in Hamburg. This instrument, one of Schnitger's finest organs,
was "rediscovered" during the third decade of the twentieth
century and extolled as an example of the ideal of the organ
building art near the turn of the eighteenth century. The
specifications are given on the next page.

Hamburg, Germany, St. Jakobi Kirche.
Built by Arp Schnitger, 1688-1692

Hauptwerk	Oberwerk
Prinzipal 16'	Prinzipal 8'
Quintatön 16'	Holzflöte 8'
Oktave 8'	Rohrflöte 8'
Spitzflöte 8'	Oktave 4'
Gedackt 8'	Spitzflöte 4'
Oktave 4'	Nasat 3'
Rohrflöte 4'	Oktave 2'
Superoktave 2'	Gemshorn 2'
Flachflöte 2'	Scharff IV-VI
Rauschpfeife III	Cymbel III
Mixtur VI-VIII	Trompete 8'
Trompete 16'	Vox humana 8'
	Trompete 4'

Rückpositiv

Brustwerk

Prinzipal 8'	
Gedackt 8'	Holzprinzipal 8'
Quintatön 8'	Oktave 4'
Oktave 4'	Hohlflöte 4'
Blockflöte 4'	Waldflöte 2'
Nasat 3'	Sesquialter II
Oktave 2'	Scharff IV-VI
Sifflöte 1 1/2'	Dulcian 8'
Sesquialter II	Trechterregal 8'
Scharff IV-VI	
Dulcian 16'	
Bärpfeife 8'	
Schalmei 4'	

Pedal

Prinzipal 32'	Rauschpfeife III
Oktave 16'	Posaune 32'
Subbass 16'	Dulcian 16'
Oktave 8'	Trompete 8'
Oktave 4'	Trompete 4'
Nachthorn 2'	Cornett 2'
Mixtur VI-VIII	

The Fantasia and Fugue in G Minor (BWV 542) is an astounding work of great proportion in its development of

content, beauty of form and order, and contrapuntal craftsmanship.   The fantasia twice balances the fugato sections
with improvisational recitatives.   The harmonic intensity,
richness, and chromatic growth in the manual parts over the
long descending Phrygian mode in the pedal is especially effective.   The fugue is based on a Dutch folksong and follows
closely the general contour of the song.   A new motive of
only four eighth-notes receives a large share of development,
which adds more interest and excitement when the new motive
is used with the principal subject.

III.   LEIPZIG (1723-1750)

When Bach left Weimar and went to Cöthen, he became a court musician, and his principal duties were to provide orchestral music.   In 1723 he became the Cantor at the
Thomaskirche in Leipzig, where his chief responsibilities
were to conduct, to compose, and to teach in the school;
an organist played under Bach's supervision, although Bach
probably played from time to time.   These facts do not suggest, however, that in the two latter periods of his life Bach
was no longer interested in the instrument, as some of his
greatest organ compositions prove.

It is interesting to study the Lutheran service in
which Bach functioned.   From the material given by Schweitzer the following annotated list of items in the order of services has been established:[8]

The service began at 7 a. m. and lasted from three to four
hours.

        Organ prelude
        Motet
        Introit
        Kyrie, sung once in German: Kyrie, Gott Vater in
            Ewigkeit; sung once in Latin: Kyrie eleison.
        Possible preludizing on the chorale Allein Gott ("To
            God Alone Be Highest Praise")
        Gloria intoned from altar, answered by choir with
            et in terra pax or by congregation with German
            Gloria in chorale form: Allein Gott
        Collect
        Epistle read or sung in old psalmody
        Organist preludized on congregational hymn
        Congregational hymn

Gospel (chanted by priest)
Credo (intoned by priest)
Organist preludized for tuning of instruments
Cantata sung by choir which lasted on the average of
    20 minutes
Hymn--German Credo: <u>Wir glauben all</u> ("We All
    Believe in One True God")
Sermon (lasted exactly one hour, from 8 to 9 a.m.)
Prayer
Blessing
Congregational hymn
Communion celebration during which German hymns
    were sung or preludizing and improvising by the
    organist took place.

Vespers at St. Thomas, Leipzig:[9]
    (Service began at 1:15 p.m.)
    Various prayers and hymns
    Sermon (usually on the Epistle)
    German Magnificat
    Hymn: <u>Nun danket alle Gott</u> ("Now Thank We All
        Our God")

The stop list below is that of the organ in the Thomaskirche at the time of Bach's tenure.

Leipzig, Germany, Thomaskirche.
Built in 1489;
rebuilt by Johann Scheibe, 1721-1722.

Hauptwerk (middle manual)	Rückpositiv (lowest manual)
Prinzipal 16'	Prinzipal 8'
Prinzipal 8'	Gedackt 8'
Quintadena 16'	Quintadena 8'
Octava 4'	Gedackt 4'
Quinta 3' (2 2/3')	Querflöte 4'
Super octava 2'	Violin 2'
Spiel-pfeife 8'	Rauschquinte II
Sesquialtera II	Mixtur IV
Mixtur VII-X	Spitzflöte 4'
	Schallflöte 1'
Brustwerk (uppermost manual)	Krumbhorn 16'
	Trommet 8'

Grossgedackt 8'   Pedal
Prinzipal 4'
Nachthorn 4'   Sub-bass 16'
Nasat 3' (2 2/3')   Posaunenbass 16'
Gemshorn 2'   Trommetenbass 8'
Zimbel II   Schallmeyenbass 4'
Sesquialtera II   Cornet 3'
Regal 8'
Geigend regal 4'

Tremulant; Vogelsang; Cymbelstern

The chorale-based organ works of Bach from the
Leipzig period include the Clavierübung, Part III (Keyboard
Practice), the six "Schübler" chorales, the Great Eighteen
chorales, and the Canonic variations on Vom Himmel hoch
("From Heaven Above to Earth I Come") (BWV 769), which
he wrote in connection with his joining the Mizler Society
for Musical Sciences in 1747.   In the canonic variations
Bach's contrapuntal ability is exhibited by his ingenious inter-
twining of all four lines of the chorale, presenting them simultaneously at the end of the fifth variation.   His unsur-
passed understanding of contrapuntal possibilities is shown
in the Art of the Fugue and the Musical Offering.

Clavierübung, Part III

The Clavierübung, Part III (BWV 669-689), was en-
graved and published in 1739.   The title page reads:

Third Part
of the
KEYBOARD PRACTICE
composed
of
several preludes
on the
Catechism and other hymns
for the organ
for music lovers
and especially for connoisseurs
of such work
composed by
JOHANN SEBASTIAN BACH
Royal Polish and Electoral Saxon
Court Composer, Capellmeister and

Director Chori Musici in Leipzig
Published by the author

This collection is sometimes called the Catechism
because of the larger chorale (pedaliter, "with pedal") settings and the smaller (manualiter, "manual alone") settings,
which might be likened to the longer and shorter Lutheran
Catechisms and because of Bach's choice of chorales representing such subjects as the Ten Commandments, the Creed,
Prayer, Baptism, Holy Communion, and Penitence. The
Clavierübung, Part III, is sometimes referred to as the organ Mass because of the settings of chorales which corre-
spond to the Lutheran Mass: the three-fold Kyrie, the Lutheran Gloria (Allein Gott in der Höh' sei Ehr--"To God
Alone be Highest Praise"), the Ten Commandments (Dies
sind die heiligen zehn Gebot--"These Are the Holy Ten Commandments"), and the Lutheran Credo (Wir glauben all' in
einen Gott--"We All Believe in One True God"). Bach's
grand design for the collection does suggest these conceptions. He also obviously hoped that it would sell well and
appeal to keyboard players other than organists. This might
be the reason he included the four duettos, which have no
liturgical significance and no connection with chorales; the
duettos strongly suggest performance on stringed keyboard
instruments. The manualiter chorale settings could also be
performed on keyboard instruments other than the organ.

The Clavierübung, Part III, offers two settings of nine
chorales and three arrangements of Allein Gott, perhaps in
honor of the three persons of the Trinity, framed by the
pieces in E-flat major, the prelude at the beginning and the
fugue at the end of the entire work. Most of the manualiter
settings are smaller compositions, which are built on only
the initial chorale phrase melody. A manualiter fugue is
based on Jesus Christus, unser Heiland ("Jesus Christ, Our
Saviour"), and a complete arrangement of one stanza of
Vater unser ("Our Father, Who in Heaven Art") is given a
beautiful setting for one manual. One admires the intense
rhythmic vigor imparted to the shorter setting of Dies sind
die heiligen zehn Gebot ("These Are the Holy Ten Commandments") and the fughetta in A major on Allein Gott ("To God
Alone be Highest Praise").

In the larger chorale settings the first ones associated
with the three persons of the Trinity are indeed profound.
Flowing counterpoint makes the large trio on Allein Gott an

absorbing piece, alternating phrases of the chorale melody
between the hands and ending with the final phrase sounded
first by the pedal and then by the right hand.   The large
setting of Dies sind die heiligen zehn Gebot presents the
chorale in canon for the left hand.   The fugue on Wir glauben
all' an einen Gott is called the "Giant" fugue because of the
sturdy strides made by the ascending broken thirds in the
pedal part, which give the work breadth and strength.   The
complex rhythms of the large work based on Vater unser
make it difficult to understand and to perform.

Aus tiefer Not ("Out of the Depths") is a work in six
voice parts.   Each chorale phrase is introduced imitatively
in most of the voice parts.   The piece was written for double
pedal;   the right foot has the melody of the chorale in augmentation.   The cantus firmus of the Communion hymn Jesus
Christus, unser Heiland ("Jesus Christ, Our Saviour") is in
the pedal part;   the other two parts are played on separate
manuals in intricate and technically demanding counterpoint.
This counterpoint begins with a broken tenth contracting to
a broken octave and then to a broken sixth, all in eighth-
notes;   this same figure is repeated three more times, each
time one step higher.   A 16th-note continuation of the line
enters soon thereafter to become a foil to the bounding
eighth-notes in the other hand.

The three principal themes of the Prelude in E-flat
might also be considered symbolic of the Trinity, as have
the three subjects of the E-flat fugue.   (The key signature
also contains three flats.)   The structure of the prelude can
be shown by the graph below.   The sections composed of
primary thematic material is indicated by the straight line.
Secondary thematic material is indicated by dotted lines and
tertiary thematic material is shown by x's.   The numbers on
the lines give the exact measure numbers in the prelude, and
the numbers in parenthesis denote the number of measures
in the section.[10]

```
1--32 33--50 51--70 71--98 99--111 112--129 130--174 175--205

_____ ...... _____ xxxxxx _____ ........ xxxxxxxx _____
 (32)   (18)   (20)   (28)   (13)    (18)     (45)     (31)
```

By using three different planes of tone quality the performer
can make a distinction between the sections so that the form

can be easily comprehended by the attentive listener.

The three expositions of the Fugue in E-flat Major
have been said to be symbolic of the three persons of the
Trinity. [11] The first subject is combined with the second
subject in the middle section, and all three themes are combined in the final section.

SIX CHORALES
of several types
to be played
on an
Organ
with two manuals and pedal
composed by
Johann Sebastian Bach
Royal Polish and Electoral Saxon Court Composer
Capellmeister and Director. Chor. Mus. Lips.
Published by Joh. Georg Schübler
at Zella in the Thuringian Forest
to be purchased in Leipzig from the Capellmeister Bach,
from his Sons in Berlin and Halle,
and from the publisher in Zella

The Six Chorales (BWV 645-650), often called the
"Schübler" Chorales, were published after 1745 by Georg
Schübler of Zella. [12] Each one of the six is a trio arrangement made by Bach of vocal movements from his own cantatas. All six pieces are for two manuals and pedal, in
which the melodies stand out distinctly from the other parts.
Wachet auf, ruft uns die Stimme ("Wake, Awake, a Voice Is
Calling") is a transcription of the tenor solo of Cantata 140.
In Wo soll ich fliehen hin ("O Whither Shall I Flee") the
frantic soul in search of refuge is musically depicted by a
nervous contrapuntal motive set against the melody in the
alto range played by a 4' pedal; the cantata from which this
movement was taken has been lost. The third chorale, Wer
nur den lieben Gott lässt walten ("If Thou but Suffer God to
Guide Thee"), is transcribed from a duet for soprano, alto,
and basso continuo from Cantata 93; the decorative counterpoint was drawn from the initial chorale phrase. The fourth
Schübler chorale is based on the German chorale arrangement of the chant tone to which the Magnificat was often sung
(Tonus Peregrinus). Meine Seele erhebt den Herren ("My
Soul Doth Magnify the Lord") is introduced by a pedal solo
passage, which is repeated at the end (ritornello). The com-

position Bach arranged is found in his Cantato 10, where it
was a duet for alto and tenor.   The counterpoint of Ach
bleib bei uns ("Abide with Us") contains large leaps over a
wide range, and sounds least appropriate of all the six chorales to the organ.   Bach's original movement was for soprano, violoncello piccolo, and basso continuo, and came
from Cantata 6.   Kommst du nun ("Praise to the Lord") is
a delightful piece which Bach transcribed from the alto solo
with violin obbligato and basso continuo from Cantata 137.
The cantus firmus is played on a 4' pedal stop with the melody in the alto range.

Eighteen Chorales

        In 1878 Wilhelm Rust assigned this title to a group of
larger chorales when he was preparing Volume XXV of the
Bach-Gesellschaft.   He patterned the title after that of the
Six Chorales.   These larger chorales have no relationship
to each other, liturgical or otherwise.   They were probably
sketched in the Weimar period and rewritten in Leipzig;   indeed, Bach worked on them shortly before his death.   Bach
dictated the last three chorale preludes to his son-in-law,
Altnikol.   The final work Bach composed was the final chorale in the collection, Vor deinen Tron tret' ich ("Before Thy
Throne I Now Appear"), because he realized that his life
was rapidly drawing to a close.   The text, which is usually
associated with this melody, is Wenn wir in höchsten Nöten
sein ("When We Are Found in Deepest Need").

        The two chorales found at the beginning of the great
Eighteen are settings of Komm, heiliger Geist, Herre Gott
("Come, Holy Ghost, Lord God").   The first setting is a
lengthy fantasia with the cantus firmus in the pedal;   the
second has the embellished melody on a separate manual.
An Wasserflüssen Babylon ("By the Waters of Babylon"), a
poetic arrangement of Psalm 137, gives the tender ornamented melody to the tenor part on a separate manual.   One
of the favorite chorales from this set is the beautiful coloratura setting of Schmücke dich, o liebe Seele ("Deck Thyself,
My Soul, with Gladness").   Trio writing at its purest is
found in Herr Jesu Christ, dich zu uns wend' ("Lord Jesus
Christ, Turn Thou to Us").   Von Gott will ich nicht lassen
("From God I Ne'er Will Turn Me") assigns the melody to a
4' stop in the pedal.   The rhythmic motive used in this piece
is called the "joy" motive, two 32d-notes followed by a 16th-
note.   One of the most exquisite pieces in all organ literature is the coloratura treatment of Nun komm der Heiden

Heiland ("Now Comes the Saviour of the Gentiles"); the ornate soprano melody spins above the moving pedal and sedate-
ly flowing alto and tenor parts. Trio and organo pleno settings of the same melody follow as numbers ten and 11 in the
series. An embellished setting, an arrangement with the
melody in the tenor disguised, and a splendid trio on Allein
Gott ("To God Alone be Highest Praise") are the next three
chorales. Two settings of Jesus Christus, unser Heiland
("Jesus Christ, Our Saviour") are numbers 15 and 16; the
first has the cantus firmus in the pedal, and the second was
written for manuals alone. The 17th chorale is an organo
pleno arrangement of Komm, Gott Schöpfer, heiliger Geist
("Come, Creator-God and Holy Ghost"), the first eight measures of which are exactly the same as the Orgelbüchlein
setting of the chorale. The composition continues in flowing
16ths and discards the off-beat pedal and rhythmic pattern of
the earlier setting.

Leipzig Period: Free Works

Forkel, Bach's first biographer, states that Bach
wrote the six sonatas for two manuals and pedal for his
eldest son, Wilhelm Friedemann.[13] They were probably
conceived for stringed keyboard instruments with pedals.
The chamber music character of the writing seems to support this thesis. The sonatas, nevertheless, are admirably
suited to the organ. In general they follow the Italian violin
concerto or the Italian instrumental trio sonata form: fast,
slow, fast. All of the movements, with the one exception of
the last movement of the first sonata, were given tempo
markings by Bach. Schweitzer has remarked that scarcely
any difficulty of old or modern organ music has not been
met in the sonatas if one has studied them thoroughly.[14] A
wide variety of moods is presented here: restrained, cheery,
graceful, lofty, lyric, vigorous, pastoral, and lustrous.

The Prelude and Fugue in G Major (BWV 541) is a
vivacious and joyous combination of two pieces which are
closely related in quality, consistent in spirit and in technical demand.

Toward the close of the Weimar period and on into
the Leipzig period Bach's preludes and fugues became more
independent of each other. Each part became longer, and
both parts tended to treat the subject material contrapuntally
throughout and concentrated on one or two motives in a consistent manner. A significant number of the later fugues

can be classified in the ricercar type in which the subjects
are composed of notes of longer duration and much less
marked rhythm than the subjects of earlier fugues.   Virtuoso
pedal passages and concertato treatment does recur from time
to time in later preludes and fugues but to a much smaller
degree than that found in the Weimar period.

        The so-called "Dorian" Toccata and Fugue in D Minor
(BWV 538) is a brilliant work, one of the few Bach organ
works in which manual changes were indicated by Bach himself.   This composition generates a vitality which continues
throughout the piece.   The subject of the fugue is much more
serious in nature than the thematic material of the toccata.
The subject ascends from D to the D an octave higher and
then descends to its starting point, frequently using syncopation.

        The Prelude and Fugue in E Minor (BWV 548) is a
great work in which the harmonic tension produced by suspensions is similar to that found in the Prelude and Fugue
in B Minor.   The fugue subject grows in everwidening broken
intervals to the distance of an octave, a fact which has
caused the fugue to be given the programmatic title of the
"Wedge" fugue.   Bach used the simple sequence and scale
in such a melodic fashion that one is scarcely aware of the
musical materials from which these mature pieces were
fashioned.   One characteristic frequently employed in the
pedal part of these later works is the 16th-note progression
downward with a step back on alternating notes.

        The Prelude and Fugue in B Minor (BWV 544) is
ornate, symmetrical, melodic, and majestic.   The performer
must allow the piece to be an expressive organo pleno.
Manual changes can clarify the structure of the prelude as
shown by the graph below.   The sections composed of primary thematic material is indicated by straight lines.   The
numbers in parentheses denote the number of measures in
each section, and the numbers on the lines give the exact
measure numbers. [15]

```
1----16        27-----42        50----72           78------85
_____ ......_____ ......_____ ........._____
         17--26            43--49            73-----78
  (16)   (10)    (16)      (7)      (23)     (5 1/2)   (7 1/2)
```

        The fugue has an unassuming subject, but it is beauti-
fully and naturally developed.   When the new theme enters

in measure 59, it is treated with so much prominence that
it might be considered a new countersubject. The architecture of the fugue is easily understood, and the episodes of
secondary subject matter, which do not call for pedal, might
suggest performance on a different manual.

The Prelude and Fugue in C Major (BWV 547) is
dated about 1744. Both the prelude and fugue are lyric in
character. The prelude is written in $\frac{9}{8}$ time and the fugue
in common meter. Each measure of the prelude is directly
related to one of four distinct ideas which are found in the
soprano part of the first four measures. The pedal part of
the fugue enters only 24 measures before the end of the 72-
measure composition, and there are over 50 appearances of
the fugue subject.

Notes

1. The order followed here corresponds with the chronology
    of works prepared by Wolfgang Schmieder in his The-
    matisch-systematisches Verzeichnis der Werke Joh.
    Seb. Bachs, Leipzig: Breitkopf und Härtel, 1950. The
    abbreviation BWV refers to a rearrangement of words
    in the title of this same index: Bachs Werke Verzeich-
    nis. The abbreviation S. refers to Schmieder and is
    sometimes used instead of BWV.
2. Hermann Keller, The Organ Works of Bach, translated
    by Helen Hewitt, New York: C. F. Peters Corp. ,
    1967; p. 176.
3. Johann Philipp Kirnberger's Collection consists of 24
    chorale settings which he copied by J. S. Bach and a
    few other composers such as Walther, J. L. Krebs,
    and Bernhard Bach. Kirnberger (1721-1783) was a
    pupil of Bach in 1749. The collection is listed in the
    Schmieder catalog as numbers 609 through 713.
4. Albert Schweitzer, J. S. Bach, London: Adam and
    Charles Black, 1923 (reprint, 1947); vol. II, p. 25-
    74. See also F. E. Kirby, A Short History of Key-
    board Music. New York: Free Press, 1966; p. 116-
    117.
5. Hermann Keller, The Organ Works of Bach, translated
    by Helen Hewitt, New York: C. F. Peters Corp. ,
    1967; p. 72.
6. Keller, op. cit. , p. 148.
7. Schmieder, op. cit. , p. 421.
8. Albert Schweitzer, op. cit. , vol. I, p. 126-129.

9. Schweitzer, op. cit., vol. I, p. 128.
10. Based on the analysis found in Keller, op. cit., p. 160.
11. The English hymntune St. Anne, first published in 1708,
    has been attributed to William Croft (1678-1727), who
    was organist of St. Anne's Church, Soho, London.
    The first subject of the E-flat Fugue has the same
    melody as the St. Anne hymntune, which is the ex-
    planation of why the E-flat Fugue is often called the
    "St. Anne" fugue. The similarity is merely coinci-
    dental because it is highly unlikely that Bach ever
    saw this particular English hymntune or that Bach
    was familiar with it. This same melody can also be
    found as the subject to Buxtehude's fugue in E major
    and in two different movements of Handel's O Praise
    the Lord with One Consent, a Chandos anthem.
12. Schübler is listed as one of the pupils of Bach in Hans
    Löffler, "Die Schüler Joh. Seb. Bachs," Bach-
    Jahrbuch, Evangelische Verlaganstalt Berlin, vol. 40
    (1953), p. 6, 10.
13. Keller, op. cit., p. 130.
14. Schweitzer is quoted in Keller, op. cit., p. 134.
15. Based on the analysis given in Keller, op. cit., p. 158.

Bibliography

Aldrich, Putnam. "On the Interpretation of Bach's Trills,"
    Musical Quarterly, vol. XLIX (1963), p. 289-310.
_____. Ornamentation in J. S. Bach's Organ Works.
    New York: Coleman-Ross Co., 1950.
Bodky, Erwin. The Interpretation of Bach's Keyboard Works.
    Cambridge, Mass.: Harvard University Press, 1960.
Clough, F. F., and G. F. Cuming. "Bach's Organ Works
    in BWV Numbering," Eighth Music Book. London:
    Hinrichsen Edition Ltd., 1959; p. 193-206.
David, Hans T., and Arthur Mendal. The Bach Reader.
    New York: W. W. Norton and Co., 1945.
Dickinson, A. E. The Art of J. S. Bach. London: Hin-
    richsen Edition Ltd., 1950; p. 67-93.
_____. Bach's Fugal Works. London: Isaac Pitman and
    Sons, 1956.
Donington, Robert. Tempo and Rhythm in Bach's Organ
    Music. London: Hinrichsen Edition Ltd., 1961.
Dufourcq, Norbert. J. S. Bach: Le Maître de l'Orgue.
    Paris: Librairie Floury, 1948.
Emery, Walter. Bach's Ornaments. London: Novello and
    Co., 1953.

_____. "On the Registration of Bach's Organ Preludes
and Fugues," Musical Times, No. 1432, vol. 103
(June 1962), p. 396; no. 1433, vol. 103 (July 1962),
p. 467.
Frotscher, Gotthold. Geschichte des Orgelspiels und der
Orgelkomposition. Berlin: Merseberger Verlag,
1959; vol. II, p. 849-969.
Geiringer, Karl. Johann Sebastian Bach--the Culmination of
an Era. New York: Oxford University Press, 1966.
Grace, Harvey. The Organ Works of Bach. London: Novel-
lo and Co. , 1922.
Heiller, Anton. "Chorales of the Clavierübung, Part 3,"
The Diapason (October 1962), p. 8.
Hinrichsen, Max, ed. Eighth Music Book. London: Hin-
richsen Edition Ltd. , 1956.
Kasling, Kim R. "Some Editorial, Formal and Symbolic
Aspects of J. S. Bach's Canonic Variations on 'Vom
Himmel hoch da komm ich her'," Diapason, Pt 1
(May 1971), p. 18; Pt 2 (June 1971), p. 16-17;
Pt 3 (July 1971), p. 20-21; and Conclusion (August
1971), p. 20-21.
Keller, Hermann. Die Orgelwerke Bachs: Ein Beitrag zu
ihrer Geschichte, Form, Deutung und Wiedergabe.
Leipzig: C. F. Peters, 1948 (English ed. , The
Organ Works of Bach, translated by Helen Hewitt,
New York: C. F. Peters Corp. , 1967).
Klotz, Hans. "Bachs Orgeln und seine Orgelmusik," Die
Musikforschung, vol. II (1950), p. 189-203.
Lawry, Eleanor. "Symbolism as Shown in Chorale Preludes
of Bach Is Studied," The Diapason (August 1949),
p. 6.
Löffler, Hans. "Die Schüler Joh. Seb. Bachs," Bach-
Jahrbuch in Auftrage der neuen Bachgesellschaft,
Alfred Dürr and Werner Neumann, eds. Berlin:
Evangelische Verlaganstalt, 1953; vol. XL, p. 5.
Moeser, James C. "Symbolism in J. S. Bach's Orgelbuch-
lein," The American Organist, vol. 47, no. 11 (No-
vember 1964), p. 14-20; vol. 47, no. 12 (December
1964), p. 14-22; vol. 48 (January 1965), p. 12-16;
(February 1965), p. 22-25; (March 1965), p. 16-22;
(April 1965), p. 14-21; (May 1965), p. 11-14;
(June 1965), p. 12-17; and (July 1965), p. 11-13.
Pirro, André. L'Orgue de J. S. Bach. Paris: Librairie
Fischbacher, 1897.
Reinburg, Peggy Kelley. "Affektenlehre of the Baroque Era
and Their Application in the Works of Johann Sebas-
tian Bach (Specifically in the Schübler Chorales),"

American Organist (June 1968), p. 15.

Richards, Ruthann. "The Orgelbüchlein--Its History and
    Cantus Firmus Treatment," _Diapason_ (October 1969),
    p. 24-25.

Riedel, Johannes. _The Lutheran Chorale: Its Basic Tradi-
    tions_. Minneapolis: Augsburg Pub. House, 1967.

Schmieder, Wolfgang. _Thematisch-systematisches Verzeich-
    nis der musikalischen Werke von Johann Sebastian
    Bach_. Leipzig: Breitkopf und Härtel, 1950.

Schweitzer, Albert. _J. S. Bach, le Musicien-Poète_. Leip-
    zig: 1905 (English ed., _J. S. Bach_, translated by
    Ernest Newman, 2 vols., London: Breitkopf und
    Härtel, 1911; reprint, London: Adam and Charles
    Black, 1947.

Spitta, Philipp. _Johann Sebastian Bach_, 2 vols. Leipzig:
    1873-1880 (English ed., _Johann Sebastian Bach: His
    Work and Influence on the Music of Germany_, trans-
    lated by Clara Bell and John Alexander Fuller-
    Maitland, 3 vols., London: Novello and Co., 1899;
    reprint, New York: Dover Pub., 1951).

Sumner, Willian Leslie. _Bach's Organ-Registration_, London:
    Hinrichsen Edition Ltd., 1961.

_____. _The Organs of Bach_. London: Hinrichsen Edi-
    tion Ltd., 1954.

Taylor, Stainton de B. _The Chorale Preludes of J. S.
    Bach_. London: Oxford University Press, 1942.

Terry, Charles Sanford. _Bach: A Biography_. London: Ox-
    ford University Press, 1928.

_____. _Bach's Chorals_, 3 vols. Cambridge, England:
    University Press, 1915-1921.

_____. _The Music of Bach: An Introduction_. London:
    Oxford University Press, 1933 (reprint, New York:
    Dover Pub., 1963).

Tusler, Robert L. _The Style of Bach's Chorale-Preludes_.
    New York: Da Capo Press, 1968.

Williams, Peter F. "J. S. Bach and English Organ Music,"
    Music and Letters, vol. XLIV (1963), p. 140-151.

9. CLASSICAL FRENCH ORGAN SCHOOL: 1600-1800

The founder of the Classical French organ school, Jehan Titelouze (1563-1633), was of English ancestry ("Title-house").[1] The family had emigrated to France by way of the Spanish Netherlands. At the age of 22 Titelouze was appointed organist of the church of St. Jean, Rouen. In 1591 he became the organist of the Rouen Cathedral, where he served until the end of his life. He became a canon there in 1610. Titelouze was a priest, scholar, teacher, performer, composer, theoretician, and expert in building organs. He carried on a lively correspondance with Mersenne, the author of Harmonie universelle and also a prominent musical theoretician.

Titelouze wrote two collections of organ music for the church. The first, Hymnes de l'Eglise pour Toucher sur l'Orgue, avec les Fugues et Recherches sur Leur Plain Chant (Balard, 1623), appeared one year before Scheidt's Tabulatura nova (1624). Titelouze's first book embraces 12 Latin hymns, each containing three or four versets. His second volume, Le Magnificat, ou Cantique de la Vierge pour Toucher sur l'Orgue, Suivant les Huit Tons de l'Eglise, appeared in 1626. This volume contained settings of six versets in all eight tones for the Magnificat: Magnificat, Quia respexit, Et misericordia, Deposuit potentes, Suscepit Israel, and Gloria Patri et Filio. Titelouze always wrote two settings of the Deposuit verse so that when the Benedictus (which needed seven organ versets) was sung to the same tune, there would be enough organ pieces provided.

The music of Titelouze, as Harvey Grace wrote,[2] is music of "austere gravity." He was faithful to the modes when the major-minor system began to take precedence. The lack of modulation, some chromaticism, and diatonic discords, are characteristics of his music. As a general practice Titelouze wrote in four parts in continuous flow, uninterrupted by cadences. Each voice usually begins by imitating the initial motive of the plainchant. The polyphony is vocal in style in the slower movements. The forms employed by

HISTORICAL BACKGROUND

1608	Champlain founded Quebec
1610-1643	Reign of Louis XIII
1612	Louvre begun
1616-1634	Richelieu became member of the Council
1621-1696	LaFontaine
1622-1673	Molière
1623-1662	Pascal
1632-1687	Lully
1635	Académie française established
1636	Mersenne Harmonie universelle
1639-1699	Racine
1643-1715	Reign of Louis XIV
1657-1726	Lalande
1682	LaSalle explored Mississippi River region
1683-1764	Rameau
1684-1721	Watteau
1694-1778	Voltaire
1709	Dispersion of nuns of Port-Royal
1712-1778	Rousseau
1714-1787	Gluck
1715-1774	Reign of Louis XV
1722	Rameau Traité de l'harmonie
1732-1806	Fragonard
1774-1792	Reign of Louis XVI
1789-1794	French Revolution

Titelouze were the plein jeu, the ricercar (he used the term recherche), and choral figuré in which the melody notes are not actually ornamented. The plainsong cantus firmus is written in notes of equal value. [3] The pedal reed often played the cantus firmus in the tenor range. The pedal division of French organs of that time was very small and usually contained only one 8' reed, one 8' Bourdon, and perhaps a 4' flute. There was no 16' sound in the pedal division. The left hand played the part which performed the bass function (the real bass part).

François Roberday (1624-1680) is a little known figure in organ history. He issued a collection, Fugues et Caprices, à Quatre Parties Mises en Partition pour l'Orgue (1660), which contained three pieces by other composers: Frescobaldi, Ebner, and Froberger. His own pieces were composed on themes given him by musical acquaintances such as Couperin, d'Anglebert, and Froberger. These polyphonic pieces incorporate thematic metamorphosis, which

Frescobaldi had so effectively employed. [4]

By 1650 French organ composers had accepted the
new musical style which established registration practices
for specific musical types on the organs whose specifications
had become rather standardized throughout France.   The didactic counterpoint of Titelouze began to be replaced by more
melodic, less austere music influences principally by Italians
such as Cavalli and Lully.   The public preferred the secular,
the music of ballet and the theater, the dance, and solo and
orchestral music.   Lute music was especially popular.   Ho-
mophony supplanted polyphony: one voice was predominant,
supported by the other voices.   The clavecin (harpsichord)
was popular with its many short programmatic pieces and
dances, all elaborately embellished.   Since organists were
often clavecinists also, the style of popular music influenced
the "old fashioned" organ music.   Organists-clavecinists
Charles Racquet, Jacques Champion de Chambonnières, and
Robert Cambert, who were active in numerous musical pur-
suits, influenced organ music.   Other organ composers were
Henri DuMont (1610-1684), Etienne Richard (d. 1669), and
Jacques-Denis Thomelin (ca. 1640-1693), the court organist
for Louis XIV and teacher of François Couperin. [5]

The accompanied solo type of instrumental composition
was incorporated into organ literature: basse de trompette
and basse de cromorne.   Clever effects such as duos, echos,
and dialogues replaced Gregorian chant.   The compositions
of Louis Couperin (1625-1661) responded to the taste of the
day in chacones, sarabandes, and fantasy pieces like Les
Carillons de Paris.   The superscription of Les Carillons
tells that it was written "to imitate the carillons of Paris
and which was always played on the organ of St. Gervais between vespers of All Saints' Day and that of the dead." Another of his compositions is the Chacone in G Minor, the refrain of which could be played on the Grand Orgue;   this
same composition was probably intended for harpsichord
originally.   French composers of this period used the term
chacone for a rondeau with several couplets and a repeated
refrain.

Jean Henri d'Anglebert (1635-1691) is noted for his
Pièces de clavessin (1689), which included a valuable table
of French ornaments.   His contrapuntal ability is shown by
five fugues based on a single subject.

Organ music of the latter half of the seventeenth

CLASSICAL FRENCH ORGAN SCHOOL: 1600-1800

1600   1650   1700   1750

1563/1564 Titelouze, J. 1633
1597 Racquet, Charles-----1664
after 1601 Chambonnières, J. -----1670/1672
1610 DuMont, Henry------1684
ca. 1621 Richard, E. 1669
1624 Roberday, François ----1680
1625 Gigault, Nicolas------1707
ca. 1626 Couperin, Louis 1661
1628 d'Anglebert, Jean-Henri-----1691
1630 Lebègue, Nicolas------1702
1632 Nivers, Guillaume------1714
? Geoffroy, Jean-Nicolas ?
ca. 1653 Jullien, Gilles ------1703
? Raison, André ----1719
ca. 1653 Boyvin, Jacques-----1706
1668 Couperin, François------1733
1669 Marchand, Louis ----1732
1672 de Grigny, N. 1703
1676 Clérambault, Louis-Nicolas-----1749
? Guilain, Jean-Adam-Guillaume ?
ca. 1676 DuMage, Pierre------1751
1682 Dandrieu, Jean-François 1738
1694 Daquin, L.-C. --1722

CHRONOLOGICAL LIST OF IMPORTANT FRENCH ORGAN BOOKS BY INDIVIDUAL COMPOSERS OF THE SEVENTEENTH CENTURY

1623	J. Titelouze	Les Hymnes pour toucher sur l'orgue avec les Fugues.
1626	J. Titelouze	Le Magnificat ou Cantique de la Vierge.
1636-1643	Ch. Racquet	Pièces d'orgue.
1656-1661	L. Couperin	Pièces d'orgue.
1660	Roberday	Fugues et Caprices.
1650-1669	E. Richard	Pièces d'orgue.
1665	G. Nivers	Premier Livre d'orgue.
1667	G. Nivers	Deuxième Livre d'orgue.
1675	G. Nivers	Troisième Livre d'orgue.
1676	N. Lebègue	Premier Livre d'orgue.
1678-1679	N. Lebègue	Troisième Livre d'orgue.
1685	N. Gigault	Livre d'orgue.
1688	A. Raison	Livre d'orgue.
1689	D'Anglebert	Fugues et Quatuor.
1689	Boyvin	Livre d'orgue.
1690	Fr. Couperin	Livre d'orgue.
1690	G. Jullien	Premier Livre d'orgue.
1699	N. de Grigny	Premier Livre d'orgue.

century in France became confined to forms which were used by all French organ composers of that period. Registration indications became titles for pieces. Most of these pieces are rather short because of the brief time allotted for organ playing between various sections of the Mass. [6]

In the Cérémoniale de l'Eglise de Paris (1662) instructions were given about the use of the organ in the Catholic Mass. In short preludes the organ gave the pitch to the choir and alternated with the choir on sections of the Kyrie, Gloria, Sanctus, and Agnus Dei. As a solo instrument the organ was allowed to play at the offertory, [7] at the elevation, and for the postlude. At vespers the organ played more frequently between psalms or in alternation with sung verses of the Magnificat. [8]

Guillaume-Gabriel Nivers (1632-1714) wrote with froideur et la grâce facile, (detachment and flowing elegance)[9] and remained faithful to the ecclesiastical modes. Nivers seemed to prefer the duo type and the reed or cornet solo (récit), which was the only ornamented part. He also

(text continued on page 127)

TITLES OF FRENCH ORGAN COMPOSITIONS OF THE SEVENTEENTH AND EIGHTEENTH CENTURIES AND EXPLANATION OF PERFORMANCE. *

Title	English Translation and Description
Basse de trompette Basse de cromorne	Trumpet (or cromorne) solo in the bass (lower) range of the keyboard. The solo would be accompanied by foundation tone in the upper two parts.
Cornet	Cornet solo (with flute accompaniment). The cornet is a compound of five different pitches (8', 4', 2 2/3', 2', 1 3/5'), usually of flute quality, played as a melody.
Cromorne en taille	Cromorne solo in the tenor (range of the keyboard, accompanied by flutes)
Dialogue	Dialogue (of alternating sections between manuals or of alternating solo colors)
Dialogue sur les grands jeux	Literally: "Dialogue on big stops." Dialogue alternating between two choruses or ensembles on different manuals, usually between <u>Grand</u> <u>orgue</u> and <u>Positif</u>.
Duo	Duo (duet). Composition for two voices, usually contrasting, for example, a reed stop with a combined sound of Bourdon 8', Doublette 2' and Larigot 1 1/3' or a similar combination.

Echo   Echo. Composition employing echo effects by using the same musical material on two or more manuals of diminishing volume and perhaps changing colors.

Fonds d'orgue   Organ foundation (tone). The combination of all principals and flutes at 16', 8', and 4' pitches was used for this type.

Fugue   Fugue. Fugues were frequently based on plainsong or Latin hymn melodies. The most frequent characteristic quality of sound used for fugues was that of the reeds.

Jeu (jeux)   Stop (stops); the word jeu (jeux) can also mean a combination of stops.

Musette (Muzète)   Musette. (Bagpipe) Composition written over a drone bass (pedal point).

Offertoire sur les Grands Jeux   Literally: "Offertory on big stops." Composition which usually falls into several contrasting sections with such inclusions as (1) alternations between manuals, (2) melody on one manual and accompaniment on another, (3) tempo and meter changes between sections, and (4) echo effects. The predominant sound of the grands jeux was a reed sound supported by foundation stops.

Plein jeu   Literally: "Full stop." A bright ensemble, full sound on Grand Orgue and Positif choruses combined with mixtures providing the characteristic color. Plein jeu at one time meant the enormous mixture called Blockwerk elsewhere.

Point d'orgue   Organ point. Composition employing a pedal- or organ-point as its principal characteristic.

Title	English Translation and Description
Tierce	Composition for a melody and accompaniment. The melody stop incorporated the Tierce 1 3/5' stop which provided its characteristic color.
Trio	Trio. Composition written for three voice parts which could be played in one of three ways: (1) all three parts on one manual, (2) two upper parts on one manual and the third part on another manual, and (3) the two upper parts on two different manuals with the third part in the pedal.
Récit - - de Basse de Trompette - de Cromorne - de Nazard - de Tierce en taille - de Voix humaine	Solo. A solo melody of individual color accompanied by flutes or sufficient foundation tone to support the solo. The solo color to be used was indicated by the stop name in the title such as "trompette," "cromorne," and "nazard."
Other French terms: à 2; à 3; à 4; à 5; à 6	The number denotes the number of voices in the composition. A Fugue à 4 would be a fugue written for four voice parts.
Premier/Dernier Kyrie Sanctus Agnus	First/Last (Final). These words were used to indicate which setting of a particular Mass movement would be played by the organ, e.g., the first Kyrie; the last Kyrie.

*For thorough discussion of these types of compositions and their registrations see Fenner Douglass, The Language of the Classical French Organ, Yale University Press, New Haven, 1969, pp. 106-114. The organs of this period are discussed in Peter Williams, The European Organ 1450-1850, B. T. Batsford Ltd., London, 1966, pp. 169-203.

alternated between manual choruses and used echo effects.
His Diminution de la Basse was replaced later by the Tierce
en taille.   Nivers wrote three Livres d'orgue (1665, 1667,
1675), and attained a fine synthesis of polyphony and homo-
phony. [10]

     Nicolas Gigault (1624-1702) published pieces for litur-
gical use in his Livre de Musique pour l'Orgue (1685).   While
Gigault was not an inspired composer, his works have a degree of interest, they are highly ornamented and make use of
quick manual changes.   The pedal supplies soft support or
sounds the plainsong themes in the tenor part. [11]

     Three Livres d'Orgue (1676, 1678-1679, 1685?) came
from the pen of Nicolas-Antoine Lebègue (ca. 1630-1702).
Lebègue wrote for the liturgical and concert organ.   For the
most part his music is tuneful and charming rather than
learned, profound, or contrapuntally developed.   Lebègue
employed the ecclesiastical modes in his organ Mass, which
contains 19 short pieces, and he also referred to the Kyrie
Cunctipotens plainsong melody in this Mass.   The Mass conformed strictly to the requirements of the Cérémoniale of
1662.   He wrote the second book for those who had only a
moderate ability (qu'une science médiocre).   Lebègue is the
first to have systematically exploited the varieties of forms
of the récit, duo, basse de trompette, dialogue, fugue grave,
and solo de cornet. [12]   As for the concert organ music,
Lebègue added great impetus to what was to become a widespread interest in imitating orchestral instruments, bells,
and, later, even extra-musical activities.   He often used the
various contrasting colors and effects of the organ combined
with dance rhythms and was one of the first to write variations on French carols (noëls).   These were written as familiar music, intimate, picturesque, very human, to suggest
Christmas characters such as the shepherds, Joseph, the
Virgin Mary, and the ordinary French citizen's naïve pleasure
at the coming of the Christmas season. [13]

     Gilles Jullien (1650-?), the organist of the Chartres
cathedral from 1663-1703, brought out his Premier Livre
d'Orgue the same year that François Couperin issued his two
organ Masses (1690).   Jullien used all the forms which were
currently being written and grouped them into suites on each
of the eight ecclesiastical modes.   That Jullien was not a
"finished" musician is revealed by a number of parallel octaves, awkward jumps, and monotonous passages.   Surpris-
ingly enough he used the récit en taille for Cromhorne or

Tierce only once each.   Jullien indicated that his four-part
fugues be performed on two manuals. [14]

André Raison (?-1719) wrote two <u>Livres d'Orgue</u>
(1688, 1714).   In his five Masses he used the forms already
in vogue and added some originality by putting the <u>trompette</u>
piece in the tenor range.   He employed quick manual changes
and wrote in "frank tunefulness."[15]   Raison's <u>Offerte</u> in the
fifth tone is one example of how the secular had entered the
church.   The tendency of secularization was to grow much
stronger and practically eliminate the organ's liturgical function in the eighteenth century.   The <u>Offerte</u> was written for
the entry of the king to the Hôtel de Ville in Paris on January 30, 1687.   Strains of <u>Vive le Roy</u> are incorporated at
the end of the piece.   Raison, the teacher of Clérambault,
wrote the <u>Trio en Passacaille</u> (<u>Christe</u> from <u>Messe du
Deuziesme Ton</u>), the theme of which J. S. Bach presumably
borrowed for his monumental <u>Passacaglia in C Minor</u> (BWV
582). [16]

Jacques Boyvin (ca. 1653-1706) also wrote series of
pieces based on the eight church tones, which seems to have
been one of the chief factors common to all French organ
books of the period.   His <u>tierces en taille</u> are well developed, and the pedal <u>trompette</u> has a prominent part in the
<u>Grand Prélude</u> in C major. [17]

Louis Marchand (1669-1732) was the organist of a
large number of Parisian churches.   He was an ill-tempered
virtuoso and rival of Couperin.   It is common knowledge that
Marchand avoided the confrontation with Bach at Dresden during his concert tour in Germany and temporary exile from
France.   The better known compositions of Marchand are the
three-voiced <u>Récit de flute</u>, the heroic <u>Dialogue</u> in C major,
and the six-part <u>Plein jeu</u>. [18]

The famous <u>Grand Jeu</u> of Pierre DuMage (ca. 1676-
1751), organist of the Collegiate Church of St. Quentin,
closes DuMage's <u>Livre d'Orgue</u> (1708).   The <u>Grand Jeu</u> is
divided into several sections: a solemn introduction, a quick,
dancing, fugal section in triple meter which incorporates
double echos, and a return to the solemnity of the first section.

The two outstanding composers of the Classical French
school at the end of the seventeenth century were François
Couperin (1668-1733) and Nicolas de Grigny (1672-1703).

Couperin was part of the family dynasty which presided at
the organ console of St. Gervais in Paris for many years.
He wrote two organ Masses, his only publications for organ.
The first Mass contains 21 pieces and is designed for the
use of parish churches (Messe pour les Paroisses).   The
Parish Mass frequently employs plainsong melodies.
The second Mass (Messe pour les Convents) is easier to
play and is designed for convent use.   There seems to be
no connection with plainchant in any of the 21 pieces in the
second Mass.   Couperin followed the examples of Titelouze
and Lebègue and never decorated the plainsong melody when
it was incorporated into his pieces, although there is a wide
use of embellishment in his works.   Couperin employed much
variety in his short works--the Kyrie fugues for reed stops,
the Chromhorne and Tierce solos, the dialogues, duos, and
plein jeu settings. [19]

     The specifications of the organ at St. Gervais, where
the Couperin family were organists from 1650 until 1826,
are typical of organs of the Classical French period, and
the stop list is given below.

Paris, France, St. Gervais.
Built by Pierre Thierry, 1649-1650; rebuilt, 1625.
Maintained by Alexandre Thierry
during the tenure of François Couperin.

First keyboard	Second keyboard
Positiv (49 notes: A, C, D-c^3)	Grand Orgue (49 notes: A, C, D-c^3)
Bourdon 8'	Montre 16'
Montre 4'	Bourdon 16'
Flûte 4'	Montre 8'
Doublette 2'	Bourdon 8'
Fourniture III	Prestant 4'
Cymbale III	Doublette 2'
Nasard 2 2/3'	Fourniture III
Tierce 1 3/5'	Cymbale III
Larigot 1 1/3'	Flûte 4'
Cromorne 8'	Grosse Tierce 3 1/5'
	Nasard 2 2/3'
Echo (37 notes: c-c^3)	Tierce 1 3/5'
	Trompette 8'
	Clairon 4'
Bourdon 8' and Flûte 4'	Voix Humaine 8'
Cymbale III	Cornet V (2 octaves)

Nasard 2 2/3'   Fourth keyboard
Doublette 2' and Tierce 1 3/5'
Cromorne 8'   Récit
                                      (3 octaves: C-c^3)
          Pédale
(29 notes: A, C, D, E, to e)   Cornet Séparé V

Flûte 8'
Flûte 4'
Trompette 8'

    Grand Orgue/ Positiv; Grand Orgue/ Pédale; Tremblant
      doux; Tremblant fort
    Changes made in 1714: removed lower octave of Echo;
      removed Flûte 4' from Grand Orgue and put in Trom-
      pette 8'

      Nicolas de Grigny (1672-1703),[20] a student of Lebègue,
was organist of Notre Dame in Rheims. Grigny's Premier
Livre d'Orgue (1699) contained about 50 pieces, which included an organ Mass and five Latin hymn settings. The
famous Récit de Tierce en Taille from the Mass is especially
beautiful. Grigny renewed the tradition of Titelouze in his
five Latin hymn arrangements and, unlike Couperin, retained
the modal character of plainsong when he utilized it as a
cantus firmus. Just as Couperin often used four voices in
many of his compositions, de Grigny frequently utilized five-
part texture. Grigny advanced the fugue development into
more extended compositions and treated the same forms and
styles of the classical school but in a more serious and intellectual way. Grigny accomplished the difficult synthesis
of liturgical and concert organ composition and also coupled
warmth with a strong sense of lyricism.

      The Premier Livre de Pièces d'Orgue by Jean-
François Dandrieu (1682-1738) appeared after his death.
Dandrieu played with great facility and had thoroughly absorbed the characteristics of music of his time. Although
his pleins jeux and fugues are majestic, the larger part
of his music is of a light, playful quality, with markings
such as vivement, tendrement, and légèrement. Duos, such
as one marked en cor de chasse (suggesting the hunting horn
by its gigue rhythm) and musettes are typical of his writing.

      Louis-Nicolas Clérambault (1676-1749) dedicated his
Premier Livre d'Orgue (1710) to Raison. His two suites

contain the usual series of short pieces, each of which shows
some Italian influence, which was widely felt in France at
that time.   The tempo indications gayement, gay, gracieuse-
ment are not those of liturgical music.   Clérambault's work
as a French polyphonist is exhibited by his fugue in the first
tone.   The familiar Basse et Dessus de Trompette comes
from the First Suite and the Caprice sur les Grands Jeux
from the second.   Each of the four suites in four different
modes by Guilain (?1600's-1700's?) contains at least one
Petit plein jeu, a Duo, a Trio, a Basse de Trompette or
Cromorne, a Dialogue, and a récit of some sort. [21]

Les Noëlistes

In the widespread attempt to please the public, both
religious and secular carols were used as themes for variations by French organist-composers about the beginning of
the eighteenth century.   The tunes were simple, easily assimilated, and remembered.   Each variation (couplet) had a change
in rhythmic treatment, usually progressing from slower to
quicker and quicker note values;   the early variation or theme
might present the melody in quarter notes, and the following
variations probably would move to even eighth-notes, to triplets, and thence to 16th-notes or a rapid rhythmic figure.
The harmony is often limited to dominant and tonic chords,
and usually no modulation is employed.   These variations
relied upon the variety of note-values and color of stops to
hold the listener's attention.   Cromhorne is answered by
cornet;   echo effects;   plein jeu, oboe, musette, clairon,
piccolo, flutes--all these colors and effects and more
charmed the audience.   As Dufourcq writes, [22] these pieces
required little imagination to compose, only spirit and fin-
gers.   Such are the noëls of Dandrieu, M. Corrette, Dornel,
and Daquin.   The noëls of Lebègue led to those of Pierre
Dandrieu and thence to those of the best of the noël writers,
Daquin, the "king of the Noëlists." [23]

Pierre Dandrieu (d. 1733), a priest, issued one organ
book containing a variety of types of pieces: Noels, O filii,
Chansons de Saint Jacques, Stabat Mater et Carillons, le
Tout Revu, Augmenté, Extrêmement Varié et Mis Pour
l'Orgue et le Clavecin (1714).   The volume contained such
carols as Joseph est Bien Marié, Jacob Que Tu Es Habile,
and Une Jeune Pucelle. [24]

Louis-Claude Daquin (1694-1722) was an outstanding
virtuoso, a court favorite, and a prominent improviser.   The

citizens of Paris flocked to hear him play his carol variations
during the Christmas season at one of the many churches in
which he held the position of organist simultaneously.   In the
Nouveau Livre de Noëls Daquin treated 12 carols in many
colorful ways.   His work exhibits charm, grace, virtuosity,
and warmth.

Michel Corrette (1709-1795), the father and son
Beauvarlet-Charpentier, and Claude Balbastre (1727-1799)
from Dijon also wrote in this simple form.   Balbastre wrote
four suites of variations on Burgundian carols. [25]

Decline of the Classical French School

The entire eighteenth century and the first half of the
nineteenth century were a secular age in France.   This was
the Age of Reason, of interest in philosophy, and of the rise
of the common man.   Music of this period was under the influence of Italian music, the theater, and ballet.   Compositions were performed during Mass which had no liturgical
significance whatsoever.   Dances, songs, marches, imitations, patriotic airs, and picturesque improvisations were
often played in this anti-ecclesiastical era.   Some improvisations depicted cannon fire and battles.   Some compositions by
Michel Corrette were entitled April Showers, Enchanted
Lovers, Seven-league Boots, Stars, The Taking of Jericho.
Chatt wrote Agriculture and The Sovereignty of the People. [26]

The Te Deum offered many opportunities in improvisation for the imaginative organist.   Mercier, in his Tableau
de Paris wrote about Daquin, "more sublime than ever,
played in the Judex crederis which carried impressions into
the hearts so vivid that everyone paled."[27]   At another time
he wrote that the organist "plays during the elevation of the
host and of the chalice some ariettas, sarabandes--hunting
pieces, minuets, romances, rigaudons."[28]   Beauvarlet-
Charpentier explained in his Te Deum that his piece ends
with "prolonged thunder at the will [of the performer] to depict the upsetting of the Universe."[29]   Michel Corrette told
how to make a storm and thunder at the organ by putting a
board across the last octave of the pedals with the trumpet
and bombarde stops drawn which the foot could play at will.
At the end, to give an imitation of a clap of thunder, one
struck the lowest keys with the elbow. [30]

Such was the degradation of the organ in France for
over a century.   Not until the middle of the nineteenth

DECLINE OF THE CLASSICAL FRENCH ORGAN SCHOOL: 1710-1850

1650	1700	1750	1800	1850

ca. 1660 Dandrieu, Pierre 1733

1684 Dagincour, François 1758

ca. 1685 Dornel, Antoine------1765

? Corrette, Gaspard ?

1709 Corrette, Michel-------------1795

(1709 Bédos de Celles, Dom F. --1779) L'Art du Facteur d'Orgues

1715 Février, Pierre-----ca. 1780

? Siret, Nicolas 1754

(? Père Pingré ?)

1727 Balbastre, Claude-Bénigne 1799

1734 Beauvarlet-Charpentier, J.-J. 1794

1740 Lasceux, Guillaume----------------1831

1745 Séjan, Nicolas-----------1819

1757 Marrigues, Jean-Nicolas -------1834

1766 Beauvarlet-Charpentier, J.-M. 1834

1786 Séjan, Louis-Nicolas 1849

century did the organ regain some of its integrity through the
unappreciated efforts of Boëly and later through the compositions of men such as Franck and Saint-Saëns.

Notes

1. Norbert Dufourcq, La Musique d'Orgue Française de
    Jehan Titelouze à Jehan Alain, Paris: Librairie Floury,
    1949; p. 37.
2. Harvey Grace, French Organ Music Past and Present,
    New York: H. W. Gray Co. , 1919; p. 5.
3. For additional study of the works of Titelouze see Willi
    Apel, Geschichte der Orgel- und Klaviermusik bis
    1700, Kassel, Germany: Bärenreiter Verlag, 1967;
    p. 488-492.
4. Dufourcq, op. cit. , p. 51, and Apel, op. cit. , p. 703.
5. Dufourcq, op. cit. , p. 53-61.
6. Dom Bédos de Celles (1709-1779) wrote about organ
    construction and registration for a large number of
    different forms and effects in his monumental L'Art
    du Facteur d'Orgues (1770).
7. In France the offertoire was a prominent part of the
    organ Mass; this was not true in organ Masses of
    other countries.
8. Dufourcq, op. cit. , p. 62.
9. Dufourcq, op. cit. , p. 61.
10. Dufourcq, op. cit. , p. 62-63; Apel, op. cit. , p. 706-
    707.
11. Dufourcq, op. cit. , p. 71-73; Apel, op. cit. , p. 709-
    711.
12. Dufourcq, op. cit. , p. 66.
13. Dufourcq, op. cit. , p. 64-70; Apel, op. cit. , p. 707-
    709.
14. Dufourcq, op. cit. , p. 76-77.
15. Grace, op. cit. , p. 29.
16. Dufourcq, op. cit. , p. 74-75; Apel, op. cit. , p. 712-
    713.
17. Dufourcq, op. cit. , p. 77-79; Apel, op. cit. , p. 713-
    715.
18. Dufourcq, op. cit. , p. 75-98; Apel, op. cit. , p. 723.
19. Apel, op. cit. , p. 716-719.
20. Norbert Dufourcq, in the Preface to his edition of the
    organ works of Nicolas de Grigny, cites a baptismal
    notice that de Grigny was baptized in Saint-Pierre-le-
    Vieil Oct. 8, 1672, not 1671, which is the date usu-
    ally given for his birth.

21. Apel, op. cit. , p. 724.
22. Dufourcq, op. cit. , p. 114.
23. Dufourcq, op. cit. , p. 114.
24. Dufourcq, op. cit. , p. 115-116; Apel, op. cit. , p. 722-723.
25. Dufourcq, op. cit. , p. 118; Apel, op. cit. , p. 723-724.
26. Dufourcq, op. cit. , p. 110.
27. Dufourcq, op. cit. , p. 121.
28. William Leslie Sumner, "The French Organ School," Hinrichsen Musical Year Book, London: Hinrichsen Edition Ltd. , 1949-1950; vol. 6, p. 284.
29. Ibid. , p. 284.
30. Dufourcq, op. cit. , p. 121.

Bibliography

Andersen, Poul-Gerhard. Organ Building and Design. New York: Oxford University Press, 1969; p. 140-156.

Apel, Willi. Geschichte der Orgel- und Klaviermusik bis 1700. Kassel, Germany: Bärenreiter Verlag, 1967; p. 487-493, 703-728.

Borrel, Eugène. L'Interpretation de la Musique Française de Lully à la Révolution. Paris: Librairie Félix Alcan, 1934.

Bouvet, Charles. Une Dynastie de Musiciens Français: Les Couperin, Organistes de l'Eglise Saint-Gervais. Paris: Bossuet, 1919.

Brunold, Paul. François Couperin, translated by J. B. Hanson. Monaco: L'Oiseau Lyre, 1949.

Citron, Pierre. Couperin. Bourges, France: Editions du Seuil, 1956.

de Wall, Marilou. "The Tonal Organization of the Seventeenth Century French Organ," American Guild of Organists Quarterly, vol. VIII, no. 1 (January 1963, p. 12; vol. VIII, no. 2, (April 1963), p. 43; vol. VIII, no. 3 (July 1963), p. 89.

_____. "Interpretation of French Organ Music of the 17th and 18th Centuries," The Diapason (April 1964), p. 42.

Douglass, Fenner. The Language of the Classical French Organ: A Musical Tradition Before 1800. New Haven, Conn. : Yale University Press, 1969.

Dufourcq, Norbert. Le Grand Orgue et les Organistes de Saint-Merry de Paris. Paris: Librairie Floury, 1947.

_____. Nicolas LeBègue (1631-1702). Paris: Librairie
    Flowry, 1954.
Fesperman, John. "Rhythmic Alterations in 18th Century
    French Organ Music," Organ Institute Quarterly,
    vol. IX, no. 1 (Spring 1961), p. 4-10; vol. IX, no.
    2 (Summer 1961), p. 13-22.
Gay, Harry W. "Saint Quentin, Its Collegiate Church and
    Pierre du Mage," The Diapason (May 1958), p. 8.
_____. "Notes upon Jean Titelouze (1563-1633)," The
    American Organist, vol. 42, no. 9 (September 1959),
    p. 299-307.
_____. "To Know Nicolas de Grigny, Perform His Many
    Pieces," The Diapason (September 1957), p. 18.
Goodrich, Wallace. The Organ in France, Boston: Boston
    Music Company, 1917.
Grace, Harvey. French Organ Music, Past and Present.
    New York: H. W. Gray Co., 1919.
Grimes, Conrad. "The Noels of Louis-Claude Daquin,"
    The Diapason (December 1968), p. 24.
Hardouin, Pierre. "Le Grand Orgue de Saint-Gervais de
    Paris," L'Orgue, 1949, p. 91.
_____. "François Roberday (1624-1680)," Revue de
    Musicologie, vol. XLV (1960), p. 44-62.
Howell, Almonte C. "French Baroque Organ Music and
    the Eight Church Tones," Journal of the American
    Musicological Society, vol. XI (1952), p. 106-108.
Mellers, Wilfrid. François Couperin and the French Clas-
    sical Tradition. London: Denis Dobson, 1950 (re-
    print, New York: Dover Pub., 1968).
Moeser, James. "French Baroque Registration," The
    American Organist, June 1967, p. 17 and July 1967,
    p. 21.
Raugel, Félix. Les organistes; Paris: H. Laurens, 1923.
Sharp, Geoffrey B. "Louis Marchand, 1669-1732," Musical
    Times, no. 1521, vol. 110 (November 1969), p. 1134.
Shay, Edmund. "French Baroque Organ Registrations," The
    Diapason (November 1969), p. 14.
Stevlingson, Norma. "Performance Styles of French Organ
    Music in the 17th and 18th Centuries," Music/The
    A. G. O. and R. C. C. O. Magazine, vol. III, no.
    2 (February 1969), p. 26.
Sumner, William Leslie. "The French Organ School,"
    Sixth Music Book. London: Hinrichsen Edition Ltd.,
    1950; p. 281-294.
Tessier, André. "Les Messes d'Orgue de Fr. Couperin,"
    Revue Musicale, vol. VI, no. 1.
_____. Couperin. Paris: Librairie Renouard, 1926.

Williams, Peter. <u>The European Organ 1450-1850</u>.   London:
B. T. Batsford, 1966; p. 169-203.

10.   ENGLAND: 1650-1800

    The seventeenth century in England witnessed many
struggles for control of the government.   The reign of the
house of Stuart, the rise of Puritanism, the establishment
of the English Commonwealth, and the restoration of a mon-
arch, the Glorious Revolution of 1688--all were events related to the political unrest of the nation.   During this period
many organs were destroyed, and most forms of music were
abolished or forbidden in worship.   This made it necessary
that keyboard music, especially organ music, be performed
on small instruments (harpsichords, clavichords, organs) in
the home rather than in church.   The English organs of this
period had no pedal board, and a performer did not change
registration during the course of a piece.

    "Father" Bernard Smith (d. 1708) and Renatus Harris
(ca. 1652-1724) were two competitive organ builders who had
been trained in their craft on the continent and who began
serious organ building in England after the Restoration of
Charles II to the throne (1660).   The German-born Smith
was probably superior in tonal matters, but Harris surpassed
Smith in mechanical ones.   Smith is given much credit,
however, for enlarging and transforming the tonal qualities
of the old English organ.   Renatus Harris built a four manual
instrument (no pedal) at Salisbury Cathedral in 1710 in which
he introduced duplexing (borrowing). [1]

    John Snetzler (1710-1785) was another foreign-born
organ builder who contributed to building pedal divisions and
increasing the number of reeds in many instruments during
the eighteenth century.   The earliest date which can be as-
certained for the introduction of pedals to English organs is
1720; the few pedals of the organ at St. Paul's Cathedral,
London, were probably pull-downs and playable by the toes
only.   Another important fact in organ history is that the
first Swell (enclosed) organ in England was built by Abraham
Jordan at the church of St. Magnus the Martyr in London in
1712.

HISTORICAL BACKGROUND

1603-1625	Reign of James I
1604	Shakespeare Othello
1605	Bacon On the Advancement of Learning
1605	Ben Jonson Volpone
1606	Shakespeare Macbeth
1611	King James version of The Bible
1625-1649	Reign of Charles I
1649-1660	English Commonwealth
1653	Oliver Cromwell dissolved Parliament
1660	Pepys Diary
1660	Restoration of Charles II to throne; ruled until 1685
1665	London plague
1666	London fire
1667	Milton Paradise Lost
1678	Bunyan Pilgrim's Progress
1675	St. Paul's Cathedral begun by Wren
1682	William Penn founded Philadelphia
1685-1688	Reign of James II
1689-1702	Reign of William and Mary
1697	Dryden Alexander's Feast
1702-1714	Reign of Anne
1711	Pope Essay on Criticism
1714-1727	Reign of George I
1719	Defoe Robinson Crusoe
1726	Swift Gulliver's Travels
1727-1760	Reign of George II
1738	Wesley's reform movement begun
1754	Samuel Johnson Dictionary
1760-1820	Reign of George III
1766	Goldsmith The Vicar of Wakefield
1770	Gainsborough The Blue Boy
1775-1781	Revolutionary War in America
1776	American Declaration of Independence
1776	Burney, general history of music
1777	Sheridan School for Scandal
1786	Joshua Reynolds The Duchess of Devonshire

Many of the organ compositions written in England
during the seventeenth and eighteenth centuries were called
voluntaries. In the seventeenth century the terms fancy,
verse, and voluntary were interchangeable. Dances, airs,
and marches were composed for either organ or harpsichord.
The early form of the voluntary was that of a through-
composed piece of moderate length. It contained much imitation between voices, texture in three parts or four parts,
and a great amount of ornamentation. The voluntary later
developed into a piece divided into two sections (slow, fast),
the first a shorter one written for diapasons, and the second
for a solo and accompaniment, including echo portions. [2]
Benjamin Rogers (1614-1698) and Matthew Locke (ca. 1630-
1677) were two composers of preludes and voluntaries from
the first half of the seventeenth century. Melothesia: or,
Certain General Rules for Playing upon a Continued-Bass
(1673), which contained seven organ pieces, was Locke's
largest opus.

English fugues of the eighteenth century can usually
be classified in two types. The first has a lively tempo,
loose construction, parts added whimsically by the composer,
and episodes built upon broken chords. The second type of
fugue conformed to the stricter rules of fugue construction
such as correct answers to the fugue subject, episodes derived from the subject, and a consistent number of voices.
The alla breve fugue, as the second type is called, was frequently written in minor keys. [3]

Dr. John Blow (1649-1708) was a teacher of Purcell
and the organist of Westminster Abbey and St. Paul's Cathedral. He composed verses, voluntaries, and preludes. His
Voluntary for Full Organ uses a rapid 16th-note figuration
which suggests toccata writing. The 16th-note figuration became a common characteristic of the voluntary in the
eighteenth century. The Verse in C Major has a number
of places which suggest manual changes for a double-organ
(an organ which had two manuals). [4]

Henry Purcell (1659-1695) was a musical genius in
seventeenth-century England. He wrote, however, less than
ten works for the organ. Hugh McLean suggests that the
best-known organ work connected with Purcell's name,
Voluntary on the Old 100th, might have been composed by
either Blow or Purcell, or even composed by Blow and altered by Purcell. [5] Although this was not the first English
prelude on a hymn-tune, it was one of the earliest. [6] It is

possible that copyists intended that the piece be played on divided stops or half-stops[7] because the left-hand accompaniment part never goes above c^1. After an introduction in which each of the three parts enter on the initial phrase melody in imitation at the octave and unison, the complete psalm-tune is presented in the lowest part. Here the registration would make the left-hand part more prominent. Later the same kind of treatment is given with the entire psalm melody in the right hand (probably on the Cornet) and with the accompaniment in the left hand.

Purcell's Voluntary for Double Organ in D Minor is a lengthy and showy piece for two manuals. This, like the other Voluntary in D Minor, contains rapid scales and running figurations in 32nd-notes with much rhythmic variety. The two verses, one in F and the other in the Phrygian mode, are shorter pieces. All the Purcell works are highly ornamented. The texture in Purcell's pieces is usually three-part and, with the exception of two voluntaries, always begins with imitation. These pieces give the impression of spontaneity and of improvisation.[8] Daniel Purcell (d. 1717), the son of Henry Purcell, wrote psalm harmonizations with interludes.

In the hands of Dr. William Croft (1678-1727) the voluntary usually took the form of a two-section work of moderate length. The first part was a slow introduction followed by a fast second part. The second section was often a fugato based on one subject, which first appeared in all voices imitatively. The counterpoint grows from the harmony, with the lower voices usually supporting the principal melody in the highest voice part. The lines are vocal, there is much stepwise movement, and a frequent use of sequence, with uncomplicated, flowing rhythms. Not all of the Croft voluntaries were in the two-part form; some are in the same tempo throughout and are unified by one theme.[9]

George Frideric Handel (German form: Georg Friedrich Händel) (1685-1759) invented the organ concerto and wrote 21 concertos for organ and orchestra.[10] These concertos were written to provide a change of fare during the intermissions in his oratorio performances. Two announcements of oratorio performances read:[11]

> "The Messiah" with organ concerto.
> "Esther" with organ concerto.

ENGLISH ORGAN COMPOSERS: 1650-1800

1600	1650	1700	1750	1800	1850

Ravenscroft, John ca.1708
1614 Rogers, B. -------- 1698
1615 Gibbons, C. 1676
ca.1630 Locke - 1677
1649 Blow, J. ---------- 1708
1659 Purcell, H. 1695
Purcell, D. -- 1717
1667 Pepusch, J. C. ------ 1752 (Ger-Eng)
ca.1670 Clarke, J. 1707
ca.1674 Barrett, J. ca.1735
1677 Reading, John ------------------ 1764
1678 Croft, Wm. 1727
1685 Handel, G. F. ------ 1750 (Ger-Eng)
1687 Hine, Wm. 1730
1690 Roseingrave, T. ------ 1766
ca.1695 Greene, M. ----- 1755
Hart, P. ---- 1749
ca.1703 Travers, J. 1758
1706 Hayes, Wm. ------ 1777
1707 Humphries, J. ca.1730
1709 Flackton, Wm. ------- 1798
1710 Avison, C. ---- 1770
1710 Arne, T. A. -- 1778
1710 Boyce, Wm. -- 1779
ca.1711 Keeble, J. ------ 1786
1713 Stanley, C. J. -- 1786

1715 Felton, W. 1769
1715 Alcock, John ------------ 1806
1715 Nares, James 1783
1724 Worgan, J. -- 1790
1725 Walond, Wm. 1770
1726 Burney, Charles ------ 1814
1726 Jones, Wm. ------ 1800
1733 Dupuis ---- 1796
1734 Cooke, B. 1793
1738 Battishill, J. -- 1801
1738 Hayes, Philip ------ 1819
Blewitt, Jonas - 1805
Goodwin, Starling
Green, George
Heron, Henry
Burgess, Henry, the younger
Thorley, Thomas
Prelleur, Peter
Long, Samuel
ca.1750 Berg, G. 1771
1750 Beckwith, J. C. 1809
1752 Marsh, John -- 1828
Kirkman, J. 1792
1757 Wesley, Charles 1834
ca.1758 Broderip, R. 1808
1765 Attwood, T. --- 1838
1766 Wesley, S. --- 1837
Guest, George - 1831
1774 Linley, F. 1800
1781 Novello, Vincent --- 1861
1790 Viner, Wm. L. - 1867

The concertos reflect tremendous assurance, vitality, fire,
and strong secular gaiety, all of which is associated with this
renowned musician.   Handel synthesized his style from native
German, Italian, and English characteristics with the purpose
of pleasing English audiences.   The concertos are virtuoso
pieces, but most of them were written for the typical English
organs without pedals.   Concerto No. 7 (the first concerto
in the second set) is the only concerto which has an independent pedal part.   This work could have been written for
performance on an organ on the continent which had pedals.
The concerto might have been played on one of Handel's
several trips away from England.   The first movement contains rocking 16th-note figurations in the pedal part on broken intervals in the harmonies and quick scale passages on
the manuals.   Many of the concertos allow the organ soloist
to extemporize cadenzas, and there is much dialogue between
the organ and the full orchestra (ripieno).   At times the organ plays with a few orchestral instruments (concertino).
Strongly contrasting dynamics also help to clarify the form.

        The orchestra consisted of strings and two oboes,
with cellos, contrabasses, and bassons on the continuo part.[12]
The continuo was also played by the left hand on the harpsichord.   The Sixth Concerto is an exception to this orchestration because it calls for harp, two flutes, and muted vio-
lins, with the violas, cellos, and contrabass all playing piz-
zicato.   The 16th concerto in F major in six movements
adds two horns to the basic orchestration already mentioned.

        Forms used in the various movements are the French
overture, recitative, fugue, variation, march, and modified
dance forms (bourée, gigue, menuet).   The general division
of the concertos into four movements is taken from the Italian
church sonatas.   The most common arrangement of the movements was slow-fast-slow-fast.   Occasionally a short, slow
interlude introduces a quick movement.   Handel often borrowed themes or whole movements from his own concerti
grossi or compositions for other media and included them
in his organ concertos.   Sometimes he left notes for the organist to improvise a complete movement.   William Felton
(1715-1769) adopted Handel's concerto form for compositions
for organ or harpsichord.

        In addition to the concertos Handel wrote fugues and
voluntaries.   Six Fugues or Voluntaries for the Organ or
Harpsichord was published by Walsh in 1735, and another
edition was published in 1784 by Harrison.[13]   Twelve Volun-

taries and Fugues for the Organ or Harpsichord ... by the
Celebrated Mr. Handel was published by Longman and Broderip.[14] The fugues are characterized by rhythmic vitality
and smooth, flowing counterpoint, although some of the fugue
subjects contain rather wide leaps. The harmonic rhythm
usually changes every beat. Three of the six fugues are
double fugues. The G major fugue subject resembles some
fugues by Buxtehude because of the use of repeated notes on
one pitch.

Handel's voluntaries are divided into two sections in
slow-fast arrangement. The slow sections (Grave, Largo)
were intended to be played on small diapasons. The fast
sections emphasized the use of solo sounds such as the cornet, trumpet, or flute, and short echo passages. The texture is nearly always two-part and three-part. Cadential
trills are the principal ornaments employed. These voluntaries do not incorporate imitation as a unifying feature.

Thomas Roseingrave (1690-1766) was organist at St.
Georges, Hanover Square. He wrote fugues and voluntaries
for the organ. His ability to improvise contrapuntally was
greatly admired, but his part writing was eccentric at
times.[15] His two books were Voluntarys and Fugues Made
on Purpose for the Organ or Harpsichord and Six Double-
fugues for the Organ or Harpsichord.

Dr. Maurice Greene (ca. 1695-1755) was the organist
of St. Paul's Cathedral, London, and a friend of Handel.
His voluntaries, like those of Handel, fall into two sections.
The figural counterpoint is derived from the harmony. There
is little ornamentation except at cadences, and most of the
voice movement is stepwise. Since there are few accidentals
or modulations the music has a bland effect. The solo sounds
indicated in the Allegro sections are cornet or trumpet, and
echo passages are occasionally incorporated. Greene's two
volumes are Ten Voluntaries for Organ or Cembalo (1770)
and Twelve Voluntaries for the Organ or Harpsichord, published by J. Bland, London (1780?).[16]

Dr. William Boyce (1710-1779) was a pupil of Greene
and Dr. John Christopher Pepusch (1667-1752), a highly
respected teacher of many of the organists of that time. Ten
Voluntaries for the Organ or Harpsichord by Boyce was published after his death in 1785. He wrote antiphonally for the
solo Trumpet and echo in a dramatic manner, and his voluntaries resemble their German counterpart, the prelude and

fugue.   The texture of the Boyce voluntaries is three-part,
and the form employed is the slow larghetto followed by a
lively fugue or trumpet and echo piece.   The compositions
of Boyce are more attractive than many of those of his contemporaries because of their fresh and interesting rhythms
and tunes.

Dr. Boyce played at All Hallows-the-Great church
between 1749 and 1769.   The specifications are given below.

London.   All Hallows-the-Great, Thames Street.
Built by Glyn and Parker, 1749.

Great	Swell
Open Diapason 8'	Trumpet 8'(G-d^3)
Stopped Diapason 8'	Cornet III (G-d^3)
Principal 4'	
Twelfth 2 2/3'	Choir
Fifteenth 2'	Open Diapason 8'
Sesquialtera IV	Stopped Diapason 8'
Cornet V (c$\sharp^1$-d^3)	Flute 4'
Trumpet 8'	Twelfth 2 2/3'
	Vox Humana 8'

The Swell and Choir were played from the same manual, and
there were no pedals.

An outstanding composer of voluntaries was the blind
genius Charles John Stanley (1713-1786).   He wrote three
sets of ten voluntaries (Op. 5, 6, and 7), which were published in 1742.[17]   These pieces exhibit a wide variety of interesting harmonic, melodic, and rhythmic features within
the two section voluntary form for three voice lines.   Small
diapason tone, clear and unforced, is used for the opening
slow movements.   The second sections call for flute, trumpet, or cornet solos, and echo passages.   William Walond
(1725-1770) was another successful composer of voluntaries.
The Oxford organist wrote Six Voluntaries for Organ or
Harpsichord, published by J. Johnson (ca. 1760).

The Wesleys were a remarkable musical family.
Charles Wesley (1757-1834) and Samuel Wesley (1766-1837)
were the sons of Charles and nephews of John Wesley, the
two clergymen whose efforts at church reform eventually
produced the Methodist Church.   Charles' music was in-

fluenced by that of Bach, whom he admired a great deal.
Some of Charles' voluntaries contained four movements and
are dated about 1815.   His Six Concertos for the Organ or
Harpsichord ... were written about 1778 and published in
1781. [18]

Twelve Short Pieces for Keyboard (there are actually
13) by Samuel Wesley appeared in 1815. These are little character pieces, [19] which were composed in various forms, such as
through-composed pieces, dances, solos for "hautboy," flute,
cornet, vox humana, fugues, and ensemble pieces for a full
sound.   Probably the best known pieces from this group are the
Air in F major and a gavotte in the same key.   Two other books
of pieces by Samuel Wesley were Six Introductory Movements for
the Organ, Intended for the Use of Organists as Soft Voluntaries,
to be Performed at the Commencement of Services (ca. 1825) and
Six Voluntaries for the Organ (1820-1830).   The meeting of
Samuel Wesley and Felix Mendelssohn was an interesting
historical event.   Wesley composed the Fugue in B minor
for the occasion and was congratulated warmly by Mendelssohn after his performance. [20]

Notes

1.   A practice in organ building whereby the organist can
      secure the (same) sound by drawing stops on two dif-
      ferent manuals, although the pipes are actually sound-
      ing in only one division and not two.
2.   For a general description of the several types of volun-
      taries see Percy A. Scholes, The Oxford Companion to
      Music, 9th ed. , London: Oxford University Press,
      1959; p. 1103.
3.   Peter F. Williams, ed. , Three Voluntaries of the Later
      18th Century (Tallis to Wesley series, No. 22), Lon-
      don: Hinrichsen Edition Ltd. , 1961; preface.
4.   Willi Apel, Geschichte der Orgel- und Klaviermusik bis
      1700, Kassel, Germany: Bärenreiter Verlag, 1967;
      p. 737-741.
5.   Hugh McLean, Henry Purcell: The Organ Works, Novello
      & Company, London, 1957, Preface, iii.
6.   McLean mentions the anonymous O Lord Turn Not Away
      in Musica Britannica, vol. I, p. 80; and The Psalms
      by Dr. Blow Set Full for the Organ or Harpsichord as
      They Are Played in Churches or Chapels, London:
      John Walsh, 1731.
7.   Half-stops were used to play the melody above middle C

as a solo in the right hand on such stops as the Cornet or Trumpet and as an accompaniment on softer
registration in the left hand below middle C.

8.   Apel, op. cit. , p. 741-744.
9.   Apel, op. cit. , p. 745.
10. Francis Routh, "Handel's Organ Works," Handel's Four
     Voluntaries for Organ or Harpsichord (Tallis to Wes-
     ley series, No. 19), London: Hinrichsen, 1961.
11. Marcel Dupré, ed. , G. F. Handel: Seize Concertos,
     vol. I, Paris: Bornemann, 1937; preface, ii.
12. Although only the bass line was written out, the con-
     tinuo player was expected to fill out the harmonies.
13. Gordon Phillips, ed. , Handel: Six Fugues or Voluntaries,
     London: Hinrichsen Edition Ltd. , 1960; preface.
14. Francis Routh, "Handel's Organ Works," George Fri-
     deric Handel: Four Voluntaries. London: Hinrichsen
     Edition, Ltd. , 1961.
15. Denis Stevens, ed. , Thomas Roseingrave: Compositions
     for Organ and Harpsichord, University Park: Penn-
     sylvania State University Press, 1964; editor's note.
16. Several other composers of this school who also wrote
     fugues, concertos, and voluntaries in groups designed
     for either organ or harpsichord are Philip Hart (d.
     1749), Charles Avison (1710-1770), Dr. Thomas
     Augustine Arne (1710-1778), John Travers (ca. 1703-
     1758), and John Keeble (ca. 1711-1786).
17. Republished in a facsimile edition by Oxford University
     Press in 1957.
18. Gordon Phillips, ed. , The Wesleys (Tallis to Wesley
     series, No. 5), London: Hinrichsen Edition Ltd. ,
     1960; preface.
19. Character pieces were short compositions which rose to
     prominence during the nineteenth century. These
     pieces are usually composed in ternary form (A B A)
     and express many different moods and emotions or
     depict objects or actions. The character piece is
     typical of the programmatic compositions of the Ro-
     mantic period in music history.
20. Gordon Phillips, ed. , Samuel Wesley and Dr. Mendels-
     sohn (Tallis to Wesley series, No. 14), London:
     Hinrichsen Edition Ltd. , 1962; preface.

Bibliography

Anderson, Poul-Gerhard. Organ Building and Design, trans-
     lated into English by Joanne Curnutt. London: Oxford

University Press, 1969; p. 169-176.
Apel, Willi. Geschichte der Orgel- und Klaviermusik bis
    1700. Kassel, Germany: Bärenreiter Verlag, 1967;
    p. 309-318, 737-745.
Clutton, Cecil, and Austin Niland. The British Organ.
    London: B. T. Batsford, 1963; p. 52-89.
Dawes, Frank. "Philip Hart," Musical Times, no. 1469,
    vol. 106 (July 1965), p. 510.
_____. "The Music of Philip Hart (c. 1676-1749)," Pro-
    ceedings of the Royal Musical Association, vol. 94
    (1967-1968).
Dupré, Marcel, ed. G. F. Haendel: Seize Concertos, vol.
    I. Paris: Bornemann, 1937; preface, ii.
Frotscher, Gotthold. Geschichte des Orgelspiels und der
    Orgelkomposition. Berlin: Merseberger Verlag,
    1959; vol. II, p. 805-848.
Hutchings, Arthur. "The English Concerto with or for
    Organ," Musical Quarterly, vol. XLVII (April 1961),
    p. 195-206.
McLean, Hugh. Henry Purcell: The Organ Works. London:
    Novello and Co. , 1957; preface, iii.
Oldman, C. B. "Thomas Attwood, 1765-1838," Musical
    Times, no. 1473, vol. 106 (November 1965), p. 844.
Phillips, Gordon, ed. Handel: Six Fugues or Voluntaries.
    London: Hinrichsen Edition Ltd. , 1960; preface.
_____. "Purcell's Organs and Organ Music," Organ and
    Choral Aspects and Prospects (Ninth Music Book).
    London: Hinrichsen Edition Ltd. , 1958; p. 133-135.
_____. Samuel Wesley and Dr. Mendelssohn (Tallis to
    Wesley series, No. 14). London: Hinrichsen Edition
    Ltd. , 1962; preface.
_____. The Wesleys (Tallis to Wesley series, No. 5).
    London: Hinrichsen Edition Ltd. , 1960; preface.
Redlich, Hans F. "Samuel Wesley and the Bach Revival in
    England," Seventh Year Book. London: Hinrichsen
    Edition Ltd. , 1952.
Routh, Francis. "Handel's Organ Works," Handel's Four
    Voluntaries for Organ or Harpsichord (Tallis to Wes-
    ley series, No. 19). London: Hinrichsen Edition Ltd. ,
    1961.
Scholes, Percy A. "Voluntary," The Oxford Companion to
    Music, 9th ed. London: Oxford University Press,
    1956; p. 1103.
Stevens, Denis, ed. Thomas Roseingrave: Compositions for
    Organ and Harpsichord. University Park: Pennsyl-
    vania State University Press, 1964; editor's note.
_____. Thomas Tomkins: Three Hitherto Unpublished

Voluntaries (Francies, Verses) (Tallis to Wesley
series, No. 17). London: Hinrichsen Edition Ltd.,
1959; preface.

West, John Ebenezer. "Old English Organ Music," Proceedings of the Musical Association, vol. XXXVII
(1911), p. 1-16.

Williams, Peter F., ed. Three Voluntaries of the Later
18th Century (Tallis to Wesley series, No. 22). London: Hinrichsen Edition Ltd., 1961; preface.

11. SPAIN, PORTUGAL, AND ITALY: 1600-1800

Spain and Portugal

The two principal forms of Spanish and Portuguese organ music of the seventeenth and eighteenth centuries were versets (versos, versillos) and tientos. Versets were composed on the various chant tones for alternation between the organ and verses sung. The tientos were usually pieces of short duration, in three of four voice parts, which were frequently introduced by imitation. The tiento had its Italian counterpart in the ricercar. Tientos were contrapuntal, but the counterpoint was derived from the simple harmonic background. The use of accidentals and modulation was infrequent, and even that resulted only when closely related keys were introduced.

A Portuguese priest, Father Manoel Rodriguez Coelho (1583-ca. 1623), composed 24 tentos in his Flores de musica para o instrumento de tecla e harpa (Lisbon, 1620), the first instrumental work which was published in Portugal.[1] Pedro de Araujo (fl. 1600's) wrote a Tento de segundo tom in this same style.

A composition which presents a number of contrasting musical ideas is the Tiento de quarto tono por E la mi a modo de Canción by Francisco Correa de Arauxo (1575/1577-1663). Three sections begin with imitative entries, but an interlude and the final section have different rhythmic and melodic character from that of the standard tiento. Most of Correa's tientos are more dignified, longer, and more developed than those of Cabezón and other sixteenth-century Iberian composers. The seventeenth-century tientos are sectional, sometimes beginning sections with imitative entries and at other times begin with two or more parts sounding simultaneously. If there are a number of sections, the meter usually changes from duple to triple meter (often $\frac{3}{2}$ time) in at least one section and returns to duple meter for the last portion of the piece. The same material is alternated between higher and lower parts of the keyboard, sug-

1588	War between Spain and England
1588	Defeat of the Spanish Armada
1605	Cervantes Don Quixote, Part I
1605	Thomas Luis da Victoria Requiem
1617-1682	Murillo
1621-1665	Reign of Philip IV of Spain
1635	Velásquez Surrender of Breda
1637-1657	Reign of Ferdinand III, Holy Roman Emperor
1656	Velásquez The Maids of Honor
1665-1700	Reign of Charles II of Spain
1678	Murillo Mystery of the Immaculate Conception
1700-1746	Reign of Philip V of Spain
1702-1714	War of Spanish Succession
1755	Lisbon earthquake
1759-1788	Reign of Charles III of Spain
1756-1763	Seven Years' War between Spain and England
1773	Pope Clement XIV dissolved Jesuit order
1788-1808	Reign of Charles IV
1805	Battle of Trafalgar
1808-1814	War for Spanish independence from France

gesting the echo effect. The texture varies from two to four parts. The little ornamentation used is found at a few principal cadences. The most common dissonances are passing tones and chains of suspensions. Other tiento composers from this period were Diogo de Alvorado (d. 1643) and Pablo (Pau) Bruna.

The versos were tiny pieces, ten to 20 measures in length. Imitation of the chant melody was the principal unifying factor, and sometimes the added voices merely harmonized. Composers such as Agostinho da Cruz (ca. 1590-1633?), Lucas Puxol, Francisco Llusá (Llissa), Cándido Eznarriaga, Gabriel Menalt (d. 1687), and Diego de Torrijos (?-1691) wrote versillos.

Bartolomeo de Olague, probably from the seventeenth-century Catalan school, wrote a composition entitled Xácara de 1º tono, a series of variations of dance-like character built on a short harmonic theme in triple meter which suggests a chaconne.

Juan Cabanilles (1644-1712) was an outstanding Spanish composer who wrote tientos, passacaglias, gagliardas, battle pieces, paseos, diferencias, toccatas, pedazo de música, gaitilla, and xácara. Cabanilles wrote with rhythmic interest and vitality and freely used 16th-note patterns in sequences. His tientos, like those of Correa de Arauxo, are developed at some length, and employ more chromaticism than in those of his predecessors. Sometimes there is a tiento conceived as an entity, but most are sectional and adopt melodic metamorphosis when progressing to a different section. The texture never exceeds that of four parts, and the tientos are not always forced into imitative counterpoint. Some begin very majestically with slow-moving, full chords. Fray (Brother) Miguel Lopez (1669-1732) composed a number of short, direct versillos, always imitative but melodic and interesting. These pieces contain active eighth-note figures.

About the turn of the eighteenth century some new forms were used: tocata, fuga, paso, sonatina, and sonata. These reflect Italian influence, which was very strong in Spain. José Elías (ca. 1675-ca. 1749) wrote an extended Tocata de Contras Quinto Tono, which contained long 16th-note scale passages in a single line or in thirds over pedal points; the harmonies seldom change.

Joaquin Martinex Oxinagas wrote several florid pieces under the title Fuga. The texture is principally three part, with sections in invertible counterpoint and with echo effects suggested. Sequences supply a large part of the unifying material. In the same Italianate style were pieces by Juan Moreno y Polo (d. 1776).

Domenico Scarlatti, the famous Italian harpsichord sonata composer, spent from 1720 or 1721 until his death in 1757 in the service of royal patrons in Portugal and Spain. His influence was powerful and made itself felt in practically all of the eighteenth-century keyboard music of Spain and Portugal. Some of the composers who were influenced by Scarlatti were José Antonio Carlos Seixas (1704-1742), Freixanet, Manuel de Santo Elias (fl. 1750's-1790's), Padre Anselm Viola (1730-1798), Joao de Souza Carvalho (1745-1798), and José Lidon (1752-1827). Lidon composed a stirring two-part Sonata da 1º Tono para clave o para organo con trompeta real. This sonata is dramatic when played on strong, fiery reed stops for which Iberian organs are famous. Many compositions by these composers are in binary form. They utilize two-voice texture and could be played on all

keyboard instruments. Rhythmic vitality, pleasing melodies
and harmony, with key relationships which clarify the structure are features of music composed under Scarlatti's influence.

Fray Antonio Soler (1720-1783) is famous for Seis
Conciertos para dos Organos. The two instruments sometimes play simultaneously, at other times antiphonally. These
concertos are all written in two movements. The first movement is in duple meter, usually in a slower tempo than the
second movement. The Minue in triple meter is the second
movement, a series of variations. A generous amount of
ornamentation is employed throughout these pieces. The concertos do not use pedal, however.

Spanish organs of the seventeenth and eighteenth centuries are especially interesting. Half-stops had become
popular in Spain by 1620, where they were used for colorful
solo sounds played by the right hand above $c\sharp^1$ and accompanied
by the left hand on the lower part of the same keyboard.

The most striking element of the Spanish organs of
this period was the inclusion of horizontal trumpets called
reeds en chamade, a French term which has no connection
with the reeds' origin or name. There are horizontal reeds
to be found on the organ in Burgos; the date of the building
of the organ might be 1636. Cavaillé-Coll, the famous nineteenth-century organ builder, was deeply impressed by the
brilliant reeds found in Spanish organs. Horizontal reeds
were easy for the tuners to reach, and they gave an even,
strong, penetrating, direct sound, which stood out above the
mild chorus stops and delicate mixtures.

Spanish baroque organ building reached its climax
during the eighteenth century in the large instruments designed for the major cathedrals. It is not uncommon to find
two organs in large Spanish churches, as the specification
schemes of two organs in the Braga Cathedral confirm. [2]
The organs, which were built in 1737-1738, were not connected. The organ on the south side of the choir has one
manual of 45 notes. The manual divided between c^1 and
$c\sharp^1$. The organ has no pedal. Stops are arranged for the
left side and for the right side of the manual and affect only
that corresponding side of the manual. Three horizontal
reeds are found on both sides, and the stop for one additional
reed (Trompeta real 8') is found on the right hand side. The
second organ (on the north side of the choir) has two manuals

SPANISH AND PORTUGUESE COMPOSERS: 1600-1800

1600	1650	1700	1750	1800	1850

1575/77 Correa de Arauxo 1663
1583 Coehlo ca. 1623?
   de Alvorado 1643
ca. 1590 da Cruz 1633
      de Araujo, Pedro
       1644 Cabanilles, J. 1712
         de Torrijos 1691
         Puxol, Lucas
         Menalt, G. 1687
         Bruno, Pablo (Pau)
         de Olague, Bartolomeo
         Llussá, Francisco
         Eznarriaga, Cándido
         Ximenes, José
         Crest, Rafael
         Andreu, Francisco
         Viladrosa, Sebastián
         Serrado, Isidoro
         Rouxa, Pablo
         Salo, Juan
           1664 Nassarre (Fray) 1724
           1669 Lopez, M. 1732
         ca. 1675 Elías, J. ca. 1749
                  Oxinagas, Joaquin Martinez
                  Moreno y Polo, Juan 1776
               1704 Seixas, J. 1742
               (1720-57 D. Scarlatti in Portugal and Spain)
               1729 Soler, Antonio 1783
            ca. 1730 Freixanet
                  de Santo Elias, Manuel
             1736 Sessé y Balaguer, Juan de
             1739 Viola, Anselm 1798
               1742 Lopez, Félix Máximo 1821
                  Baptista, Francisco Xavier
                  Conceiçao, Diogo da
                  Silva, João Cordeiro da
                  Silva, Alberto José Gomes da 1795
                  Olagué, Martinho Gracia de (Portu-
                     guese)
                  Rodriguez, Vicente
                  Jacinto (Frei)
             1745 Carvalho, João 1798
               1752 Lidon, José 1827
                  Carrera y Lanchares, Pedro

and pedal.   The stops are either halved or available on only
the treble or bass side.   Part of the stops for the second
manual form an Echo division inside the case.   The pedal
has only one stop, the Contras 16'.

Italy

        Seventeenth-century Italian composers continued to
write ricercars, canzonas, fugues, toccatas, Mass movements, Magnificat versets, and organ hymns.   Two new
forms which were introduced during this period were the
pastorale and sonata.

        Michel Angelo Rossi (ca. 1600-ca. 1674) published two
books: Toccate e corrente per organo, o cembalo (1657)
and Toccate e corrente d'intavolatura d'organo e cimbalo.
Among his compositions is a Partite sopra La Romanesca,
a series of four variations on a famous secular tune.   Rossi
continued the toccata tradition of his predecessors but cast
his toccatas in the form of three sections.   Each section is
introduced by sustained chords before beginning the running
sixteenth-note figures and fugato passages.   If the pedal is
used, long, sustained notes are held as pedal-points to support the active manual voices.   Rossi also composed versetti.

        Vagueness of terminology still existed.   There was a
close relationship between the sectional canzona and the sonata
in which sections are written in different meters, but the
sections are based on related thematic material.   A sonata
of this type is the Sonata chromatica by Tarquinio Merula
(ca. 1590-after 1652).   Ambiguity also appears again in the
works of Carlo Francesco Pollaroli (1653-1722), whose capriccio and sonata exhibit no stylistic differences.   Pollaroli's
Fuga is an extended work constructed on one subject.

        Annuale, Che contiene tutto quello che deve fare un
organista per risponder al choro tutto l'anno by Giovanni
Battista Fasolo (early seventeenth century) appeared in Venice
in 1645.   This book provided organ pieces to play in response
to the sung portions of the Te Deum, Masses, the Magnificat,
and organ hymns.   All of these pieces are necessarily short
and in four parts.   The parts sometimes enter imitatively or
as simple, harmonizing voices.

        Bernardo Pasquini (1637-1710) wrote sectional toccatas
which change meter at the different sections and frequently

HISTORICAL BACKGROUND

1503-1707	Naples belonged to Spain
1600	Galileo law of falling bodies
1621-1623	Reign of Pope Gregory XV
1637	First public opera house, Venice
1642	Monteverdi L'Incoronazione di Poppea
1643	Death of Frescobaldi
1650	Carissimi Jephtha
1662	Cavalli Ercole amante
1681	Corelli trio sonatas
1698	Torelli violin concertos, Op. 5
1707	A. Scarlatti Mitridate eupatore
1733	Pergolesi La Serva padrona
1735-1759	Reign of Charles, King of Naples
1760	Villa d'Este erected in Tivoli
1763	Excavations begun at Pompeii and Herculaneum
1769	Mozart travelled in Italy
1778	La Scala opened in Milan
1792	Cimarosa Il Matrimonio segreto
1796	Napoleon's battles in Italy

have 16th-note activity occurring in one part. Pasquini's Introduzione e pastorale is long and contains an introduction which is in the rocking, dotted rhythm associated with the siciliano. Some of Pasquini's sonatas appeared in Sonate da organo di vari autori, edited by Aresti around 1687.

Giovanni Maria Casini (1670?-1714) composed Pensieri per l'organo in partitura (1714). The eighth pensiero from Book Two is in three separate sections, but all three parts are based on the same melodic material. The third section is a lively gigue. Much of the voice movement is stepwise, and there are many parallel thirds and sixths and much chromaticism. Sonatas and toccatas by Azzolino Bernadino della Ciaja (1671-1744) appeared in his Sonate per cembalo ... e grave stile ecclesiastico, per grandi organi (1727).

The opera composer Nicolo Antonio Porpora (1686-1766) and Giuseppe Bencini (fl. early 1700's) contributed fugues. Porpora's fugue writing, however, suggests composition for strings rather than for organ.

Domenico Zipoli (1688-1726), the organist of the Jesuit church in Rome and a missionary to Argentina, wrote a two-part work called Sonate d'intavolatura per organo, o

ITALIAN ORGAN COMPOSERS: ca. 1600–1850

    1600   1650   1700   1750   1800

Rossi, Michel Angelo
Salvatore, Giovanni -- 1688?
Merula, T. ------ 1652
Fasolo, G. B.
  1590 Vitali, Filippo 1653
fl. 1599 Gussago, Cesario
  1600/01 Battiferri, L. 1682?
 ca. 1600 Fantini, G. ?
        Giustiniani, Michele
  1605 Carissimi, Giacomo 1674
 ca. 1620 Ziani, P. A. 1684
        1637 Colonna, G. P. 1695
        1637 Pasquini, Bernardo 1710
           Fontana, Fabrizio 1695
           Aresti, Giulio Cesare
           Storace, Bernardo
           1653 Pollaroli, C. F. 1722
          ca. 1657 Bassani, G. B. 1716
             1661 Perti, Jacopo Antonio 1756
          ca. 1667 Lotti, Antonio 1740
             1670? Casini, G. M. 1714
             1671 della Ciaja, A. B. 1744
           ca. 1673 Aldrovandini, G. 1708
             1673 Feroci, Francesco 1750
             1678 Vivaldi, Antonio 1741
               1684 Durante, Francesco 1755
               (1685 Scarlatti, Domenico 1757)
               1686 Porpora, Nicolo Antonio
               1686 Marcello, B. 1739
               1688 Zipoli, D. 1726
                  Santini, Giuseppe Maria
                  Marzola, Pietro
                  Palafuti
                  Bencini, Giuseppe
                  Jacchini, Giuseppe
               1693 Sammartini, Giuseppe 1750
              ca. 1704 Pescetti, Giovanni B. 1766
                1706 Martini, Giovanni Battista 1784
                1710 Pergolesi, G. B. 1763
                  1721 Gasparini, Q. 1778
                  ca. 1735 Monza, Carlo 1801
                  ca. 1735 Cattenacci, G. D. ca. 1800
                     Franzosini, Bartolomeo
                     1750 Salieri, Antonio 1825
                     1759 Gherardeschi, G. 1815
                       1760 Valeri, Gaetano 1822
                       1762 Santucci, Marco 1843
                       1762 Gervasoni, Carlo 1819
                          Consolini, Luigi

cimbalo (1716). Part One contained seven types of organ
composition: verset, toccata, canzona, elevation, post-
communion, offertory, and pastorale. Part Two contained
only two types, suites and variations. Zipoli's writing is
easy and direct. The phrases are evenly matched, and simple harmonies change at regular intervals. The versetti are
a bit more extended than others had been before Zipoli's
time; the canzona is in two forms, through-composed and
sectional. The Pastorale, probably Zipoli's best-known composition, is in three sections. The slow first and last sections are written in $1\frac{2}{8}$ time, and the middle section contrasts by being quick and in a dotted rhythm.

Benedetto Marcello (1686-1739) wrote vocal settings
for one to four voices with basso continuo for Giustiniani's
paraphrases of the first 50 Psalms. [3]

The outstanding eighteenth-century Italian organ composer was Padre Giovanni Battista (Giambattista) Martini
(1706-1784), a Franciscan with whom Mozart studied. Martini had two volumes published, Sonate d'intavolatura per
l'organo, e'l cembalo (1742), and a collection, Sonate per
l'organo e il cembalo (1747). Most of his compositions suggest writing for the cembalo rather than for the organ.

Several books of versetti were written during the
eighteenth century: Libro di Sonate d'organo d'intavolatura
... fatto per comodo da sonare alle Messe, Vespri, com-
piete, ed altro (1720) by Giuseppe Maria Santini (1778-1862);
Versetti in tutti li tuoni Coralli by Pietro Marzola (fl. 1700's);
and 112 Versetti per organo per rispondere al coro in tutti
i tuoni del canto fermo by Marco Santucci (1762-1843). An
unusual composition is the Sonata a 3 organi col basso by
Carlo Zenolini (Zanolini) (fl. 1700's).

Notes

1. M. S. Kastner, ed. , Cravistas Portuguezes, vol. I,
    Mainz, Germany: B. Schott's Söhne, 1935; preface.
    Also see Willi Apel, Geschichte der Orgel- und
    Klaviermusik bis 1700, Kassel, Germany: Bärenreiter
    Verlag, 1967; p. 507-613.
2. Peter Williams, The European Organ 1450-1850, London:
    Batsford, 1966; p. 245-260.
3. Organ transcriptions of Psalms 19 and 20 have been
    made by such editors as Guilmant and Biggs.

Bibliography

SPAIN AND PORTUGAL

Andersen, Poul-Gerhard. Organ Building and Design, trans-
    lated into English by Joanne Curnutt. New York: Ox-
    ford University Press, 1969; p. 159-169.
Apel, Willi. Geschichte der Orgel- und Klaviermusik bis
    1700. Kassel, Germany: Bärenreiter Verlag, 1967;
    p. 507-537, 751-754.
Williams, Peter. The European Organ 1450-1850. London:
    B. T. Batsford Ltd. , 1966; p. 243-261.
Wyly, James. "The Pre-Romantic Spanish Organ: Its
    Structure, Literature, and Use in Performance. " Un-
    published Ph. D. dissertation, University of Missouri,
    1964.

ITALY

Andersen, Poul-Gerhard. Organ Building and Design, trans-
    lated into English by Joanne Curnutt. New York: Ox-
    ford University Press, 1969; p. 115-121.
Apel, Willi. Geschichte der Orgel- und Klaviermusik bis
    1700. Kassel, Germany: Bärenreiter Verlag, 1967;
    p. 473-747, 476-479, 677-682.
Williams, Peter. The European Organ 1450-1850. London:
    Batsford, 1966; p. 212-230.

12. GERMANY AFTER BACH: 1725-1800

Although Bach exerted a strong influence upon his pupils, the taste of the music-loving public was rapidly changing. Polyphonic elements and forms were incorporated, but other styles of music such as the style galant took precedence. The importance of chorale settings and polyphonic forms, which had reached their zenith in the works of Bach, was greatly diminished. Chorale settings were written by few composers; the few settings were not convincing and lacked the strength and energy of pure contrapuntal works because of the secular style in which they were written. [1]

Johann Ludwig Krebs (1713-1780) was the outstanding pupil of Bach. [2] Krebs' artistic compositions owe much to his famous teacher and show that he probably was an able performer, if we can judge by the active and demanding pedal solos and the carefully wrought, technically challenging writing for manuals in his works. Krebs also composed for solo instruments and organ. He assigned the chorale melody to the oboe or trumpet, and a contrapuntal trio of interweaving voices was written for the organ. Krebs' Fantasie for oboe and organ is a beautiful free work in ternary form.

Bach's sons made few contributions to organ literature. Wilhelm Friedemann Bach's chief musical ability was improvisation. Carl Philipp Emanuel Bach (1714-1788) wrote Preludio e sei Sonate per Organo (1790) for house organ. Other sons who wrote organ compositions were Johann Christoph Friedrich Bach (1732-1795) and Johann Christian Bach (1735-1782).

Johann Christian Kittel (1732-1809), one of the last pupils of Bach, became an influential teacher. Among his writings are a three-part organ method Der angehende praktische Organist, Vierstimmige Choräle mit Vorspielen (1803), Vierundzwanzig kurze Choralvorspiele, and Grosse Präludien. [3]

Even though Wolfgang Amadeus Mozart (1756-1791) wrote that he was very fond of the organ, he left few organ

1725	Fux Gradus ad Parnassum
1740-1786	Reign of Frederick the Great of Prussia
1742	C. P. E. Bach Prussian Sonatas
1742-1745	Reign of Charles VII, Holy Roman Emperor
1745	Stamitz went to Mannheim
1748	War of Austrian Succession ended
1750	Quantz flute concertos
1752	First German Singspiele
1753	C. P. E. Bach Versuch über die wahre Art
1755	Graun Der Tod Jesu
1755	Haydn first quartets
1764	Winckelmann Geschichte der Kunst der Altertums
1769	Mozart travelled in Italy
1781	Kant Critique of Pure Reason
1782	Mozart Die Entführung
1782	Schiller Die Räuber
1786-1797	Reign of Frederick Wilhelm II of Prussia
1786	Mozart Le nozze di Figaro
1787	Goethe Iphigenia
1789-1794	French Revolution and rise of Napoleon
1791	Mozart Requiem
1792	Beethoven went to Vienna
1800	Haydn Seasons

compositions. His sonatas for several combinations of small instrumental ensembles and organ contain elements of the church trios and other keyboard forms. The organ, however, supplies little more than a figured bass with a few solo passages. These sonatas were written to be used as interludes between the Epistle and Gospel at High Mass when Mozart was serving at the Salzburg Cathedral. He called them "sonata all'epistola." The archbishop had ruled that the service should last no longer than 45 minutes, thus limiting the length of time available for music to a few minutes.

Mozart's two Fantasias in F Minor (K. 608 and K. 594) were written during the last two years of his life for a mechanical flute organ in a large clock. The naïve Andante in F Major was also written for a musical clock. The two fantasias are technically quite difficult, especially since some adapting must be done in order that they can be performed on the modern organ. The fantasias were commissioned by Count von Deym for his museum-art gallery in Vienna. The

larger fantasia (K. 608) is in three sections. Massive chords
separated by flourishes, which suggest the French overture,
introduce the first and third sections. The Andante section in
the middle is a series of variations in A-flat major. Stirring
fugal parts are found in the center of the two outer sections and
draw the whole fantasia to a brilliant close. The other, less frequently played but quite beautiful, Fantasia in F Minor(K. 594)
is also in large ternary form. The first theme of the opening
and closing parts is played by the pedal, which outlines the harmonies sustained on the manuals. The middle division of the
fantasia is in the parallel major key and contrasts a strong rhythmic and chordal motive with quick-flowing streams of parallel
thirds, sixths, and tenths in 16th-notes.

Franz Joseph Haydn (1732-1809) wrote 32 tiny pieces for
a mechanical flute organ in a clock (Spieluhrstücke). He also
wrote three concertos in C major about 1760. The concertos
are written for organ (or cembalo), two oboes, and string orchestra. There is no organ pedal part, nor are the oboes used
in the slow movements. The three movements are arranged in
fast-slow-fast order.

Johann Christoph Oley (1738-1789), a pupil of J. S. Bach,[4]
composed chorale preludes in the stolid, learned style. [5]

Justin Heinrich Knecht (1752-1817) gave his pieces
dramatic titles and subjective markings such as Sehnsuchts-
voll (full of yearning) and Etwas feurig und doch angenehm
(rather fiery and yet pleasing), and musical characteristics
of broken chords, colorful, romantic chromaticism, and
orchestral effects. One of his compositions was entitled
Die Auferstehung Jesu ("The Resurrection of Jesus") with
subtitles such as schauervolle Stille des Graves (dreadful
stillness of the grave), das Zurückstürzen der römischen
Schaar (the falling backwards of the Roman troops) and
Triumphgesang der Engle (angels' song of triumph). Knecht
is also known for his Orgelschule des Choral (1795-1798).

Abbé Georg Joseph Vogler (1749-1814) was a man of
many talents: writer, acoustician, inventor, teacher, composer, virtuoso organist, and priest. His conceptions of
organ building were not successful, although many of them
were cordially received. At his recitals his improvisations
included fantastic effects like Seeschlacht mit Trommelrühren
(sea battle with drum rolls), Geschrei der Verwundeten (cries
of the wounded), Jauchzen der Sieger (shouts of the victor),
and Das Wetter in April (April Weather). His performance

GERMANY AFTER BACH: 1725-1825

        1700   1750   1800

1673 Grunewald, G. 1739
1675 Justinus a Desponsatione 1747
ca. 1678 Peyer, J. B. 1733
     (1685 Bach, Johann Sebastian 1750)
     1685 Kirchhoff, Gottfried 1746
     1688 Fasch, Johann Friedrich 1758
       1690 Krebs, Johann Tobias 1762
       1690 Stölzel, G. H. 1749
    ca. 1690 Nauss, Johann Xaver 1761
    ca. 1695 Molter, Johann Melchior 1765
       1696 Vogler, Johann Caspar 1763
       1699 Hasse, Johann Adolf 1783
        ca. 1700 Kniller, Anton ?
           1701 Agrell, J. J. 1765 (Swedish)
           1702 Eberlin, Johann E. 1762
           1702 Schneider, Johann 1788
           1702 Maichelbeck, F. A. 1750
           1705 Kellner, Johann Peter 1772
           1708 Scheibe, Johann Adolf 1776
               1710 Bach, Wilhelm Friedemann 1784
               1713 Krebs, Johann Ludwig 1780
               1714 Homilius, Gottfried 1785
               1714 Bach, Carl Philipp Emanuel 1788
               1715 Doles, Johann Friedrich 1797
               1716 Seger, Joseph F. 1782 (Bohemian)
               1717 Stamitz, J. W. A. 1757
               1717 Mozart, Leopold 1787
               1718 Marpurg, Friedrich Wilhelm 1795
               1719 Monn, G. M. 1750 (Austrian)
                  1720 Agricola, J. F. 1774
                  1721 Kirnberger, Johann P. 1783
                  1727 Hertel, Johann Wilhelm 1789
                      Hugl, Franz Anton
                      1730 Pasterwitz, Georg von 1803
                      1732 Bach, J. C. F. 1795
                      1732 Kittel, Johann Christian 1809
                      1732 Haydn, Franz Joseph 1809
                      1735 Bach, Johann Christian 1783
                      1736 Albrechtsberger, Johann G. 1809
                      1737 Schneider, Franz 1812
                      1737 Haydn, Johann Michael 1806
                      1738? Oley, Johann C. 1789
                          1740 Schnizer, Franz Xaver 1785
                          1744 Prixner, Peter S. 1799
                          1748 Stadler, Maximilian 1833
                          1748 Telemann, Georg Michael 1831
                          1749 Vogler, Georg Joseph 1814
                              1750 Vierling, J. G. 1813
                              1752 Knecht, J. H. 1817
                              1753 Ruppe, Christian Friedrich 1826
                              1756 Mozart, Wolfgang A. 1791
                                  1760 Grätz, Joseph 1826
                                  1767 Schwenke, C. F. G. 1822
                                    1770 Beethoven Ludwig van 1827

of H. H. Knecht's Pastoral Festival Interrupted by a Storm
stirred the imagination of the sensation-seeking public.   The
great array of combinations and color possibilities of the organ (which often fascinate laymen) were exploited by both
Knecht and Vogler and anticipated and contributed to the de-
cadent organ style and the decline of the influence of the organ which marked a major portion of the nineteenth century. [6]

Ludwig van Beethoven (1770-1827) wrote very few organ works.   They consist of Zwei Praeludien durch alle Dur-
tonen für Orgel (auch für Klavier), Op. 39 (1789), Zweistim-
mige Fuge für Orgel (D major) (1783), and three short pieces
which can be played as a group: Adagio, Scherzo, and Allegro
(1799).   The last three pieces were composed for a mechanical organ in a clock at the request of Count von Deym, the
same man who commissioned Mozart's fantasias. [7] A principal theme is the unifying item in each of the two preludes
which progress through all major keys.   The short Fugue in
D Major is in two voices, with additional voices added for
the last 15 measures to strengthen the final cadence.   This
piece was composed when Beethoven was only 13 years of
age.

The Bohemian (Czech) school of organ composers is
a small one, which is related to the stronger schools in Germany and Italy.   Bohuslav Czernohorský (1684-1742), a Mi-
norite friar, was the first important composer and teacher in
the school.   He was followed by Jan (Johann) Zach (1699-
1773), Joseph Seger (Seeger) (1716-1782), František Xaver
Brixi (1732-1771), Jan Křtitel Vanhal (1739-1813), and Jan
Křtitel Kuchař (1756-1829).   Anton Rejcha (Reicha) (1770-1836)
was a Bohemian teacher whose pupils such as Liszt, Gounod,
Franck, and Berlioz became far better known than he.   Lighthearted organ music of the Czech school was written in forms
such as the fugue, toccata, prelude, and pastorale. [8]

Notes

1.   Composer-pupils of J. S. Bach who wrote a few chorale
     settings are Johann Kaspar Vogler (1693-1763), Johann
     Schneider (1702-1788), Johann Tobias Krebs (1690-1762),
     the father of Johann Ludwig Krebs, Heinrich Nicolaus
     Gerber (1702-1755), Johann Peter Kellner (1705-1722),
     Johann Trier (1716-1789/1790), Johann Friedrich Agri-
     cola (1720-1774), Johann Philipp Kirnberger (1721-1783),
     Gottfried August Homilius (1714-1785), Johann Friedrich
     Doles (1715-1797), and Johann Gottfried Müthel (1728-
     1788).

2. Bach himself said, in making a pun on their names, that
    his pupil was the best crab (Krebs) in the brook (Bach).
3. Some less significant composers: Johann Scheibe (1708-
    1776), Johann Eberlin (1702-1762), and Johann Albrechts-
    berger (1736-1809), one of Beethoven's teachers. Eber-
    lin, under the influence of Bach's Wohltemperirte Clavier,
    issued IX Toccate e fughe per l'organo (1747).
4. Hans Löffler, "Die Schüler Joh. Seb. Bachs," Bach-
    Jahrbuch im Auftrage der Neuen Bachgesellschaft, Al-
    fred Dürr and Werner Neumann, eds. , Berlin: Evangel-
    ische Verlaganstalt, Vol. XL (1953), p. 6, 26.
5. For an interesting comment on the music of this period
    see the General Preface to J. G. Oley, Four Chorale
    Preludes, London: Novello and Co. , 1958.
6. William Leslie Sumner, The Organ: Its Evolution, Prin-
    ciples of Construction, and Use, London: Macdonald
    and Co. , 1952 (2nd ed. , 1955); p. 206.
7. Ludwig Altman, ed. , Beethoven Organ Works, London:
    Hinrichsen Edition Ltd. , 1962; preface.
8. A Century of Czech Music, 2 vols. , Karel Paukert, ed. ,
    Chicago: H. T. FitzSimons Co. , 1965.

Bibliography

Altman, Ludwig, ed.   Beethoven Organ Works.   London:
    Hinrichsen Edition Ltd. , 1962; preface.
Biba, Otto.   "The Unknown Organ Music of Austria,"
    Diapason (January 1971), p. 10.
Emery, Walter, ed.   J. G. Oley Four Chorale Preludes.
    London: Novello and Co. , 1958; general preface.
Frotscher, Gotthold.   Geschichte des Orgelspiels und der
    Orgelkomposition.   Berlin: Merseberger Verlag, 1959;
    vol. II, p. 1048-1122.
Harmon, Thomas.   "The Performance of Mozart's Church
    Sonatas," Music & Letters, vol. 51, no. 1 (January
    1970), p. 51.
Löffler, Hans.   "Die Schüler Joh. Seb. Bachs," Bach-Jahr-
    buch im Auftrage der Neuen Bachgesellschaft, Alfred
    Dürr and Werner Neumann, eds.   Berlin: Evangelische
    Verlaganstalt, Vol. XL (1953), p. 6, 26.
Mansfield, Orlando A.   "Mozart's Organ Sonatas," Musical
    Quarterly, vol. VII (1922), p. 566-594.
Mulbury, David.   "Bach's Favorite Pupil: Johann Ludwig
    Krebs," Music/the A. G. O. Magazine, vol. II, no. 2
    (February 1968), p. 24.
Paukert, Karel, ed.   A Century of Czech Music, 2 vols.

Chicago: H. T. FitzSimons Co. , 1964.
Sumner, William Leslie. "Beethoven and the Organ," Musical Opinion, no. 1110, vol. 93 (March 1970), p. 323-325.

_____. The Organ: Its Evolution, Principles of Construction, and Use. London: Macdonald and Co. , 1952 (2nd. ed. , 1955); p. 205-208.
Tangeman, Robert. "Mozart's Seventeen Epistle Sonatas," Musical Quarterly, vol. XXXII (October 1946), p. 588-601.

13.   GERMANY AND ENGLAND: 1800-1900

Germany

The two most prominent organ building firms in Germany during the nineteenth century were the Schulze and Walcker companies.   J. A. Schulze and his son J. F. Schulze did not break with tradition, but the theories of Abt Vogler and Knecht did influence them somewhat.   Eight-foot stops predominated on the manuals;   mutations and mixtures were used less and less because they were not well made and sometimes contained a tierce which did not blend well with the ensemble.   Schulze also employed free reeds, increased the wind-pressure, and developed a solo manual.[1]

The Walcker firm began building organs in the eighteenth century.   In 1820 E. F. Walcker moved the firm to Ludwigsburg where he built many organs, some of the largest in the world, along dark, somber tonal schemes.   One unusual characteristic of some of Walcker's organs was the inclusion of two pedal boards.   One of the most important nineteenth-century instruments built by this firm was erected in Paulskirche, Frankfurt.[2]   The specifications are given below.

Frankfurt, Germany, Paulskirche.
Built by E. F. Walcker, 1827-1833.

Hauptwerk (I)	Oberwerk (II)	Manual (III) (enclosed)
Untersatz 32'	Bourdon 16'	Quintatön 16'
Prinzipal 16'	Prinzipal 8'	Prinzipal 8'
Viola da Gamba 16'	Salizional 8'	Harmonica 8'
Tibia major 16'	Dolce 8'	Bifra 8'
Oktave 8'	Gedackt 8'	Hohlflöte 8'
Viola da Gamba 8'	Quintatön 8'	Lieblich Gedackt 8'
Jubalflöte 8'	Quinteflöte 5 1/3'	Dolcissimo 8'
Gemshorn 8'	Oktave 4'	Spitzflöte 4'
Quinte 5 1/3'	Flauto traverso 4'	Lieblich Gedackt 4'
Oktave 4'	Rohrflöte 4'	Flûte d'amour 4'

HISTORICAL BACKGROUND

1797-1828	Schubert
1797-1856	Heine
1801	Haydn Seasons
1804	Schiller William Tell
1804	Beethoven "Eroica" Symphony
1806	Holy Roman Empire dissolved
1806	Goethe Faust
1808	Beethoven "Pastoral" Symphony
1813-1883	Wagner
1814	Beethoven Fidelio
1815-1866	German Confederation
1822	Schubert "Unfinished" Symphony
1823	Beethoven Ninth Symphony
1844-1900	Nietszche
1845	Wagner Tannhäuser
1847	Communist Manifesto
1854	Hanslick On the Beautiful in Music
1858	Brahms Ein deutsches Requiem
1859	Wagner Tristan und Isolde
1862	Bismarck became chancellor of Prussia
1867-1916	Reign of Franz Joseph I of Austria-Hungary
1871	Bismarck became chancellor of Germany
1888-1918	Reign of Kaiser Wilhelm II
1888	Hugo Wolf Mörike Lieder
1895	R. Strauss Till Eulenspiegel

Hohlpfeife 4'	Quinte 2 2/3'	Nasard 2 2/3'
Fugara 4'	Oktave 2'	Flautino 2'
Tierce 3 1/5'	Mixtur V	Hautboy 8'
Quinte 2 2/3'	Posaune 8'	Physharmonika 8'
Oktave II	Vox humana 8'	
Waldflöte 2'		Pedal II (upper)
Tierce 1 3/5'		
Oktave 1'		Violon 16'
Mixtur V		Subbass 16'
Scharff IV		Prinzipal 8'
Cornet V		Flöte 8'
Tuba 16'		Flöte 4'
Trompete 8'		Waldflöte 2'
		Fagott 16'

Pedal I (lower)		Couplers
Subbass 32'	Tierce 6 2/5'	Oberwerk to Hauptwerk
Contrabass 32'	Quinte 5 1/3'	Manual to Hauptwerk

Prinzipal 16'	Oktave 4'	Manual to Oberwerk
Oktave 16'	Posaune 16'	Pedal I to Pedal II
Violon 16'	Trompete 8'	Hauptwerk to Pedal I
Quinte 10 2/3'	Clarine 4'	Oberwerk to Pedal II
Oktave 8'	Clarinetto 2'	
Violoncello 8'		

Slider chests; mechanical action

One of the major expressions of Romanticism in German organ music is found in the organ compositions of Felix Mendelssohn (1809-1847), which include Three Preludes and Fugues, Op. 37 (C minor, G major, D minor), and Six Sonatas. The preludes and fugues were dedicated to Thomas Attwood, the London organist, and were composed between 1835 and 1837. Mendelssohn's interest in earlier music, especially the music of Bach, suggested the prelude and fugue form. He employed harmonically determined counterpoint in these pieces.

The English publishers Coventry and Hollier commissioned Mendelssohn to write three voluntaries for the organ. Since Mendelssohn was not familiar with the voluntary form, he chose to name his compositions sonatas, even though no movement is in sonata-allegro form.[3] Sonata No. 3 in A major was composed in August, 1844, and the other five (No. 1 in F minor, No. 2 in C minor, No. 4 in B-flat major, No. 4 in D major, No. 6 in D minor) were all composed within two months, December, 1844, and January, 1845. Most of the slow movements were cast in simple binary form; several movements approached a rondo form. The Allegretto (Sonata No. 4) resembles many of Mendelssohn's songs without words. The first movement of the Sixth Sonata is a series of variations on the chorale Vater unser im Himmelreich ("Our Father, Who in Heaven Art"). Musical inspiration seems to have guided the form of these pieces rather than any predetermined mold. Another chorale, Aus tiefer Not ("Out of the Depths"), appears in the first movement of the third sonata. The use of chorales suggests that Mendelssohn intended these sonatas for church performance.[4] He also decided to close the third and sixth sonatas with slow, soft movements, an unusual procedure.

Remarkable features of the sonatas include: close imitation between parts; use of pedal points and sequences; fugues of loose construction; crossing parts; combination of themes; filling out of harmonies with added voices and un-

resolved discords at the ends of phrases; melodies built on
arpeggio or scale figures; phrases sometimes repeated an octave above or below; phrased pedal part, sometimes using
staccato articulation for a complete section, with a number of
pedal scales; and manual technique calling for a toccata touch.
Mendelssohn's other organ compositions include a Fugue in F
Minor (1830), Praeludium in C Minor (1841) and Two Pieces:
Andante con variazione in D Major [and] Allegro in B-flat
Major (1844).

Mendelssohn's enthusiasm for the music of Bach encouraged him to perform the following recital of Bach organ
works in St. Thomas' Church, Leipzig, on August 6, 1840:

> Fugue in E-flat Major
> Schmücke dich
> Prelude and Fugue in A Minor
> Passacaglia and Fugue in C Minor
> Pastorale
> Toccata in F Major

The most prominent pupil of Johann Christian Kittel
(a pupil of Bach) was Johann Christian Heinrich Rinck (1770-
1846).   Rinck's organ music, which is designed for concert
use, is melodious and charming and contains many figurations
on harmony and sequences.   Adolphe Hesse (1809-1863) admired Bach's organ works and encouraged many pupils to
study them.   Hesse's own compositions contain elements of
imitation, but are homophonic in character.

Robert Alexander Schumann (1810-1856) composed
three sets of pieces in 1845 which can easily be played on
the organ, although he wrote them for the pedal-piano (Pedal-
flügel).   These compositions include the Studies (Etudes),
Op. 56, Sketches, Op. 58, and Six Fugues on the Name of
BACH, Op. 60. [5]   The six studies (C major, A minor, E
major, A-flat major, B minor, and B major) are written in
the form of canons.   Some of the studies resemble such
divergent works as those of Bach or Mendelssohn's Songs
without Words.

The four Sketches (C minor, C major, F minor, and
D-flat major) are pianistic in nature.   Schumann's six fugues
(B-flat major, B-flat major, G minor, B-flat major, F
major, and B-flat major), the subjects of which spell Bach's
name musically, were inspired by the counterpoint of Bach.

GERMAN ORGAN COMPOSERS: 1800-1900

    1800   1820   1840   1860   1880   1900   1920

1770 Rinck, J. C. --------- 1846
1779 Aiblinger, Johann Caspar ------ 1867
    1786 Schneider, Friedrich - 1853
    1787 Gebhardi, Ludwig Ernst --- 1862
    1788 Ett, Johann 1814
    1788 Sechter, Simon ---------- 1867
        1790 Assmayer, Ignaz ----- 1862
        1791 Czerny, Carl ----- 1857
        1791 Töpfer, Johann Gottlob ---- 1870
        1796 Bach, August Wilhelm - 1869
        1797 Schubert, Franz Peter 1828
            1801 Stolze, H. W. ---- 1868
            1803 Lachner, Franz -------------- 1890
            1804 Becker, Carl F. ------ 1877
            1805 Schneider, Julius ---------- 1885
            1808 Richter, E. F. E. ---- 1879
            1809 Mendelssohn, F. 1847
            1809 Hesse, Adolphe --- 1863
                1810 Schumann, R. 1856
                1811 Liszt, Franz ---------- 1886 (Hungarian)
                1811 Ritter, August G. ------ 1885
                1812 Hanisch, Joseph ---------- 1892
                1812 Flügel, Gustav ---------------- 1900
                1812 Volckmar, W. A. V. -- 1887
                1817 Zahn, Johannes ----------- 1895
                1818 Kullak, Theodor ------- 1882
                    1821 Rebling, Gustav ----------- 1902
                    1822 Fink, Christian -------------- 1911
                    1823 Faisst, I. G. F. ------ 1894
                    1824 Goltermann, Georg E. - 1898
                    1824 Bruckner, Anton ------- 1896
                    1827 Merkel, Gustav Adolph 1885
                        1832 Bibl, Rudolf ---------- 1902
                        1833 Brahms, Johannes - 1897
                        1833 Habert, Johann E. - 1896
                        1834 Palme, Rudolf -------- 1909
                        1834 Becker, A. E. A. 1889
                        1834 Reubke, J. 1858
                        1835 Piel, Peter ----------- 1904
                        1839 Dienel, Otto ---------- 1905
                        1839 Rheinberger, Joseph --- 1901
                            1842 Thomas, G. A. 1870
                            1842 Labor, Josef -------------- 1924
                            1843 Neruda, Franz Xaver - 1915
                            1843 Blumenthal, Paul -------------- 1930
                            1844 Flugel, Ernst --------- 1912
                            1846 Piutti, Karl ------- 1902
                            1847 Forchhammer, Theophil ---- 1923
                            1848 Singenberger, Johann ------- 1924
                                1850 Oechsler, Elias --- 1917
                                1850 Rudnick, Wilhelm ------ 1927
                                1850 Reimann, H. -- 1906
                                1855 Wolfrum, Philipp -- 1919
                                1856 Wolfrum, Karl ------------- 1937
                                    1863 Kaun, Hugo ------------ 1932
                                        1873 Reger, Max 1916
                                        1877 Karg-Elert, Sigfrid - 1933
                                        1874 Schmidt, Franz ----- 1939

Franz Liszt (1811-1886), the famous Hungarian virtuoso pianist, composed three large works for organ, a few
short pieces, and an organ Mass (1879). Liszt's interest in
the organ is indicated by his purchase of a pedalboard in
1854, his visit with Franck at Ste. Clotilde in 1866, and his
examination of the newly installed Cavaillé-Coll organ at the
Trocadéro in Paris in 1878. His interest in orchestral music and his own dazzling keyboard technique gave the predominant character and form to the three larger organ works.
The Fantasy and Fugue on Ad nos, ad salutarem undam
(1850), the theme of which was taken from the choral of the
three Anabaptists in Meyerbeer's opera Le Prophète, is a
long, rhapsodic work, full of pianistic arpeggios, pedal trills,
key changes, double-pedaling, virtuoso cadenzas, and many
tempo changes. Alexander Winterberger (1834-1914), a pupil
of Liszt, played the first performance at Merseburg in 1855. [6]

The Prelude and Fugue on B-A-C-H was composed in
1855. The piece was intended for the organ inauguration at
the Merseburg Cathedral, but it was not completed in time
for the celebration. A second version appeared in 1870.
Although the Prelude and Fugue is similar to the "Ad nos"
fantasy, it is much shorter.

Liszt's third large composition is the Variations on
Weinen, Klagen, Sorgen, Zagen, based on the basso ostinato
of the first chorus of Bach's cantata for the third Sunday
after Easter and the basso ostinato of the Crucifixus from
Bach's Mass in B Minor. The variations were composed in
1863.

Liszt's Messe für die Orgel zum gottesdienstlichen
Gebrauch contains the following pieces to be played during
Mass but not for alternation with a choir: Kyrie, Gloria,
Graduale, Credo, Offertorium, Sanctus, Benedictus, and
Agnus Die. Liszt also wrote an organ Requiem zum gottes-
dienstlichen Gebrauch containing an Adagio; Dies irae; Re-
cordare, pie Jesu; Sanctus; Benedictus; Agnus Dei; and Post-
ludium.

Julius Reubke (1834-1858), the son of an organ
builder and a pupil of Liszt, lived only 24 years, but he
left one of the finest Romantic works for organ, a large
fantasy, The Ninety-Fourth Psalm (Sonata). This one composition is in three movements based on one theme (idée
fixe) in two segments, the first a rhythmic idea, and the
second, a chromatically descending theme. The sonata is

a virtuoso work which closes with a brilliant fugue.   The "program" for the sonata is a selection of nine verses from Psalm 94.   The brooding grave introduction and larghetto is based on the text verses beginning, "O God, to whom vengeance belongeth, show thyself ..." and "... how long shall the wicked triumph?"   A supple manual technique is required to execute the broken chords (the diminished seventh chord is used often), scale passages in 16th-notes, the variety of articulations, and rhythms, all of which are balanced by an active pedal part, wherein the sonata motive frequently appears.   A short grave section returns to the mood of the opening section and diminishes in sound and animation in order to introduce the soft adagio movement.   Restless chromaticism and modulations constitute the treatment of the sonata motive in the slow movement, which is based on the text verse beginning, "In the multitude of my cares within me thy comforts delight my soul."

The (Allegro) fugue in C minor employs the sonata motive as the subject and the answer, which is real (i. e., an exact transposition of the fugue subject into the dominant key).   The excitement rises and subsides frequently in order to interpret, "But the Lord is my defence.... And he ... shall cut them off in their own wickedness...."   Jagged, dotted rhythms and a change to a quicker triplet rhythm in the piu mosso section further heighten the fierce climax which closes the final movement with a thrilling, virtuoso pedal part under brisk, manual chords.

Josef Anton Bruckner (1824-1896), the famous Austrian symphonist, was best known in the organ field as an improviser.   Bruckner organ compositions include two preludes in E-flat written about 1836 and 1837, two Orgelstücke in D minor (ca. 1846), a Prelude and Fugue in C Minor (ca. 1847), and a Fugue in D Minor (1861/62).

Gustav Adolph Merkel (1827-1885) was a Dresden organist who wrote some 60 volumes of organ works in a combination of Baroque and Romantic styles. [7]   His pieces include naïve, easy, melodic pastorales, chorale preludes which suggest concert performance, songs without words, and organ forms especially connected with the Baroque period such as passacaglias, fugues, and canons.   The nine organ sonatas by Merkel were all composed in three movements and in minor keys.   The Sixth Sonata contains two chorale melodies, Aus tiefer Not ("Out of the Depths") and Wie schön leuchtet der Morgenstern ("How Brightly Shines the Morning Star").

A great composer of symphonic and piano works who
wrote organ compositions was Johannes Brahms (1833-1897).
Brahms' earlier compositions for the organ were written in
Düsseldorf and were primarily contrapuntal in character.
These include the Chorale Prelude and Fugue on O Traurigkeit, O Herzeleid (early 1856), two preludes and fugues in
A minor and G minor (1856/1857), and the Fugue in A-flat
Minor (April 1856). The G minor prelude contains many
different elements and suggests a fantasy. The A-flat minor
fugue employs rich harmonies and a moderate use of chroma-
ticism. The cross-rhythms of the chorale prelude on O
Traurigkeit anticipated this same characteristic used in some
of the chorale settings Brahms wrote 40 years later.

The Eleven Chorale Preludes, Op. 122, were Brahms'
final compositions. These pieces were written during his
last summer (1896) at Ischl in Upper Austria (and perhaps
at Carlsbad) when he was in a somber frame of mind, ill,
tired, and bereaved at the loss of several close friends.
(He had written the Vier ernste Gesänge upon Clara Schumann's death.) These chorale preludes are personal and
are written about life in retrospect and life after death.

Some of the preludes suggest Brahms' interest in
Bach by their contrapuntal nature: Schmücke dich ("Deck
Thyself, My Soul, with Gladness") and Mein Jesu der du
mich ("My Jesus Calls to Me"). Herzlich thut mich erfreuen
("My Faithful Heart Rejoices") is quite pianistic. Rich har-
monies abound in Es ist ein Ros' entsprungen ("Lo, How a
Rose E'er Blooming"), the two settings of Herzlich thut mich
verlangen ("O Sacred Head, Now Wounded"), and two of O
Welt, ich muss dich lassen ("O World, I Now Must Leave
Thee"). These miniatures contain much rhythmic and melo-
dic imitation: Herzliebster Jesu ("Ah, Blessed Jesus") and
Herzlich thut mich verlangen [I] ("O Sacred Head, Now
Wounded"); echo passages: O Welt, ich muss dich lassen
[II] ("O World, I Now Must Leave Thee") and Herzlich thut
mich erfreuen ("My Faithful Heart Rejoices"); and the use
of unifying elements such as the diminished fifth interval in
melodic form, often inverted, in Herzliebster Jesu ("Ah,
Blessed Jesus"). O wie selig ("O How Blessed Are Ye
Faithful Souls") is a chorale which expresses exaltation of
life beyond death.

Joseph Gabriel Rheinberger (1839-1901) was a prolific
composer who wrote 20 organ sonatas in as many keys and
a large number of meditations, character pieces, monologues,

fughettas, trios, two organ concertos (Op. 137 in F and Op.
177 in G minor), some suites for organ, violin and cello,
Op. 149, and two suites for violin and organ, Op. 150 and
Op. 166. Seventeen of the sonatas contain fugues. Rheinberger was able to write original and expressive music in
such strict contrapuntal forms as canon, fugue, and ground
bass. [8] Perhaps Rheinberger's best compositions are the
Sonata in F-sharp Major, Op. 111, Sonata in D-flat Major,
Op. 154 (1888), the first movement of the C Major Sonata,
Op. 165, Fantasie-Sonata in B Major, Op. 181, and Cantilena
from Sonata 11 in D Minor, Op. 148, the Twelve Monologues,
Op. 162, and the Ten Trios, Op. 189. Rheinberger's organ
works were conceived in the classic trandition and for a
classic organ, although his compositions have sometimes
been considered of mediocre quality, sentimental, and un-
imaginative. Rheinberger's organ had no swell division;
changes of dynamics could be observed only by adding or
taking off stops. The dynamic indications in his music must
not be taken too literally but in a relative manner, according
to the music's demands. Rheinberger disliked ostentation and
avoided dramatic writing; there is only one toccata in nearly
200 pieces.

German Romanticism in organ music reached a high
point in the works of Max Reger (1873-1916). Reger's music
is popular in Germany, and most organ recitals there contain
at least one of his compositions. He employed traditional
forms such as toccata, trio, passacaglia, chorale-fantasia,
and especially fugue. Reger frequently used contrapuntal devices such as imitation, sequence, and canon. The texture,
however, tends to become thick, the harmonic rhythm rapid,
and the use of chromaticism extreme. A highly developed
keyboard technique is necessary in order to perform the complex chords, which frequently involve octaves and constantly
changing rhythms.

There are 29 opus numbers (at least 220 compositions)
of organ works, a quantity of unnumbered ones, and at least
20 arrangements of Bach works for the organ. At least eight
opus numbers are collections of both character pieces and
compositions written in old forms. The Benedictus, Op. 59,
No. 9, is probably Reger's best known organ composition in
America. The Introduction and Passacaglia in D Minor, Op.
59, No. 5, are also well known. Reger's Opus 59 contains
three pieces inspired by texts from Mass Ordinary sections:
Kyrie eleison (No. 7), Gloria in excelsis (No. 8), and
Benedictus (No. 9). These pieces incorporate fragments of

plainsong melodies associated with the Latin texts.

An extraordinary ability to develop thematic material
is exhibited in the larger, virtuoso works, which are rather
orchestral in character (Variations and Fugue on an Original
Theme in F-sharp Minor, Op. 73; the chorale fantasias Ein'
feste Burg, Op. 27, Freu dich sehr, Op. 30, Wie schön
leuchtet and Straf mich nicht, Op. 40, Alle Menschen, Wachet auf, and Hallelujah! Gott zu loben, Op. 52). Reger's
smaller and easier cantus firmus compositions on chorale
melodies treat single stanzas in reharmonization, as solo
melody with accompaniment, echo phrases, and melody in
canon (Leicht ausführbare Vorspiele, Op. 67, Kleine Choralvorspiele, Op. 135a).

Although Franz Schmidt and Sigfrid Karg-Elert lived
well into the twentieth century, their music is late Romantic
in style. Franz Schmidt (1874-1939), a famous Austrian
teacher and composer, wrote in an appealing style similar
to that of Brahms and Reger. Schmidt wrote eight long works,
six chorale settings, and a group of four short preludes and
fugues. The most frequent organ forms he used include toccata, prelude, chaconne, variation, fugue, and chorale prelude. A tonal center is often established without chromaticism; as the piece progresses, chromaticism is gradually
added. A bravura style characterizes the fourth (D major)
of the Vier kleine Praeludien und Fugen and the much longer
Toccata in C major (1924). The four short chorale preludes
are consistent in style, and the chorale melodies are treated
in conventional ways.

Sigfrid Karg-Elert (1877-1933) was encouraged by
Reger to write for the organ. He approached composition for
the organ through an understanding of wind instruments, as a
pianist of brilliant technical ability, and as a student and ad-
mirer of Bach.[9] Many times Karg-Elert's compositions seem
to be sentimental and contain bizarre registration indications,
which denote an imperfect understanding of the tonal possibilities of the organ.[10]

Karg-Elert's 13 opus numbers contain works for the
harmonium, for which instrument both French and German
composers have written a considerable amount of material of
delicate or intimate nature. Many of these short compositions
are character pieces such as the Aquarelles, miniatures,
monologues, Intarsien (inlaid work), consolations, portraits,
impressions, and romanesque pieces. Karg-Elert's organ

works are original and include a wide variety of forms such
as cantus firmus settings of both chorale and plainsong melodies, character pieces, passacaglias, chaconnes, fugues,
canzonas, and partitas.   Karg-Elert's works may be grouped
into five musical categories: simple harmonic, contrapuntal
(historical), mixed styles, tone paintings (with involved harmonic structures), and final phase.

Many organists are familiar with only one or two of
the chorale-improvisations, the large chorale-improvisation
on In dulci jubilio ("In Sweetest Joy"), and perhaps one of
the selections from Cathedral Windows or one of the Pastels
from Lake Constance. The chorale-improvisations and pieces
from Cathedral Windows lend themselves to use in the church
service because of the basic chorale and plainsong melodies.
Op. 65 and Op. 78 contain 66 and 20 chorale settings, re-
spectively, for different seasons of the church year.   Probably Karg-Elert's most familiar piece is the Marche Triom-
phale on Now Thank We All Our God, Op. 65, No. 59.
Canons, trios, echo phrases, extremely chromatic writing,
pianistic passages, tender and slow treatments which contrast with strong and rugged settings, siciliennes, and solo
airs are utilized by Karg-Elert in Op. 65.   His seven Pastels from Lake Constance, Op. 96 (1919) are German Impressionism at an advanced stage.   The altered chords arranged in rapid harmonic rhythm make a strong impression,
and the score calls for kaleidoscopic registration changes.

England

Some of the first organ compositions published in
England in the nineteenth century were Charles Wesley's
voluntaries (ca. 1815) and Samuel Wesley's Twelve Short
Pieces (1815), Six Introductory Movements (ca. 1825), and
the Six Voluntaries (1820/1830).   Samuel Wesley showed
remarkable musical ability at an early age and was examined
by experts who were interested in exceptionally talented youth
such as Mozart and Crotch, who were also prodigies. [11]
Samuel admired Bach intensely and worked to introduce
Bach's music to the English people.   In 1810 Wesley and
C. F. Horn published Bach's Well-Tempered Clavier in the
first English edition.   These two men also published the
Bach trio sonatas in a piano duet version. [12]

Samuel Sebastian Wesley (1810-1876) was a brilliant
performer.   He became the organist of a succession of

HISTORICAL BACKGROUND

1788-1824	Byron
1791	Boswell Life of Johnson
1794	Haydn visited London for the second time
1792-1822	Shelley
1795-1881	Carlyle
1800-1859	Thomas Macaulay
1805	Battle of Trafalgar
1810	Scott The Lady of the Lake
1812	Bryon Childe Harold
1813	Philharmonic Society of London founded
1812-1815	War of 1812
1813	Jane Austen Pride and Prejudice
1815	Battle of Waterloo
1821	Constable The Hay Wain
1833	Oxford movement began in Church of England
1836	Dickens Pickwick Papers
1837-1901	Reign of Victoria
1843	Dickens Christmas Carol
1848	Thackeray Vanity Fair
1853	Crimean War began
1859	Tennyson Idylls of the King
1859	Darwin Origin of the Species
1864	Lewis Carroll Alice in Wonderland
1868	Browning The Ring and the Book
1883	Stevenson Treasure Island
1885	Gilbert and Sullivan The Mikado
1891	Doyle Adventures of Sherlock Holmes
1893	Oscar Wilde Salomé
1894	Kipling Jungle Book
1898	Boer War

---

several cathedrals and had high musical standards, which he would not compromise. His compositions contain frequent use of chromaticism, altered and seventh chords, and feminine cadences. Most of his music falls into neat, four-measure phrases. His best known organ composition is probably the Choral Song and Fugue from the First Set of Three Pieces for Chamber Organ. A Second Set of Three Pieces, for a Chamber Organ was issued by Sacred Music Warehouse Novello, Ewer and Co. , between 1867 and 1876. [13]

Thomas Attwood Walmisley (1814-1856) was the organist of Trinity and St. John's Colleges at Cambridge University. His compositions are melodic, flowing, and employ a small amount of chromaticism. The Prelude and Fugue in

E Minor is a solid, well-designed piece and is written in
rhythmic simplicity, which is characteristic of much English
organ music of the nineteenth and twentieth centuries.

In 1829 Mendelssohn made his first trip to England.
He performed Bach's organ works and later his own, both of
which needed an adequate pedal board and pedal division.
Mendelssohn's playing and interest in organ music helped to
establish a new conception of the organ and its music in
England.

Between 1830 and 1850 the organ building firm of
William Hill and Dr. Henry John Gauntlett attempted to extend the ability of the English organ to reach the capabilities
of continental instruments. One of their major contributions
was an adequate, independent pedal organ and enlarged Swell
division which could perform the function of accompanying,
serve as a German Positiv, or as a solo division. It is indeed regrettable that the improvements and superior design
of instruments such as the one at George Street Chapel,
Liverpool, which was built by Hill and Gauntlett, were not
appreciated and not accepted as examples to be followed
after 1850. [14]

The Great Exhibition of 1851 introduced organs which
were built by the Swiss-German Edmund Schulze, by Aristide
Cavaillé-Coll, and by Henry Willis. Probably the outstanding
contribution which Schulze made to English organ building was
large diapason tone, which seems to have appealed enor-
mously to English taste, a proclivity which has survived for
at least 100 years. As a result of his instrument shown at
the 1851 Exhibition Willis was commissioned to build the
100-stop organ for St. George's Hall, Liverpool. This instrument had complete diapason and reed choruses, a modern
console, and a heavy-pressure wind supply, which was provided by a steam engine. Toward the end of his life "Father"
Willis included fewer and more subdued mixtures in his designs and used a standard wind pressure of 3 1/2", 7", and
15" for his reeds. [15]

During the nineteenth century many organs were built
in cathedrals and town halls such as St. George's Hall,
Liverpool, where William Thomas Best (1826-1897) served
as organist from 1855 to 1894 and played weekly recitals.
These programs were very well attended, and Best, the
leading English concert organist of the nineteenth century,
frequently performed his transcriptions of orchestral works

which introduced fine orchestral music to Liverpool audiences.
The listeners would not have been able to hear such music
otherwise due to the lack of orchestras in many cities of that
period.   Although Best did not compose much organ music,
his Christmas Fantasy on Old English Carols contains some
pedal passages which demand more from the performer than
had been required before from either English organists or
organs by English composers.

Best was also the organist of a parish church.   A
brief analysis of the specifications of the organ, which are
given below, reveals that there was only one mutation on the
entire organ, one mixture on both manuals, nine of the 26
stops on the organ were reeds, and that there were only four
pedal stops (two of them reeds).

Wallasey, England, Parish church.
Built by Henry Willis, 1861. [16]

Great	Swell	Pedal
Double diapason 16'	Open diapason 8'	Open diapason 16'
Open diapason 8'	Stopped diapason 8'	Bourdon 16'
Flute 8'	Principal 4'	Trombone 16'
Gamba 8'	Harmonic Flute 4'	Bassoon 8'
Dulciana 8'	Mixture III	
Principal 4'	Contra fagotto 16'	
Harmonic flute 4'	Trumpet 8'	
Twelfth 2 2/3'	Oboe 8'	
Fifteenth 2'	Vox humana 8'	
Mixture IV		
Trumpet 8'		
Clarion 4'		
Clarinet 8'		

Toward the end of the nineteenth century Robert Hope
Jones, an electrical engineer, made many changes in the
mechanical and tonal features of organs in both England and
America, which, unfortunately, effectively altered (ruined?)
the taste of many organists, organ builders, and organ audiences for perhaps more than one generation.   His alterations
included an electric action, developed high pressure reeds to
an excessive degree, took out all brightness of diapason tone
by covering the upper lips of the pipes with leather, invented
large-scale clarabellas (which he called tibias), completely
suppressed reed tone in the pedal, and allowed no stop above

ENGLISH ORGAN COMPOSERS: 1800-1900

      1800   1820   1840   1860   1880   1900   1920   1940

ca. 1770 Webbe, Samuel --- 1843
   1775 Crotch, William -- 1847
   1777 Russell, W. 1813
      1785 Adams, Thomas --- 1858
         1809 Hatton, John Liptrot ------ 1886
           1810 Wesley, S. S. ---- 1876
           1813 Macfarren, G. A. ---- 1887
           1814 Walmisley, T. A. 1856
           1816 Elvey, George Job -------- 1893
           1818 Hopkins, Edward John --------- 1901
           1819 Stirling, Elizabeth -------- 1895
              1821 Stephens, Charles Edward 1892
              1823 Spark, William ------- 1897
              1823 Chipp, Edmund T. - 1886
              1826 Best, William Thomas - 1897
              1826 Hiles, Henry ------------- 1904
              1827 Calkin, John Baptiste ----- 1905
              1829 Calkin, George ?
                 1831 Westbrook, W. J. - 1894
                 1834 Bunnett, Edward -------------- 1923
                 1835 Turpin, Edmund Hart - 1907
                 1838 Archer, Frederick ---- 1901
                    1840 Clark, F. S. 1883
                    1841 Saint-George, George ----- 1924
                    1841 Roberts, John Varley ----- 1920
                    1844 Peace, Albert Lister -- 1912
                    1845 Gladstone, Francis Edward - 1928
                    1847 Rogers, Roland ----------- 1927
                    1848 Nicholl, Horace Wadham -- 1922
                    1848 Frost, Charles Joseph - 1918
                    1848 Parry, Charles H. H. - 1918
                       1851 Foster, Myles Birket - 1922
                       1852 Booth, Josiah ?
                       1852 Stanford, Charles V. -- 1924
                       1853 Bridge, Joseph Cox --- 1929
                       1855 King, Oliver A. ------- 1923
                       1856 Pearce, Charles William 1928
                       1857 Elgar, Edward ------------ 1934
                       1858 Sibley, Churchill ?
                       1859 Strelezki, Anton 1907
                       1859 Haynes, Walter B. 1900
                       1859 Harwood, Basil -------------- 1949
                          1864 Blair, Hugh ?
                          1865 Wolstenholme, W. ----- 1931
                          1865 Brewer, Alfred H. 1928
                          1866 Archer, J. Stuart ?(after 1920)
                          1866 Duncan, William E. 1920
                          1866 Wood, Charles ---- 1926
                          1869 d'Evry, Edward ?
                             1875 Coleridge-Taylor, S. 1912

a two-foot piccolo in his design. [17]

One of England's most distinguished composers of the late nineteenth century was Sir Edward Elgar (1857-1934). His Sonata in G Major, Op. 28, was composed in 1895 and dedicated to Dr. C. Swinnerton Heap. The influence of Romantic orchestral composers combined with his own individual taste and ability is expressed in frequent key and meter changes, a great sense of tone-color and harmony, and a wide variety of rhythmic patterns. This was one of the best English organ works of the nineteenth century of larger dimension.

The organ works of Basil Harwood (1859-1949) were influenced by German Romanticism and contain the type of chromaticism and tunefulness which is associated with Mendelssohn and Rheinberger. In larger forms Harwood composed two organ sonatas and an organ concerto.

Three composers closely connected with the Anglican church are Sir Charles Villiers Stanford (1852-1924), Sir C. Hubert H. Parry (1848-1918), and Charles Wood (1866-1926). Stanford is famous for his choral music for the church; perhaps his best known organ composition is the Prelude and Fugue in E Minor. Parry exhibited much more color and imagination in his hymn-tune settings than does Charles Wood. Wood's arrangements have a monotonous quality because his rhythms seem to be limited to quarter-note and eighth-note movement, and his harmonies stay within simple diatonic triads and seventh chords. Wood also chose to use manual and pedal parallel octaves a great deal. Parry, however, displayed rhythmic, tempo, and harmonic variety, changes in manual and pedal articulations, interesting registration possibilities and appropriate writing based on the hymn texts. At the beginning of each prelude Parry listed the specific lines of the hymn which inspired his writing.

Notes

1. Peter Williams, The European Organ 1450-1850, London: B. T. Batsford, 1966; p. 165-167.
2. Ibid. , p. 94-95.
3. In brief, sonata-allegro (sonata) form consists of three sections: exposition, development, and recapitulation. The first theme, usually dramatic, is connected to the second, often lyric, theme by a modulatory bridge.

Many types of treatment such as melodic fragmentation
and rhythmic alteration are given to the themes in the
freely composed development section before a restate-
ment of both themes of the exposition recur in the
tonic key.   A coda often sums up the thematic material and closes the movement.

4.   Orlando A. Mansfield, "Some Characteristics and Pecu-
     liarities of Mendelssohn's Organ Sonatas," Musical
     Quarterly, vol. III (1917), p. 526-576.
5.   The name of Bach can be spelled musically in German
     musical notation because B signifies the English B-flat
     and the German H indicates the English B-natural.
     As a melody the name would be arranged thus: B-
     flat, A, C, B-natural.
6.   Marcel Dupré, ed., Trois Oeuvres pour Orgue de Franz
     Liszt, Paris: S. Bornemann, 1941; preface.
7.   Gotthold Frotscher, Geschichte des Orgelspiels und der
     Orgelkomposition, Berlin: Merseberger Verlag, 1959;
     vol. II, p. 1173.
8.   Harvey Grace, The Organ Works of Rheinberger, Lon-
     don: Novello and Co., 1925; p. 120.
9.   Godfrey Sceats, The Organ Works of Karg-Elert, Lon-
     don: Hinrichsen Edition, 1940; p. 5. (rev. ed.,1950.)
10. Ibid., p. 8.
11. Thomas Armstrong, "The Wesleys, Evangelists and
     Musicians," Organ and Choral Aspects and Prospects,
     London: Hinrichsen Edition Ltd., 1958; p. 99.
12. Ibid., p. 100.
13. Peter F. Williams, ed., The Wesleys, Set Two, Lon-
     don: Hinrichsen Edition Ltd., 1961; preface.
14. Cecil Clutton and Austin Niland, The British Organ,
     London: B. T. Batsford Ltd., 1963; p. 91-94.
15. Ibid., p. 100.
16. Clutton and Niland, op. cit., p. 103.
17. Clutton and Niland, op. cit., p. 106-107.

Bibliography

GERMANY

Bacon, Allan. "The Chorale Preludes of Max Reger," The
     Diapason (February 1962), p. 30-31.
Bakken, Howard, "Liszt and the Organ," The Diapason (May
     1969), p. 27-29.
Barker, John Wesley, "Reger's Organ Music," Musical
     Times, no. 1496, vol. 108 (October 1967), p. 939;

no. 1498, vol. 108 (December 1967), p. 1142; no.
1500, vol. 109 (February 1968), p. 170.
Dupré, Marcel, ed. Trois Oeuvres pour Orgue de Franz
Liszt. Paris: S. Bornemann, 1941; preface.
Frotscher, Gotthold. Geschichte des Orgelspiels und der
Orgelkomposition. Berlin: Merseberger Verlag, 1959;
vol. II, p. 1122-1195.
Gay, Harry W. "Study of Brahms' Works Expanded by Vivid
Detail," The Diapason (March 1959), p. 38.
Gibson, David. "Franz Liszt's Christmas Tree," The Dia-
pason (December 1970), p. 28.
Gotwals, Vernon. "Brahms and the Organ," Music/The
A. G. O. and R. C. C. O. Magazine (April 1970), p. 38-55.
Grace, Harvey. The Organ Works of Rheinberger. London:
Novello and Co. , 1925.
Hathaway, J. W. G. Analysis of Mendelssohn's Organ Works:
A Study of the Structural Features. London: Reeves,
1898.
Klotz, Hans. "Gedanken zur Orgelmusik Max Regers,"
Mitteilungen des Max-Reger-Instituts, vol. VII (1958).
Mansfield, Orlando A. "Some Characteristics of Mendels-
sohn's Organ Sonatas," Musical Quarterly, vol. III
(1917), p. 562-576.
Sceats, Godfrey. The Organ Works of Karg-Elert, London:
Orphington, 1940 (rev. ed. , London: Hinrichsen Edi-
tion Ltd. , 1950).
Trevor, C. H. "The Organ Music of Max Reger and Its
Performance," Organ and Choral Aspects and Pros-
pects. London: Hinrichsen Edition Ltd. , 1958; p. 78.
Walsh, Stephen. "Schumann and the Organ," Musical Times,
no. 1529, vol. 111 (July 1970), p. 741-743.
Williams, Peter F. The European Organ 1450-1850. Lon-
don: B. T. Batsford, 1966; p. 94-95.

ENGLAND

Armstrong, Thomas. "The Wesleys, Evangelists and Musi-
cians," Organ and Choral Aspects and Prospects.
London: Hinrichsen Edition Ltd. , 1958; p. 99.
Clutton, Cecil, and Austin Niland. The British Organ. Lon-
don: B. T. Batsford Ltd. , 1963; p. 89-107.
Williams, Peter F. , ed. The Wesleys, Set Two. London:
Hinrichsen Edition Ltd. , 1961; preface.

14.   FRANCE: 1800-1900

From the degradation to which organ composition in
France had sunk for nearly a century and a half only one
man appeared who made an earnest attempt to improve the
situation, Alexandre Pierre François Boëly (1785-1858).
Boëly's admiration for the organ music of Bach and classic
masters is evident in his compositions in which he combined
contrapuntal techniques and forms with harmonic materials
of his own time.   The works of Boëly have been divided into
four books.   The first book contains his youthful works in
the forms of preludes, fugues, canons, and free pieces.   The
contents of the second book include preludes, versets based
on plainsong, offertories, and pieces published after Boëly's
death.   Preludes, hymn versets, and noëls from the period
1828-1854 are found in the third book, and, in the fourth,
various pieces for the harmonium,[1] organ, or pedal piano.
Probably the best known composition by Boëly is the Fantaisie
et Fugue in B-flat major.   Boëly's compositions in this combination form probably gave rise to similar works by his
pupil Camille Saint-Saëns and later Gigout.   Boëly deserves
much credit for bringing back to French organ music the
seriousness of purpose and dignity which it had lost after
the death of Grigny.[2]

A few music editors such as Niedermeyer, d'Ortigue,
Boëly, Miné, and Fessy exhibited interest in better music of
the polyphonic school.   It was the Belgian Jacques-Nicolas
Lemmens (1823-1881), however, who encouraged more study
of classic masters.   Lemmens' deep interest in Bach and
his own scholarly approach made his teaching at the Brussels
Conservatoire influential in both Belgium and in France
through pupils such as Guilmant and Widor.   Another pupil,
Clément Loret, was an effective teacher in the Niedermeyer
school in Paris.[3]

The music of Louis James Alfred Lefébure-Wély
(1817-1869) and Antoine Edouard Batiste (1820-1876) was
published in many nineteenth- and early twentieth-century
collections in France, England, and America.   Even though

HISTORICAL BACKGROUND

1796-1875	Corot
1803	Purchase of Louisiana from France
1804	Napoleon became emperor
1810-1849	Chopin
1811-1886	Liszt
1814	Napoleon exiled to Elba
1815-1824	Reign of Louis XVIII
1815	Napoleon defeated at Waterloo
1818-1893	Gounod
1824-1830	Reign of Charles X
1829	Balzac La Comédie Humaine
1830-1848	Reign of Louis-Philippe
1831	Victor Hugo Notre Dame de Paris
1834-1917	Degas
1837	Berlioz Requiem
1838	Daguerre took first photographs
1839-1906	Cézanne
1840-1917	Rodin
1841-1919	Renoir
1841	Saxophone invented
1844	Dumas Three Musketeers
1844-1924	Anatole France
1851-1931	Vincent d'Indy
1852-1870	Napoleon III and Second Empire
1857	Flaubert Madame Bovary
1857	Baudelaire Les Fleurs du Mal
1859	Gounod Faust
1861	Paris Opéra built
1862	Hugo Les Misérables
1863	Manet Olympia
1870-1871	Franco-Prussian War
1871	National Society for French Music founded
1873	Degas Place de la Concorde
1875	Bizet Carmen
1878	Renoir Madame Charpentier et Ses Enfants
1879	Pasteur vaccines
1880	Rodin The Thinker
1880	Zola Nana
1884-1920	Modigliani
1885	de Maupassant Contes et Nouvelles
1889	Eiffel Tower finished
1890	Valéry Narcissus
1892	Debussy Afternoon of a Faun (1st ed.)
1892	Toulouse-Lautrec Au Moulin-Rouge
1894	Schola Cantorum founded
1896	Gaugin Maternité
1899	Ravel Pavane pour une infante défunte

the quality of this music might be questioned today, perhaps these men were part of the effort to improve organ music of that period.

The works of Camille Saint-Saëns (1835-1921) are conceived in classical forms, balanced, logically developed, and often pianistic in nature. His Fantaisie in E-flat major is probably his best known piece.

The "symphonic" school of nineteenth-century French organ composition was encouraged by the orchestral organs of Aristide Cavaillé-Coll (1811-1899). The Cavaillé-Coll company built organs from about 1840 until about 1900 and exerted much influence upon the organ writing of such composers as Franck, Widor, Guilmant, Gigout, Dubois, Boëllmann, and Vierne, and less significant composers such as Samuel Rousseau (1853-1904) and Théodore César Salomé (1834-1896). The manual divisions of Cavaillé-Coll organs are dominated by brilliant, high-pressure reeds. Other characteristics are harmonic flutes, orchestral reeds, and strings. Cavaillé-Coll generally suppressed the inclusion of mutations and mixtures, a practice which transformed the basic character of the organ from a polyphonic instrument to a homophonic, orchestral one. C. S. Barker patented his pneumatic lever in France in 1839; Cavaillé-Coll used the Barker lever extensively in his organs. The use of ventils made groups of stops in the various divisions usually reeds, available as a body, to be added or discarded according to the will of the performer. The practice of adding the reeds from the Swell (Récit), Great (Grand Orgue), or Positif division(s) to the foundation stops already drawn is still common in twentieth-century French organ music. Gradual crescendos and diminuendos became much more easily manipulated by the use of coupling devices.

One of the most significant changes made in the design of organs by Cavaillé-Coll was in the pedal division. In the Classical French organ there were rarely more than three pedal stops, an eight-foot reed, an eight-foot flute, and perhaps a four-foot flute. The pedal part often sounded the plainsong melody in long notes on the trumpet or played a soft part in trios. The only way a 16-foot sound could appear in the pedal was through the Great to pedal coupler (tirasse). The left hand part performed the real bass function on the manuals most of the time. The nineteenth-century change, however, increased the size of the pedal division considerably and moved the voice which performed

the bass function into the pedal, where the bass had been
played in German and Dutch organs for 200 years. [4]   Cavaillé-
Coll built a number of organs in England and made his influence felt there as well as in France.

One of Cavaillé-Coll's best known instruments is the
organ found at the Church of Ste. Clotilde, Paris, where
Franck played for 31 years.   The specifications are given
below.

Paris, Ste. Clotilde.
Built by Aristide Cavaillé-Coll, 1859.

Récit (upper manual)

Bourdon 8'	Basson-Hautbois 8'
Flûte harmonique 8'	Voix humaine 8'
Viole de gambe 8'	Trompette 8'
Voix celeste 8'	Clairon 4'
Flûte octaviante 4'	
Octavin 2'	

Positif (middle manual)

Montre 8'	Bourdon 16'	Clarinette 8'
Prestant 4'	Gambe 8'	Trompette 8'
Quinte 2 2/3'	Flûte harmonique 8'	Clairon 4'
Doublette 2'	Bourdon 8'	
	Salicional 8'	
	Flûte octaviante 4'	

Grand Orgue (lower manual)

Montre 16'	Bourdon 16'	Bombarde 16'
Montre 8'	Gambe 8'	Trompette 8'
Prestant 4'	Flûte harmonique 8'	Clairon 4'
Octave 4'	Bourdon 8'	
Quinte 2 2/3'		
Doublette 2'		
Plein-jeu V		

Pédale

Sub-bass 32'	Flûte 8'	Basson 16'
Contrebasse 16'		Bombarde 16'
Octave 4'		Trompette 8'
		Clairon 4'

FRENCH ORGAN COMPOSERS: 1800-1950

1800	1850	1900	1950

1785 Boëly, Alexandre 1858
  1801 Bellini, Vincenzo 1835
  1809 Levadé, Charles Gaston ?
    1811 Thomas, Ambroise 1896
    1813 Alkan, Charles 1888
    1817 Leybach, Ignace 1891
    1817 Lefébure-Wély 1869
    1818 Battman, Jacques-Louis 1886
    1818 Gounod, Charles François 1893
       1820 Batiste, Antoine 1876
       1822 Franck, César-Auguste 1890
             Grison, Julius
          1833 Loret, Clément 1909
          1834 Salomé, Théodore 1896
          1835 Saint-Saëns, Camille --- 1921
          1837 Chauvet, Charles 1871
          1837 Dubois, François-Clément-Théodore 1924
          1837 Guilmant, Alexandre 1911
             1844 Widor, Charles-Marie -- 1937
             1844 Gigout, Eugène ----- 1925
             1846 Périlhou, Albert -------- 1936
             1849 Dallier, Henri ---------- 1934
             1849 Klein, Franz Aloÿs 1889
                1850 Thomé, François 1909
                1851 Wachs, Paul Etienne Victor 1915
                1851 d'Indy, Vincent ------ 1931
                1852 Hillemacher, Paul --- 1933
                1853 Rousseau, Samuel 1904
                1857 Chaminade, Cécile ------- 1944
                1858 Erb, Marie-Joseph ------ 1944
                   1861 de Bréville, Pierre --- 1949
                   1862 Boëlmann, Léon 1897
                   1863 Pierné, Gabriel -- 1937
                   1864 Ropartz, Joseph-Guy-Marie 1955
                   1865 Marty, Adolphe ------- 1942
                   1867 Koechlin, Charles -------- 1950
                   1869 Decaux, Abel --------- 1943

Pédales de combinaison

Tirasse Grand Orgue	Octaves graves Récit
Tirasse Positif	Anches Pédale
Tirasse Récit	Anches Grand Orgue
Grand Orgue sur machine	Anches Positif
Copula Positif sur Grand Orgue	Anches Récit
Copula Récit sur Positif	Tremblant du Récit
Octaves graves Grand Orgue	Expression du Récit
Octaves graves Positif	

   The greatest organ composer of the French school in
the nineteenth century was César Auguste Franck (1822-1890).
A Belgian by birth, but French by education and adoption,
this modest man exerted a profound effect upon his pupils and
the development of organ music.   The organ compositions of
"Père Franck" were composed with the Cavaillé-Coll organ
at Ste. Clotilde in mind.   Franck was organist there from
1859 until his death.   As the organ professor at the Paris
Conservatoire, Franck emphasized the study of composition
in his organ teaching.   An early and perhaps trite work, the
Andantino in G minor, was composed in 1858 but was not
published until 1889.   Six Pièces (1862), compositions of
somewhat uneven quality, appeared when the composer was
40 years old.

   The first of the Six Pièces, the Fantaisie, Op. 16,
in C major, contains four sections.   The melodic line of the
opening section is primarily drawn from the tonic chord;   the
second theme enters as a canon.   The final section of the
Fantaisie is a serene Adagio, which is based (like the first
section) both harmonically and melodically to a great degree
on the C major chord.

   The Grande Pièce Symphonique, Op. 17, the precursor
of all later organ "symphonies,"[5] is a major work in three
large movements.   After a lengthy introduction, a pedal solo
presents the principal theme followed by a dignified, legato
second theme.   The movement closes softly after a passage
which functions as a bridge to the lyric second movement.
The Andante movement is in three sections.   The first and
third parts in B major have a stately melody which, in the
first section, is frequently treated in short echo phrases.
The middle section in B minor is the caprice or scherzo
section of the "symphony" in which Franck used one of his
most frequent unifying devices, a canon, between outer voice
parts.   In the final section of the movement there is a re-

turn to the thematic material of the beginning section with
the addition of a double pedal part.   An extended interlude
after the second movement incorporates four different themes
from the preceding two movements to introduce the final
movement.   The last movement utilizes the principal theme
of the first movement in its parallel major key (F-sharp
major) over an active pedal part in eighth-notes.   A fugue
closes the entire work.

The Prélude, Fugue et Variation, Op. 18, is one of
Franck's loveliest compositions.   The cantabile melody of
the prelude in B minor is presented over a simple accompaniment.   A short interlude of nine measures' length anti-
cipates the fugue subject and returns the tonality to B minor.
In the latter part of the fugue, the primary musical accent
seems to fall on the second beat of several successive bars.
After the climactic end of the fugue, the serene melody of
the prelude returns over a flowing 16th-note middle voice
part.

Franck dedicated the Pastorale, Op. 19, in E major,
to his friend Aristide Cavaillé-Coll, the organ builder.   The
tripartite composition opens with a melodic four-measure
theme which is followed by a chordal theme.   Crisp, staccato
chords against a legato melody and a fughetta are the principal material found in the quicker middle section.   In the
final section the two themes of the first section are sounded
simultaneously, and the piece closes in the same style with
which it began.

The Prière, Op. 20, is a reserved and noble composition in which the opening section states harmonies in a
somewhat choral fashion without employing the pedal.   In
the second section melodic phrases are exchanged between
the pedal and uppermost voice of the manual parts, a technique Franck also used in the Grande Pièce Symphonique.

The Final, Op. 21, one of Franck's less inspired
works, introduces long pedal solo passages and several
bravura sections for the manuals alone.

The Trois Pièces were written for the inauguration of
the large organ at the Trocadéro at the exhibition in 1878.
The Fantaisie in A major has four themes;   the first and
second themes are sounded simultaneously toward the end.
The Cantabile in B major alternates a two-measure chordal
theme with a lyric one of the same length in the beginning

section.   Franck used a canon as a unifying device in this
composition, too.   Pièce Héroïque is one of the most popular
organ pieces written by Franck.   The principal theme is
martial in quality and suggests orchestral brasses.   The effect of timpani is suggested by alternating tonic and dominant
pitches in the pedal range.   A canonic section, alteration of
themes into parallel major or minor keys, and a full organ
harmonization of the second principal theme at the close--
all contribute to maintaining the interest of the listener.

Franck's final major works for the organ are the
three chorals composed during the last year of his life (1890).
These three fantasias of large design are not built upon a
pre-existing chorale melody, but they do contain sections
which suggest hymn writing.   The Choral No. 1 in E major
opens with a stately harmonized melody which Franck developed according to the cellule génératrice technique, in which
the entire piece grows from the same motivic material.   The
dignified "choral" theme, which enters in measure 46, is
diatonic and presented in phrases of approximately equal
length.   Some of the ways in which the thematic material is
varied are as solo and accompaniment in the original key
and in the parallel minor mode and as alternating phrases
of the theme progressing back and forth from the soprano
range to the tenor range.   The First Choral closes with a
climactic version of the choral theme, in which the first
three phrases of the choral melody are repeated in the pedal
part after their statement in block chords on the full organ
sound.

Choral No. 2 in B minor, like the First Choral, is
in a variation form, that of a modified passacaglia.   The
first two chorals also contain interludes in recitative or
free fantasy style, which interrupt the series of variations
but which provide a refreshing, brief change in the musical
material.   Two sections, which resemble portions of Franck's
Symphony in D minor, softly close the two large sections
of the Second Choral;   these same soft parts are examples
of the type of musical writing which suggests the mysticism
and religious idealism reflected in Franck's works.

Perhaps the most popular of Franck's Trois Chorals
is the Choral No. 3 in A minor.   This choral is in large
ternary form.   The center section is an extended, lyric
Adagio which contrasts with the fiery first and final sections.
Franck frequently used changes of key in order to keep the
restatements of the themes effective.   Chords which demand

wide stretches of the hands are often found in Franck's works
because he had such large hands.

L'Organiste is the title of a collection of 59 short
pieces by Franck for harmonium or organ, which were written, like the chorals, during the last year of his life. [6]

Characteristics which recur frequently in Franck's
organ music are repetition of the same melodic figure with
slight chromatic changes (as from minor to major thirds),
wedge-like, widening melodic interval changes, the use of
sharp keys, canons, pedal points, the frequent use of chromaticism, and rich harmonies.

Félix Alexandre Guilmant (1837-1911) as a composer
owed much to his being a famous recitalist; he was the first
French concert performer to tour in America.   He wrote
much for the concert organ repertoire, a number of offertories, elevations, communions on noëls, and some pieces on
Gregorian themes.   Guilmant wrote his organ sonatas between 1874 and 1907.   He often added a Grand Choeur or a
fugue to the standard group of pieces in the sonatas.   Noël
Languedocien (1886) is one of his better known pieces.   Guilmant, as a music editor in collaboration with the musicologist
André Pirro, edited with scholarly competence the complete
works of composers such as Titelouze, Clérambault, and
Scherer in the Archives des Maîtres de l'Orgue series.

Charles-Marie Widor (1844-1937), a Romanticist by
nature, wrote for the symphonic organ.   Widor had a sense
of style and grandeur which was most appropriate to the instrument.   He contrasted sonorities well, changed manuals
for dramatic effect, and, like Lemmens, used a staccato
touch for brilliance.   Inverted pedal point and double pedaling
were other devices adopted by him.

Widor wrote ten organ symphonies between 1876 and
1900.   The first four (C major, D major, E major, and F
major) make up Opus 13, and the next four (F major, G
major, A major, and B major), Opus 42.   Widor, like Guilmant, added other forms such as pastorales, toccata-preludes,
chorals, variations, marches, intermezzos, scherzos, and
finales to the standard set of sonata movements.   The last
two symphonies are the Symphonie Gothique, Op. 70 (1895)
and the Symphonie Romane, Op. 73 (1900), which are mature
works of a more liturgical character than the first eight
symphonies.   The Christmas introit Puer natus est and the

Easter gradual Haec dies are two Gregorian themes used in
these two final large works.   Widor wrote Sinfonia Sacra,
Op. 81, for organ and orchestra, and Domine salvum fac
populorum for organ and brass.

Many French organ composers of the nineteenth century wrote collections of pieces in which less imaginative
writing was employed.   Théodore Dubois (1837-1924), one
time director of the Paris Conservatoire and successor to
Saint-Saëns at the Church of the Madeleine, wrote several
books of organ pieces. [7]   Eugène Gigout (1844-1925), the
organist of St. Augustin, Paris, for over 60 years, had a
great interest in plainsong.   This interest in plainsong inspired him to write some 600 pages of short pieces in
Gregorian modes for harmonium or organ. [8]   His other compositions include works for pipe organ such as the Toccata
in B minor (1892) and the famous Grand-Choeur Dialogué,
which was especially effective when divisions of the organ
were played antiphonally across the nave in St. Augustin.

Léon Boëllmann (1862-1897) was a student of Gigout
who became an adopted member of Gigout's family.   He is
famous for the Suite Gothique, which was popular in America
in the earlier part of the twentieth century.   His compositions include other suites, a Fantasia in A major, an Offertoire on two noëls, a Fantasia Dialoguée for organ and orchestra, Heures Mystiques, and many shorter pieces.

Notes

1. Toward the later part of the nineteenth century, small
    organs for the home called harmoniums or melodians
    became popular.   These instruments did not have a
    pedal board.   A number of French composers wrote
    collections of pieces for these instruments.
2. Norbert Dufourcq, A. P. F. Boëly: Oeuvres complètes
    pour Orgue, vol. 1, Paris: Editions musicales de la
    Schola Cantorum, preface, p. 2.
3. Norbert Dufourcq, La Musique d'Orgue Française de
    Jehan Titelouze à Jehan Alain, Paris: Librairie Floury,
    1949; p. 172.
4. Peter Williams, The European Organ 1450-1850, London:
    B. T. Batsford Ltd. , 1966; p. 201-203.
5. These "symphonies" are actually sonatas in several move-
    ments written for orchestral organs.   They incorporate
    forms commonly found in nineteenth-century symphonic

writing such as movements written in sonata-allegro,
variation, or song forms, and dance movements such
as scherzos. The symphony of from four to six pieces
usually closed with a stirring, brilliant toccata. Organ
"symphonies" also equaled some of their orchestral
counterparts in length. [See Dufourcq, op. cit. , p.
144-158.]

6. Franck had planned to compose 91 in all. Four manuscript pieces, which were intended to be published with
the 59 but which Franck did not have time to copy for
the original publisher (Enoch), are found in Pièces
Romantiques Ignorées, No. 17, in the L'Organiste Litur-
gique series, Schola Cantorum, Paris.

7. In the March of the Magi Kings by Dubois a high pitch is
sustained throughout the composition to signify the star
leading the wise men to Bethlehem.

8. Dufourcq, op. cit. , p. 166.

Bibliography

Cavaillé-Coll, Cécile, and Emmanuel Cavaillé-Coll. Aristide
    Cavaillé-Coll: Ses Origines, Sa Vie, Ses Oeuvres.
    Paris: Librarie Fischbacher, 1929.
Davies, Laurence. César Franck and His Circle. Boston:
    Houghton Mifflin Co. , 1970.
Demuth, Norman. César Franck. New York: Philosophical
    Library, 1949.
Dufourcq, Norbert. A. P. F. Boëly: Oeuvres Complètes
    pour Orgue, vol. 1. Paris: Editions musicales de la
    Schola Cantorum, preface.
    _____. César Franck. Paris: Editions du Vieux Colom-
    bier, 1949.
    _____. La Musique d'Orgue Française de Jehan Titelouze
    à Jehan Alain. Paris: Librairie Floury, 1949.
Gastoué, A. "A Great French Organist: A. Boëly and His
    Works," Musical Quarterly, vol. XXX, No. 3 (July
    1944), p. 336-344.
Grace, Harvey. French Organ Music, Past and Present.
    New York: H. W. Gray Co. , 1919.
    _____. The Organ Works of César Franck. London:
    Novello and Co. , 1948.
d'Indy, Vincent. César Franck, translated by Rosa Newman.
    Reprint, New York: Dover Publ. , 1965.
Pruitt, William. "Charles Tournemire and the Style of
    Franck's Major Organ Works," Diapason (October 1970),
    p. 17.

Smith, Rollin. "Camille Saint-Saëns," Music/The A. G. O.
    and R. C. C. O. Magazine, vol. 5, no. 12 (December
    1971), p. 24-26.
Sumner, William Leslie. "The French Organ School," Sixth
    Music Book. London: Hinrichsen Edition Ltd. , 1950;
    p. 281-294.
Tournemire, Charles. César Franck. Paris: C. Delagrave,
    1931.
Williams, Peter. The European Organ 1450-1850. London:
    B. T. Batsford Ltd. , 1966; p. 201-203.

15. GERMANY AND AUSTRIA SINCE 1900

In 1896 Albert Schweitzer examined a new organ in the Liederhalle of Stuttgart and drew conclusions that the sound he had heard there was indeed no forward step in organ conception and construction but actually a backward one. This experience encouraged Schweitzer to listen for several years to many instruments and to study organ building practices seriously. In 1906 Schweitzer wrote of the conclusions and observations he had made in the pamphlet The Art of Organ Building and Organ Playing in Germany and France. This pamphlet condemned the commercialism and indifference of organ builders to craftsmanship and tonality and defined his thoughts about what the ideal organ should be and how it should sound. Schweitzer's pamphlet became the earliest and basic writing on which the Orgelbewegung, the German organ reform movement, was founded, a movement which has greatly affected organ building in Europe and North America in the twentieth century. Several factors, which Schweitzer deemed of great importance, were the use of the slider chest, mechanical key action, lower wind pressures, and high and free placement of the instrument.

Another event which gave impetus to the organ reform movement occurred in Germany--the so-called "Praetorius" organ was built in the Music Institute at the University of Freiburg im Breisgau in 1921 under the supervision of Professor Willibald Gurlitt according to specifications given by Praetorius in the Syntagma Musicum, Vol. 2, De Organographia (1619). The specifications are given below.

Freiburg im Breisgau, Germany.
Music Institute, University.
Built by Walcker Company, 1921.

Oberwerk	Rückpositiv
Principal 8'	Quintadeena 8'
Octava 4'	Blockflöit 4'
Mixtur IV	Gemshörnlein 2'

HISTORICAL BACKGROUND

1870	Franco-Prussian War
1875-1955	Thomas Mann
1898-1956	Bertolt Brecht
1900	Schoenberg Gurre-lieder
1905	R. Strauss Salomé
1912	Schoenberg Pierrot Lunaire
1914-1918	World War I
1916	Freud Introduction to Psychoanalysis
1919-1933	German Republic
1921	Construction of "Praetorius" organ in Freiburg
1923	Rilke Sonette an Orpheus
1923	Hitler's Munich Putsch
1925	Kafka Der Prozess
1925	Berg Wozzeck
1926	Freiburg Organ Conference
1928	Kurt Weill Three-Penny Opera
1933-1939	Thomas Mann Joseph und seine Brüder
1933-1945	Third Reich under Hitler
1939-1945	World War II
1941	Franz Werfel Song of Bernadette
1949	Federal Republic of Germany established
1949-1963	Adenauer, chancellor of Germany
1963	Rolf Hochhuth Der Stellvertreter
1963-1966	Erhard, chancellor of Germany
1966-1969	Kiessinger, chancellor of Germany
1969-	Brandt, chancellor of Germany

Grob Gedact/Rohrflöit 8'
Nachthorn 4'
Schwiegelpfeiff 1'
Rancket oder stille
  Posaun 16'
Gemshorn 4' (added to
Praetorius specification)

Zimbel doppelt, gar klein
  und scharff
Spitzflöit oder
  Spillflöit 4'
Krumbhorn 8'

In die Brust

Klein lieblich Gedactflöit.
  Rohrflöit 2'
Baerpfeiff 8'
Geigend Regal 4'

Pedal

Untersatz starck 16'
Posaunen Bass 16'
Singend Cornet 2'
Dolzianbass 8' (added to
Praetorius specification)

This instrument became the center of interest for the famous

Freiburg Organ Conference in 1926. Christhard Mahrenholz,
one of the leaders of the conference, emphasized the close
relationship of the organ reform to the music and liturgy of
the church.

    In addition to those factors listed above, which were
stressed by Schweitzer in his pamphlet of 1906, the Deutsche
Orgelbewegung decided that the following points should also
be emphasized: the organ, which is primarily a polyphonic
instrument, should be developed for the literature to be
played on it; stop names should be appropriate to function,
pipe construction, or tone quality; the tonal design should
be developed along the "Werk principle" (completeness of
each division and contrast between divisions, placement of
the divisions, and their architectural appearance); and
acoustics of the room should be natural and allow for suitable
reverberation.

    During the third decade of the twentieth century a few
renowned teachers and organists became aware that their
Romantic performances had violated the conception and artistic styles of music from early periods of musical composition.   One of the most striking admissions of error and
of change toward producing a faithful performance enlightened
by study was that made by Dr. Karl Straube.   In the Fore-
word to his Neue Folge (new series) of Alte Meister des
Orgelspiels (Early Masters of Organ Performance) (1929).
Straube admitted that the opinions he had expressed in the
preface to his edition of Alte Meister of 1904 were no longer
valid and that the real aim of performance should be an
artistic reproduction of a work of musical art as it was
originally conceived, in direct relation to the precepts of its
period of composition and for instruments built according to
similar principles of construction of a particular era.
Straube's thoughts were shared by Günther Ramin, the organist of St. Thomas Church, Leipzig (the church Bach had
served), and Hans Henny Jahnn.   These men discovered in
1922 that the St. Jakobi organ built by Arp Schnitger in Hamburg was an excellent example of the best of organ building.

    The rise of musicological research and a great re-
awakening of interest in early music, especially from the
Renaissance and Baroque periods, deeply influenced such
outstanding twentieth-century German composers as Distler
and Hindemith to write in what might be called a neo-
Baroque style.   This objective type of composition and organ
performance also gained support from a strong reaction

against the overemotional and extremely subjective expressions of the nineteenth century at which time organs were
unashamedly built as orchestral substitutes.[1]

The specifications given below are those of a new
von Beckerath instrument, which was built recently in the
United States.

New Haven, Conn. , Dwight Chapel, Yale University.
Built by von Beckerath, 1971. Mechanical action.

Great	Positiv	Swell
Bourdon 16'	Gedackt 8'	Gedackt 8'
Principal 8'	Quintadena 8'	Principal 4'
Rohrflöte 8'	Principal 4'	Waldflöte 2'
Octave 4'	Rohrflöte 4'	Sifflöte 1'
Spielflöte 4'	Octave 2'	Terzian II
Nasat 2 2/3'	Quinte 1 1/3'	Cymbel III
Octave 2'	Sesquialtera II	Trichterregal 8'
Flachflöte 2'	Scharf IV	Tremolo
Tierce 1 3/5'	Rankett 16'	
Mixture V	Cromorne 8'	
Trumpet 8'	Tremolo	

Pedal

Principal 16'
Subbass 16'
Octave 8'
Gedackt 8'
Octave 4'
Hohlflöte 4'
Nachthorn 2'
Mixture V
Posaune 16'
Trumpet 8'
Schalmei 4'
Tremolo

Two principal composition techniques are evident in
twentieth-century German organ music. One is that of traditional polyphonic forms clothed in contemporary counterpoint
and harmony. The forms used are those of the prelude,
fugue, canon, toccata, chorale-based works such as chorale
prelude, fantasia, and partita, variation, passacaglia,

GERMAN AND AUSTRIAN ORGAN COMPOSERS: 1860--

1860   1880   1900   1920   1940   1960   1980

1860 Fielitz, Alexander von -1930
1860 Fährmann, Hans ---------- 1940
1861 Thuille, L. 1907
1861 Jung, Richard -------- 1932
1861 Franke, Friedrich Wilhelm 1932
1962 Gulbins, Max --------- 1932
1862 Klose, Friedrich ---------- 1942
1866 Schumann, Georg Alfred ------ 1952
1869 Prohaska, Carl --- 1927
        1874 Schoenberg, Arnold ------- 1951 (Austrian-American)
        1874 Schmidt, Franz --- 1939 (Austrian)
        1874 Schmid, Heinrich Kaspar -- 1953
        1879 Weismann, Julius --------- 1950
        1879 Haas, Joseph ----------------- 1960
            1881 Knab, Armin --------- 1951
            1881 Weigl, Karl ------ 1949
            1881 Simon, Josef ----- 1940
            1882 Braunfels, Walter ---- 1954
            1883 Hasse, Karl -------------- 1960
            1883 Stögbauer, Isidor ?
            1885 Windsperger, L. 1935
            1885 Poppen, Hermann Meinhardt 1956
            1886 Kaminski, Heinrich 1946
            1886 Unger, Hermann ------ 1958
            1886 Grabner, Hermann -------- 1969
            1887 Landman, Arno ----------- 1966
            1887 Tiessen, Heinz --------------- 1971
            1887 Koch, Karl ------------------- 1971
            1888 Geierhaas, Gustav?
            1889 Schindler, Hans ------ 1951
                1890 Philipp, Franz ------------ 1972
                1891 Pfeiffer, Hubert 1932
                1891 Lechthaler, Josef 1948
                1891 Hoyer, Karl 1936
                1891 Drischner, Max ----------- 1971
                1892 Jarnach, Philipp (French-German)
                1893 Pisk, Paul Amadeus
                1893 Blume, Friedrich --------- 1975
                1893 Kickstat, Paul ?
                1894 Roeseling, Karl ------ 1960
                1895 Hindemith, Paul ------ 1963
                1895 David, Johann Nepomuk --- 1977
                1895 Gothe, Georg
                1896 Wenzel, Eberhard
                1896 Piechler, Arthur ---------- 1973
                1896 Doebler, Curt ------------ 1970
                1896 Abendroth, Fedor Georg Walter 1973
                1897 Gebhard, Hans
                1897 Högner, Friedrich ------------ 1981
                1897 Heiss, Hermann ------ 1966
                1897 Weyrauch, Johannes Wilhelm Robert 1977
                1897 Marx, Karl
                1898 Werner, Fritz ------------ 1977

GERMAN AND AUSTRIAN ORGAN COMPOSERS: 1860-- (continued)

1860	1880	1900	1920	1940	1960	1980

1898 Jochum, Otto
1898 Eggermann, Fritz
1899 Ramin, Günther -- 1956
1899 Schäfer, Karl Heinrich ---- 1970
1899 Wegner, Richard
   1900 Klotz, Hans
   1900 Krenek, Ernest (Austro-American)
   1901 Humpert, Hans 1943
   1901 Pepping, Ernst ------------ 1981
   1901 Vörding, August ------ 1973
   1901 Beckerath, Alfred von
   1902 Poppen, Hermann 1956
   1902 Marckhl, Erich ----------- 1980
   1902 Micheelsen, H. F. ---- 1973
   1902 Schwartz, Gerhard von
   1902 Spitta, Heinrich ------- 1972
   1902 Krieger, Fritz ---- 1963
   1902 Chemin-Petit, Hans H. ---- 1981
   1903 Raphael, Günter -- 1960
   1903 Thörner, Helmut
   1904 Ahrens, Joseph
   1904 Schroeder, Hermann
   1904 Adam, Fritz
   1904 Quack, Erhard
   1905 Wittmer, Eberhard Ludwig
   1905 Kraft, Walter -------- 1977
   1906 Bloch, Waldemar (Austrian)
   1906 Bornefeld, Helmut
   1907 Bialas, Günter
   1907 Reichelt, Herbert
   1907 Fortner, Wolfgang
   1907 Höller, Karl
   1907 Walcha, Helmut
   1908 Distler, Hugo 1942
   1908 Mohler, Philipp
   1908 Leinert, Friedrich
   1908 Hessenberg, Kurt
   1908 Wellesz, Egon ------- 1974 (Austrian)
   1908 Fiebig, Kurt
   1908 Görner, Hans-Georg
   1908 Kraft, Karl ---------- 1978
   1908 Bauernfeind, Hans (Austrian)
   1909 Thieme, Karl
   1909 Borlisch, Hans
   1909 Schneider, Michael
   1909 Schindler, Walter
   1909 Genzmer, Harald
      1910 Joachim, Otto
      1910 Oertzen, Rudolf von
      1911 Bossler, Kurt ---- 1976
      1911 Stein, Max Martin
      1912 Wagner, Hans-Joachim
      1912 Gwinner, Volker

GERMAN AND AUSTRIAN ORGAN COMPOSERS: 1860-- (continued)

1860   1880   1900   1920   1940   1960   1980

1912 Fussan, Werner
1913 Schollum, Robert
1913 Franz, Siegfried Walter
1913 Hiltscher, W. 1941
1914 Kukuck, Felicitas Kestner
1914 Collum, Herbert
1914 Rohwer, Jens
1914 Metzger, Hans Arnold
1914 Zipp, Friedrich Otto Gottfried
1916 Reda, Siegfried 1968
1916 Eder, Helmut (Austrian)
1916 Haase, Hans-Heinz
1917 Pröger, Johannes
1917 Yun, Isang (Korean)
1917 Baumann, Max
1918 Doppelbauer, Josef Fr. (Austrian)
1918 Baur, Jürg
1918 Pirckmayer, Georg
1919 Köhler, Karl
1919 Nussgruber, Walther
1919 Schoendlinger, Anton (Yugoslavian)
  1920 Krol, Bernhard
  1920 Roevenstrungk, Bernhard
  1921 Klein, Richard Rudolf
  1921 Bonitz, Eberhard
  1921 Driessler, Johannes
  1921 Geissler, Fritz
  1922 Korn, Peter Jona
  1922 Rapf, Kurt
  1923 Ligeti, György (Romanian)
  1923 Blume, Joachim
  1923 Schmeel, Dieter
  1923 Manicke, Dietrich
  1923 Heiller, Anton 1979 (Austrian)
  1924 Heilmann, Harald
  1924 Becker, Günther Hugo
  1925 Klebe, Giselher
  1925 Lampe, Günter
  1925 Doerr, Ludwig
  1925 Hummel, Bertold
  1925 David, Thomas Christian
  1926 Schweppe, Joachim
  1926 Kameke, Ernst-Ulrich von
  1926 Vogel, Ernst
  1926 Koerppen, Alfred
  1926 Padrós, Jaime
  1926 Peter, Herbert
  1926 Zechlin, Ruth
  1927 Angerer, Paul
  1927 Barth, Hans Joachim
  1927 Schilling, Hans-Ludwig
  1927 Barbe, Helmut
  1928 Schubert, Heino

GERMAN AND AUSTRIAN ORGAN COMPOSERS: 1860-- (continued)

1860	1880	1900	1920	1940	1960	1980

1928 Haselböck, Hans (Austrian)
1928 Kern, Matthias
1928 Motte, Diether de la
1928 Petersen, Winfried
1928 Bauszern, Dietrich Edler von
1928 Gerlach, Günter
1928 Kluge, Manfred 1971
1929 Romanovsky, Erich
1929 Stadlmair, Hans
   1930 Tachezi, Herbert
   1930 Voss, Friedrich
   1930 Zimmerman, Heinz Werner
       Timme, Traugott
       Engelmann, Johannes
       Reimerdes, Friedrich
       Witt, Günter de
   1930 Giefer, Willy
   1930 Schneidt, Hanns-Martin
   1931 Stockmeier, Wolfgang
   1933 Graap, Lothar
   1933 Linke, Norbert
   1933 Callhoff, Herbert
   1934 Wiemer, Wolfgang
   1934 Thiele, Siegfried
   1935 Seckinger, Konrad
   1935 Mai, Peter Bernhard
   1936 Reimann, Arinert
   1936 Sengstschmid, Johann
   1936 Urbanner, Erich
   1936 Wegner, Heinz
   1936 Bertram, Hans Georg
   1936 Zender, Hans
   1938 Helmschrott, Robert Maximilian
   1939 Huber, Nicolaus A.
   1939 Bräutigam, Volker
      1940 Schoof, Armin
      1940 Acker, Dieter (Romanian)
      1943 Darmstadt, Hans
      1943 Radulescu, Michael (Romanian)
      1945 Wittinger, Robert (Austrian)
      1947 Planyavsky, Peter Felix
      1947 Redel, Martin Christoph

chaconne, sonata, suite, concerto, and organ Mass, which is
sometimes freely composed, sometimes based on plainsong.
Hindemith and Distler have exerted the strongest influence in
this objective style of writing.   Dissonance and lean contrapuntal lines are principal factors in this music.   Although a
tonal center is usually understood, melodic intervals of
seconds, fourths and fifths, quartal harmony, and a modal
character are emphasized.

     The second principal composition technique is the 12-
tone (serial) technique.   Schoenberg and Křenek are the chief
exponents of this type.   This technique ackowledges no tonal
center, since each of the 12 tones is of equal value and is
used in a predetermined order, either singly or in any combinations desired.   In addition to the two principal techniques
discussed, contemporary German composers have devised
modified forms and styles which incorporate various devices
and techniques.   Jazz rhythms (one of the chief elements in
the composition style of Heinz Werner Zimmermann), modal
melodies, and distinctive harmonies are a few examples of
some of the characteristics they have chosen to use.

     There are few compositions written for organ in the
serial technique.   Variations on a Recitative, Op. 40 (1940),
by Arnold Schoenberg (1874-1951) is based on the 12-tone
technique modified, but it suggests a tonal center of D.   This
work was first performed by Carl Weinrich in March, 1944,
for the International Society for Contemporary Music.   To
choose a recitative melody as a thematic basis for ten variations, a cadenza, and a section beginning in imitative style
is unusual.   Extremely complex rhythms, constant dissonance,
tempo and meter changes, all permit few moments of regu-
larity and normal pulse.   A performance of the Variations is
an intellectual achievement and a feat of industriousness for
an organist.

     Ernst Křenek (1900-   ), an Austro-American convert
to Schoenberg's dodecaphonic system, has written a Sonata,
Op. 92 (1941), in one movement for organ.   The form is
sonata-allegro with an interpolated Andante section in A-B-A
form and a scherzo finale.   Although there are many meter
changes, the basic time unit is usually a quarter-note, which
gives coherence to the composition.   The lines are more
vocal than those found in Schoenberg's Variations and the
rhythms much less complex, both of which allow this piece
to be much more easily comprehended.   Two young Germans
in the contemporary group who write in atonal style are

Giselher Klebe (1925-   ) and Arinert Reimann (1936-   ).

The Sieben Orgelchoräle (Seven Organ Chorales) by
Armin Knab (1881-1951) are tonal settings of familiar chorale
melodies such as "O Sacred Head Now Wounded," "Now
Thank We All Our God," and "How Brightly Shines the
Morning Star." The principal contrapuntal device used is
the canon, and the harmonic background for the counterpoint
is strong. Scarcely any accidentals are found in these
traditionally conceived works. Karl Hasse (1883-   ) and
Heinrich Kaminski (1886-1946) have both written chorale
preludes. Hasse, a pupil of Straube and Reger, has composed in the larger forms of fantasy and fugue, suite, and
sonata. Kaminski was a pupil of Hugo Kaun and was one
of Carl Orff's teachers. In addition to the chorale arrangements, he has written a toccata and fugue, an andante, and
three pieces for organ and violin.

Johann Nepomuk David (1895-   ) has been a prolific
composer for the organ. He has written a large body of
chorale arrangements which he has entitled Choralwerk.
He has also composed in the larger forms of chaconne,
fugue, fantasy, prelude and fugue, ricercar, and toccata and
fugue. His works are tonal but not romantic, and he employs a contemporary contrapuntal style.

Paul Hindemith (1895-1963) as a teacher and composer has been a strong stimulus for neo-Baroque composition in twentieth-century Germany. His own organ contributions are limited to three sonatas and two concertos. The
first two sonatas were written in 1937 and the third in 1940.
The first concerto was written in 1928 for the dedication of
the new organ at the Frankfurt radio station, and the second
was composed in 1962 for the new organ at Lincoln Center
Philharmonic Hall in New York City. [2]

The sonatas were conceived in the neo-Baroque style
with conventional but diversified and energetic rhythmic
character. Lean contrapuntal lines coupled with untraditional
harmonic progressions and phrases of irregular length make
these pieces for organ especially interesting. The melodies
are warm, a quality that many other contemporary works
lack. "Hindemith generally avoided any triadic outlines in
his melodies, and the frequent use of melodic fourths and
seconds (and their inversions, melodic fifths and sevenths)
were an aid to this endeavor." [3] Hindemith frequently employed the device of a melody in octaves, or sometimes

separated a melody in exact parallel motion by two octaves.
Incomplete triads and the use of chords constructed of super-
imposed fourths are two of his harmonic characteristics.
Although the meter is changed from time to time in the sonatas of Hindemith, this practice is quite frequent in his
second concerto.   Hindemith employed surprising changes of
tonal centers.

Forms used by Hindemith in the sonatas include
sonata-allegro, binary, ternary, fantasy, rondo, and fugue
forms.   The Phantasie, frei section from the First Sonata
is an exciting one, probably the most passionate movement
in all three sonatas.   Sonata II ends with a fugue in rondo
form, only one example of Hindemith's frequent use of imitation.

Hindemith selected three folk songs, "Ach Gott wem
soll ich's klagen," "Wach auf, mein Hort," and "So wunsch
ich ihr," which are included in his The Craft of Musical
Composition, Book II, as bases for the three movements of
Sonata III. [4]

There are few registration indications in the first
concerto or in the sonatas, but explicit registrations are
given for the second concerto.   As in many Baroque works,
the registration of the sonatas can indicate the structure of
the work.   Hindemith wanted the tempos exact, even though
he allowed divergence in registrations. [5]

Ernst Pepping (1901-) has written many organ works
which have been influenced by his study of sixteenth- and
seventeenth-century music.   He is probably best known for
his Grosses Orgelbuch (Large Organ Book), which contains
chorale settings in both Vorspiel (prelude) and Orgelchoral
(organ choral) forms, and Kleines Orgelbuch (Small Organ
Book) (1940), which contains shorter and easier chorale settings.   The chorale melody is clearly set apart in one voice
most of the time.   These pieces are contrapuntal, contain
much rhythmic variety, and the phrasings and articulations
are meticulously indicated.   Accidentals are frequent, since
Pepping does not employ key signatures.   He has written
several chorale partitas, some manualiter chorale settings,
two concertos, fugues, and sonatas.

Hans Friedrich Micheelsen (1902-) has composed
seven organ concertos, Das Holsteinische Orgelbüchlein
(pieces for small organ) and Choralmusik.   The concerto

on Es sungen drei Engel has probably received the largest
number of performances.

Joseph Ahrens (1904-) has been Professor of Church
Music at the Berlin Hochschule für Musik since 1950.   His
organ works are neo-Baroque in character.   Ahrens' organ
hymn Pange lingua (1936) has settings of four stanzas (two
with the cantus firmus in the pedal, one in motet style, and
a version with the cantus in long notes in the uppermost part
and an Amen section).   Thirteen imaginative variations are
found in the Lobe den Herren partita (1947).   Several bicinia,
a drone bass variation, quick ascending scale passages, rolled chords, and a wide variety of interesting rhythmic treatments are found in the partita.

Hermann Schroeder (1904-) is one contemporary
German composer who is well-known in America.   His tonal
compositions in traditional forms are interesting and make
excellent teaching material because most of them are short
and only moderately difficult.   He has written three organ
sonatas.   Cantus firmus works include an organ Mass (Orgel-
Ordinarium) based on the Kyrie Cunctipotens genitor Deus
plainsong, Orgelchoräle in Kirchenjahr, a partita on Veni
Creator Spiritus, and Six Organ Chorales on Old German
Sacred Folksongs, Op. 11, on tunes such as In dulci jubilo
and Schönster Herr Jesu.

Helmut Bornefeld (1906-) has limited himself in
organ composition to chorale-based works.   His works are
tonal and are cast in the form of chorale preludes or chorale
partitas.   The three volumes of chorale settings by Helmut
Walcha (1907-), the famous teacher and organist at the
Dreikönigskirche, Frankfurt, have been popular in the United
States.   These imaginative chorale preludes are excellent
service and teaching material in contemporary contrapuntal
tonal writing.

Hugo Distler (1908-1942) was one of the most dis-
tinguished twentieth-century German composers.   He wrote
the two splendid partitas Nun komm der Heiden Heiland,
Op. 8, No. 1 (1933), and Wachet auf, Op. 8, No. 2 (1935),
the Kleine Orgelchoral Bearbeitungen, Op. 18, No. 3 (1938)
(Small Chorale Arrangements), the trio Sonate, Op. 18,
No. 2, (1939), and Dreissig Spielstücke (Thirty Pieces),
Op. 18, No. 1 (1938), for the little organ at St. Jakobi
Church in Lübeck.   Distler served this church from 1931
to 1937. [6] He put a contemporary spirit into Baroque forms

by employing cross-rhythms, complex subdivisons of beats,
and syncopation. The contrapuntal lines are diatonic, modal,
and contain many melodic seconds and fourths. The major
and minor third is avoided in both melody and harmony. The
Spielstücke and Sonate were composed on the little chamber
organ Distler ordered built for use in his home in Stuttgart. [7]

One of Distler's pupils was Siegfried Reda (1916-1968),
who has written similar linear music. Inspired by chorales
Reda's organ works contain four chorale concertos, chorale
preludes, an Adventspartita on Mit Ernst, o Menschenkinder
(1952), and a Choral-Spiel-Buch. Other forms he has used
have been the prelude, fugue, and the sonata. The pains-
taking articulation, the complex subdivisions of the beat,
unbarred sections, the pedal solos, the absence of key signatures and many meter changes are some of the characteristics common to both Reda and Distler.

The writing of Kurt Fiebig (1908-   ) is more conventional than that of Reda or Distler. His Prelude and Fugue
in B-flat (1948) and the Triosonate utilize regular meters and
common rhythms. The Viennese teacher and concert organist
Anton Heiller (1923-   ) has written sonatas, partitas, and
settings of Ecce lignum crucis and Salve regina melodies.
A very active pedal part, cross-rhythms, frequent meter
changes, a fugal section, and pedal point are factors that
characterize the first sonata, a work in three movements.
The second movement is for manuals alone, and the third is
in toccata style. Heiller's Second Sonata was composed in
1953.

The Hungarian composer Zoltán Kodály (1882-1967)
wrote a setting of Pange lingua for chorus with a prominent
organ part. Kodály's pupil Josip Slavenski (1896-1955) composed a Sonata religiosa for organ and violin. Two younger
Hungarian composers, who have written in traditional forms
such as the passacaglia, fugue, and sonata, are Erzsébet
Szönyi (1924-   ) and Hidas Frigyes (1928-   ).

Notes

1.   Leading organ building forms of the twentieth century in
     Germany are those of Rudolf von Beckerath (Hamburg),
     Karl Schuke (Berlin), and the Walcker company (Lud-
     wigsburg). These builders have erected some distin-
     guished instruments in Germany and in the United States.

The leading Austrian organ builder is the Rieger firm in Schwarzach.
2.   See the unpublished doctoral thesis of Albert George Bolitho, "The Organ Sonatas of Paul Hindemith," Michigan State University, 1968, for a longer analysis of all the organ works of Hindemith.
3.   Ibid. , p. 30.
4.   A source of these tunes is Franz M. Böhme Altdeutsches Liederbuch, reprinted by Breitkopf und Härtel, Wiesbaden, 1966. Hindemith composed the complete sonata within a day and a half.
5.   He had the habit of carrying a pocket metronome to check tempos.
6.   Not 1933 as is given in Die Musik in Geschichte und Gegenwart.
7.   Larry Palmer, Hugo Distler and His Church Music, St. Louis: Concordia Pub. House, 1967; p. 93.

Bibliography

Brinkmann, Reinhold.   "Einige Bermerkungen zu Schönbergs Orgelvariationen," Musik und Kirche, vol. 29, no. 2 (March-April 1969), p. 67.
Brown, Rayner.   "Some New German Organ Music," The American Organist, May 1966, pp. 12-14.
_____. "Some More German Organ Music," The American Organist, July 1969, p. 16-17.
Gehring, Philip.   "Distler's Organ Works," The American Organist, vol. 46, no. 7 (July 1963), p. 14.
Gibson, Emily Cooper.   "A Study of the Major Organ Works of Paul Hindemith," Diapason (February 1971), p. 22-24.
Newlin, Dika.   "Schoenberg's Variations on a Recitative," Organ Institute Quarterly, vol. 6, no. 1 (Spring 1956), p. 16-18.
Noss, Luther.   "Arnold Schoenberg: Variations on a Recitative for Organ," Notes, vol. IV, no. 4 (Sept. 1947), pp. 485-486.
Walker, John.   "Schoenberg's Opus 40," Music/The A. G. O. - R. C. C. O. Magazine, vol. IV, no. 10 (October 1970), p. 33.

16. FRANCE SINCE 1900

At least five different styles can be identified in twentieth-century French organ composition: symphonic writing, literature based on Gregorian melodies, program music (both religious and secular), colorist or impressionistic composition, and compositions constructed in new, advanced techniques of the twentieth century.

One of the organ works which was composed in a rather free rhythm is the Messe des Pauvres by the unconventional Erik Satie (1866-1925). With one exception, the "Mass" does not employ traditional Mass sections. All of the six movements are of moderate and short duration. In connection with the Kyrie is Dixit Domine, which is followed by the Prière des Orgues, Commune qui Mundi Nefas, Chant Ecclésiastique, Prière pour les Voyageurs et les Marins en Danger de Mort, and Prière pour le Salut de Mon Ame.

Louis Vierne (1870-1937) is the outstanding organ symphonist of the early twentieth century. This blind organist of Notre Dame Cathedral was influenced by Franck, Widor, and Debussy, but he developed his own distinct but not extreme harmonic and melodic idioms. His music is technically demanding, sometimes pianistic, and is consistently orchestral in character. Vierne's compositions are original, well developed, vigorous, and tuneful; most of them are concert music. His harmonies are rich, he shows a skillful use of contrapuntal devices, and his striking themes are evenly balanced.

Vierne's music can be divided into three composition periods. The first period (1895-1905) includes the first two organ symphonies. The second period (1905-1917) encompasses music of more spontaneity and grace than that found in the first period, with themes of greater breadth and picturesque harmony found in the Third Symphony and the 24 Pièces en Style Libre. The third period, during which Vierne's writing seems more active and agitated (1917-1931), includes the last three symphonies and the descriptive Pièces de Fantaisie.[1]

HISTORICAL BACKGROUND

1900	Charpentier Louise
1902	Debussy Pélléas et Mélisande
1902	Curies discovered radium
1904	Rolland Jean Christoph
1905	Cézanne Grandes Baigneuses
1905	Dubussy La Mer
1909	Gide La Porte Etroite
1910	Stravinsky Firebird
1911	Ravel L'Heure Espagnole
1913	Stravinsky Le Sacre du Printemps
1913-1927	Proust A la Recherche du Temps Perdu
1914-1918	World War I
1917	Valéry La Jeune Parque
1919	League of Nations formed
1920	Ravel La Valse
1921	Honegger King David
1929	Cocteau Les Enfants Terribles
1930	Stravinsky Symphonie des Psaumes
1931	Saint-Exupéry Vol de Nuit
1932	Gertrude Stein Matisse, Picasso and Gertrude Stein
1933	Colette La Chatte
1935	Honegger Jeanne au Bucher
1938	Dufy Regatta
1939-1945	World War II
1941	François Mauriac La Pharisienne
1943	Sartre L'Etre et le Néant
1943	Chagall Crucifixion
1946	Giraudoux La Folle de Chaillot
1947-1958	Fourth Republic
1951	NATO formed
1957-1958	Malraux La Métamorphose des Dieux
1957	Poulenc Dialogues des Carmélites
1958-1969	DeGaulle, President of the Fifth Republic
1959	Anouilh Becket
1969-	Pompidou, President

Vierne added extra pieces to the four standard movements generally found in sonatas in his six symphonies,
which were written between 1899 and 1931: a prelude and a
fugue to the First; a choral to the Second; a cantilène to
the Third; a prelude and a menuet to the Fourth; a prelude to the Fifth, and an aria to the Sixth. The slow movements were given titles such as romance, larghetto, and
intermezzo.

The better known selections from the 24 Pièces en
Style Libre are the Carillon, Berceuse, Divertissement,
Arabesque, and Lied. From the larger fantasy pieces come
the beautiful Carillon de Westminster and Naïades.

Charles Arnould Tournemire (1870-1939) was a pupil
of Franck and the organist of Ste. Clotilde, a post he held
for over 40 years. Tournemire was a master of improvisation; the freedom of expression found in improvisation is
also contained in Tournemire's compositions. His originality
was inspired by Gregorian propers in the liberal paraphrases
named L'Orgue Mystique, which he grouped into 51 cycles
(255 pieces) for the liturgical year. These pieces were to
be played at Mass but not in alternation with the choir. Each
individual cycle consists of five pieces: prelude, offertory,
elevation, communion, and postlude. Since the first four
pieces in each cycle were associated with a liturgical function, the length of the music was governed by the function.
The preludes and elevations are brief, the communions
moderately long, the offertories longer than the communions,
and the postludes were as long as Tournemire saw fit to
make them.

The forms used by Tournemire in L'Orgue Mystique
are choral-paraphrases, versets, chorals, interludes, fantasies, fugues, variations, rhapsodies, and free forms. The
improvisatory spirit, which is supported by a rubato style
of playing, seems to flow freely through all these forms.
The music in these pieces is based on the chant modes,
both harmonically and melodically. Tournemire frequently
employed major and minor seconds in harmony and melody
and avoided thirds; his compositions often end on open fifths
or unison pitches. Parallel movement at various intervals
and note clusters are two other musical characteristics of
Tournemire's organ music. [2]

Tournemire's other compositions include some "symphonic" pieces and religious program music based upon the

seven last words of Christ.   Maurice Duruflé has reconsti-
tuted five of Tournemire's improvisations.

Joseph Bonnet (1884-1944), like Guilmant, was an
organist who was a better performer and teacher than composer.   Most of his compositions are programmatic concert
pieces such as Elfes, Chant du Printemps, and Lied des
Chrysanthèmes.

Ermend Bonnal (1880-1944) composed a Symphonie
"Media Vita" and at least three suites of programmatic
"landscapes."   Georges Jacob (1877-1950) is best known for
his 12 impressionistic, secular pieces Les Heures Bourgui-
gnonnes, based on pastoral pictures of Maurice Lena.   Religious program music was composed by Daniel-Jean-Yves
Lesur (1908-   ), who was Tournemire's assistant at Ste.
Clotilde.   Two titles of compositions by Lesur are Scène de
la Passion (1931) and La Vie Intérieure (1932).

One of the finest single organ compositions of the
twentieth-century French school is the Pastorale by Jean-
Jules-Aimable Roger-Ducasse (1873-1954).   This piece,
which is conceived in the Romantic tradition, is a series of
variations which contains a masterful use of organ colors
and demands a virtuoso technique for performance.   The
theme is presented in four different time values simultaneously in one variation, and the pedal part sounds the theme
in quick 16th-notes over most of the pedal board while the
hands alternate chords in another variation.

The organ works of Henri Mulet (1878-1967) have been
warmly received in America.   Especially popular are his
Carillon-Sortie and the Tu es Petra toccata from the Es-
quisses Byzantines (Byzantine Sketches).   This group of programmatic sketches describes different parts of a cathedral
such as the nave, stained glass, and rose window, and religious cermonies which take place in such an edifice.

One of the outstanding figures of twentieth-century
French organ music is Marcel Dupré (1886-1971).   This
internationally renowned musician's career encompassed that
of composer, music editor, author, teacher, Director of the
Paris Conservatoire, and the successor to Widor as organist
of St. Sulpice.   Dupré's non-programmatic works include the
Trois Préludes et Fugues (1920).   Religious program music
embraces the Vêpres du Commun de la Vierge (1920), Cortège et Litanie (1923), the four-movement Symphonie-Passion

FRENCH ORGAN COMPOSERS SINCE 1900

	1870	1900	1930	1960	1980

1866 Satie, Erik ---------- 1925
1870 Tournemire, Charles Arnould ---------- 1939
1870 Vierne, Louis ---------- 1937
1870 Schmitt, Florent ---------- 1958
1873 Quef, Charles ---------- 1931
1873 Roger-Ducasse, Jean-Jules-Aimable ---------- 1954
1874 Pierné, Paul ---------- 1952
1875 Reuchsel, Amédée ---------- 1931
1877 Jacob, Georges ---------- 1950
1878 Mulet, Henri ---------- 1967
1880 Bonnal, Ermend ---------- 1944
1880 Fourdrain, Félix ----------1923
1880 Reuchsel, Maurice ---------- 1968
1883 Barié, Augustin -- 1915
1883 Cellier, Alexandre-Eugène ---------- 1968
1884 Bonnet, Joseph ---------- 1944
1884 Mignan, Edouard-Charles-Octave ---------- 1969
1885 Chaix, Charles ---------- 1973
1886 Dupré, Marcel ---------- 1971
1886 Saint-Martin, Léonce de ---------- 1954
1891 MacMaster, Georges
1892 Honegger, Arthur ---------- 1955
1892 Milhaud, Darius ---------- 1974
1893 Benoit, Paul
1896 Rivier, Jean
1899 Poulenc, Francis ---------- 1963
1901 Tomasi, Henri ---------- 1971
1901 Kauffmann, Leo J. --------- 1944
1903 Fleury, André
1903 Duruflé, Maurice

1905 Jolivet, André --- 1974
1907 Langlais, Jean
1907 Desportes, Yvonne
1908 Messiaen, Olivier
1908 Lesur, Daniel-Jean-Yves
1909 Litaize, Gaston
     Lanquetuit, Marcel
     Reboulot, Antoine
1910 Puig-Roget, Henriette
1911 Grünenwald, Jean-Jacques ------------------------ 1982
1911 Alain, Jehan Ariste 1940
1912 Françaix, Jean
1915 Girod, Marie-Louise
     1920 Falcinelli, Rolande
     1920 Gelineau, Joseph
     1921 Demessieux, Jeanne ----- 1968
     1922 Xenakis, Iannis (Greek)
     1924 Cochereau, Pierre
     1924 Ballif, Claude
     1925 Chaynes, Charles
     1925 Philippot, Michel
     1926 Smit, Andre-Jean
     1927 Englert, Giuseppe Giorgio (Italian)
          1930 Guillou, Jean
          1933 Charpentier, Jacques
          1934 Darasse, Xavier
          1934 Henry, Jean-Claude
          1935 Isoir, André
          1935 Werner, Jean-Jacques
          1936 Amy, Gilbert
          1937 Ourgandijian, Raffi (Lebanese)
               1942 Roth, Daniel F.

(1924), and Le Chemin de la Croix (1932). His symphonic
works include the organ concerto (1939) and the Deuxième
Symphonie (1929). The popular 11 Variations sur un Noël,
Op. 20, was written in Montreal while Dupré was playing a
series of all-Bach programs there.

Dom Paul Benoit (1893-   ), organist of the Benedictine
Abbey of St. Maurice and St. Maur in Clervaux, Luxembourg,
has composed Noël Basque (eight variations on a familiar
carol tune) and Au Soir de l'Ascension du Seigneur (which
refers to Gregorian melodies supported by richly chromatic
harmonies).

Arthur Honegger (1892-1955) has written two pieces
for organ, a Fugue in C-sharp minor and Choral. The fugue
is a warm, Romantic development of a short, chromatic subject. One of Honegger's associates in the French group
"Les Six," Darius Milhaud (1892-   ), has written a short
Pastorale, Neuf Préludes, and a three-movement Sonata.
Francis Poulenc (1899-1963), another member of the "Six,"
wrote the tuneful and exciting Concerto in G minor in one
movement for organ, string orchestra and timpani.

Maurice Duruflé (1903-   ), organist of St. Etienne-
du-Mont, Paris, has not composed many pieces for the organ.
The Suite (1934) contains three movements, one of them the
brilliant and challenging Toccata. The Prélude et Fugue sur
le Nom d'Alain, which was written in memory of Jehan Alain,
incorporates some strains from Alain's Litanies. The subtle
registration and impressionistic harmonies found in Duruflé's
compositions, such as the three movements based on Veni
Creator, resemble compositions by Fauré, one of Duruflé's
teachers.

Most of the organ works of Jehan Ariste Alain (1911-
1940) were written for the tracker organ built in the home by
Jehan and his father, Albert Alain (1880-   ), who was a student of Guilmant, Dupré, and Bonnet. The father had carefully studied Dom Bédos' writings when he was constructing
the organ and designed it to include classical French stops.

The Postlude pour l'Office de Complies was Alain's
earliest composition and was written for an organ in the
eighteenth-century Abbey of Valloires in northern France
while the composer was there on retreat. In 1932 Alain was
deeply impressed with the displays and performances presented at the French colonial exhibition in Paris. The dances,

unusual rhythms, and melodies which employed microtones he
heard and saw there inspired him to write Deux Danses à
Agni Vavishta.   The Variations sur un Thême de Clément
Jannequin are actually written on a tune by an anonymous
composer, which Alain found in an early book of French folk
songs.   Litanies has been extremely popular for use as a
toccata in organ recitals.

        The composition styles of Alain encompass the free,
improvisatory type, impressionistic works, and pieces influenced by plainsong.   Although Alain was a composition
pupil of Dukas, Alain did not like to be restricted to prescribed forms.   In his mind he heard irregular divisions of
beats, but found it impossible to transcribe to paper what he
heard.   Alain disliked the 16' sound in the pedal so he frequently registered sounds in that division at only the 8' level.

        Jean Langlais (1907-   ) is the present organist of
Ste. Clotilde, Paris.   Many of his works have these characteristics: brightly colorful registration;   through-composed
pieces with sharply contrasting sections;   irregular rhythms
and meter changes;   poetic and directly appealing melodies;
rich harmonies (frequent use of harmonic progressions employing chromatic mediants);   virtuoso pedal work;   bitonality;
incorporation of plainsong themes;   and early forms treated
in contemporary styles.

        Most of Langlais' colorful works are pieces of mod-
erate length grouped in suites or collections such as the programmatic Trois Poêmes Evangeliques, Trois Paraphrases
Grégoriennes, Neuf Pièces, Suite Brève, Suite Française,
and Hommage à Frescobaldi.   Fête and Incantation pour un
Jour Saint are only two of many individual pieces which are
widely used as recital pieces.   The Première Symphonie
(1941-1942) is his only effort so far in a larger form.   Langlais wrote the Suite Médiévale in the form of a low Mass and
incorporated incidentally the melodies of the Asperges me
(Entrée), Kyrie-Fons bonitatis (Offertoire), Adoro te devote
(Elévation), Ubi caritas (Communion), and Christus vincit
(Acclamations sur le Texte des Acclamations Carolingiennes).

        One of the most significant and influential composers
of the twentieth century is Olivier Messiaen (1908-   ), a
highly idiomatic and individualistic composer.   In the Preface
to his book The Technique of My Musical Language Messiaen
listed a number of people and things tangible and intangible
which have affected him and his music.   Among others were

Dukas, Dupré, members of his family, Shakespeare, Claudel, holy scripture, birds, Russian music, plainsong, Hindu rhythms, the mountains of Dauphiné, and his musical interpreters.

Among the earliest of Messiaen's pieces for organ are three of short or moderate length: Le Banquet Céleste (1928), Diptyque (1930), and Apparition de l'Eglise Eternelle (1932). The Celestial Banquet is based upon the text from the Gospel according to St. John which begins, "He who eats my flesh ...," which refers to the Holy Eucharist (Holy Communion, The Last Supper). All three of these pieces conform to regular pulse (meter). The registration suggested by the composer for Diptyque and Apparition is rather traditionally French, but the Banquet calls for Prestant 4' and Piccolo 1' coupled to the pedal without any pedal stops drawn until the final chord. Repetition in Messiaen's works provides gathering intensity and the suggestion of eternal concept which transcends time.

L'Ascension (1933) is a suite in four movements based upon texts associated with the ascension of Christ and the Mass of the Ascension. The first and fourth movements are very slow and majestic. The Serene Alleluias pictures the soul as it flutters and trembles in joyful anticipation of being received into spiritual realms. Cross-rhythms and buoyant melody give this movement its primary motion and interest. The third movement, Outburst of Joy, contrasts the full Great organ against the full Swell, sharp, staccato chords against legato pedal melody and a series of triplets, and, further, cadenzas, chords alternated between hands in toccata style, to express the deep happiness of the soul before the glory of Christ.

La Nativité du Seigneur ("The Nativity of the Lord") (1935) is a suite of nine meditations which depict various personages who were present at the nativity (the virgin and Child, shepherds, angels, wise men) and also several significant meanings of the event (eternal purposes, the Word, God among us). Messiaen treated his approach to the subject with emotion and sincerity but also with the attempt to communicate with the listener from three points of view: theological, instrumental, and musical. Many unusual and perhaps exotic timbres and colors are indicated. Often the 8' pitch is omitted and various combinations of mutations are desired. Transpositions, different modes, and added rhythms are only three of the musical techniques used by Messiaen in his carefully defined and intellectual conception of composition.

Les Corps Glorieux (1939) is a group of seven visions of the life of the resurrected ones. These highly imaginative pieces sometimes employ single line, one melody in octaves, or two-part textures for extended portions of the movements. The music in these pieces is constructed from the same musical materials as those used in the Nativity.

Messe de la Pentecôte (1950) was inspired by texts appropriate to Pentecost and deal with subjects such as the tongues of fire which descended upon the apostles; "things visible and invisible" (from the Nicaean Creed); the gift of wisdom; "springs of water and birds of heaven, bless the Lord"; and the rushing wind filled all the house." Three elements used by Messiaen in this suite of five movements are bird calls, changing note durations in ascending and descending degrees, and three Hindu rhythmic modes: one which does not change, one which gains value each time it is presented, and one which diminishes in value each time it is sounded.

Livre d'Orgue (Organ Book) (1951) contains seven pieces which embody a great use of polyrhythms, asymetric and symetric enlargement of rhythmic cells, bird calls, unusual combinations of mutations and stops of octave displacement, along with inspiration of various scriptural texts, and cluster appogiaturas. The most recent organ work by Messiaen is a shorter one, the Verset pour la Fete de la Dédicace (1960), which was composed as a test piece for the Paris Conservatory.

Notes

1. Norbert Dufourcq, La Musique d'Orgue Française de Jehan Titelouze à Jehan Alain, Paris: Librairie Floury, 1949; p. 186.
2. William Pruitt, "Charles Tournemire 1870-1949," The American Organist, August 1970, p. 20-25.

Bibliography

Alain, Marie-Claire. "The Organ Works of Jehan Alain," translated by Irene Feddern, The Diapason, pt I (January 1970), p. 20-21; pt II (February 1970), p. 22-25;

and pt III (March 1970), p. 6-8.

Cohalan, Aileen. "Messiaen: Reflections on Livre d'Orgue," Music/The A. G. O. and R. C. C. O. Magazine, vol. II (July 1968), p. 26; November 1968, p. 28; and December 1968, p. 28.

Delestre, R. L'Oeuvre de Marcel Dupré. Paris: Procure Générale du Clergé, 1952.

Doyen, Henri. Mes Leçons d'Orgue avec Louis Vierne: Souvenirs et Témoignages. Paris: Editions Musique Sacrée, 1966.

Dreisoerner, Charles, "The Themes of Langlais' Incantation," Music/The A. G. O. -R. C. C. O. Magazine, vol. 6, no. 4 (April 1972), p. 41-44.

Dufourcq, Norbert. "Panorama de la Musique d'Orgue Francaise au XXe Siècle," Revue Musicale, vol. XIX, no. 184 (June 1938), p. 369-376; vol. XIX, no. 185 (July 1938), p. 35-44; vol. XIX, no. 186 (September 1938), p. 120-125; and vol. XX, no. 189 (March 1939), p. 103-115.

_____. La Musique d'Orgue Française au XXe Siècle. Paris: Librairie Floury, 1939.

_____. La Musique d'Orgue Française de Jehan Titelouze à Jehan Alain. Paris: Librairie Floury, 1941 (2 ed. , 1949).

Gavoty, Bernard. Louis Vierne, la Vie et l'Oeuvre. Paris: Albin Michel, 1943.

Goléa, Antoine. Rencontres avec Olivier Messiaen. Paris: René Julliard, 1960.

Hassman, Carroll. "Messiaen: An Introduction to his Compositional Techniques and an Analysis of 'La Nativité'," Diapason, pt 1 (December 1971), p. 22-23; and pt 2 (January 1972), p. 26-27.

Hesford, Bryan. "Dupré's 'Stations of the Cross'," Musical Times, vol. 102, no. 1425 (November 1961), p. 723-724.

Kasouf, Richard J. "Louis Vierne and His Six Organ Symphonies," The American Organist (November 1970), p. 20-26.

Klinda, Ferdinand. "Die Orgelwerke von Olivier Messiaen," Musik und Kirche, vol. 39 (January-February 1969), p. 10.

Long, Page C. "Vierne and His Six Organ Symphonies," The Diapason, pt I (June 1970), p. 23; pt II (July 1970), p. 7; and pt III (August 1970), p. 8.

Lord, Robert Sutherland. "Organ Music of Jean Langlais: Comments on performance style," The American Organist, (January 1968), p. 27-32.

_____. "Sources of Past Serve Langlais in Organ Works,"

The Diapason (January 1959), p. 24; and February
    1959, p. 24.
Messiaen, Oliver.   Technique de Mon Langage Musical,
    Paris: Leduc, 1944; The Technique of My Musical
    Language, translated into English by John Satterfield,
    Paris: Leduc, 1956.
Pruitt, William.   "Charles Tournemire 1870-1939, " The
    American Organist (August 1970), p. 20-25.
Raugel, Félix.   Les Grandes Orgues des Eglises de Paris.
    Paris: Librairie Fischbacher, 1927.
Samuel, Claude.   Entretiens avec Olivier Messiaen.   Paris:
    Editions Pierre Belfond, 1967.
Sumner, William Leslie.   "The French Organ School, " Sixth
    Music Book.   London: Hinrichsen Edition Ltd. , 1950;
    p. 281-294.
Thomerson, Kathleen.   "Errors in the Published Organ Com-
    positions of Jean Langlais, " American Guild of Organ-
    ists Quarterly, vol. X, no. 2 (April 1965), p. 47-54.

17. ENGLAND AND CANADA SINCE 1900

England

During the first half of the twentieth century English organ builders constructed Romantic, orchestral instruments. The organ reform movement, which became strong in Germany in the 1920's, is beginning to affect English organ building slowly. Examples of a more classic concept of organ design than that exhibited earlier in this century are the organs at the Royal Festival Hall, London (1954), and the first new tracker-action organ in London City Church of St. Vedast (1961). The most prominent English organ builders today are Harrison and Harrison, William Hill & Son and Norman & Beard, J. W. Walker & Sons, and N. P. Mander.[1]

Although many twentieth-century English composers have written for the organ, no single composer has composed a great deal. Much of the literature which has been written is based upon hymn-tunes, although the pieces may be called "chorale" preludes and employ the same techniques as those applied to chorale settings for several hundred years. Although it is not true of all contemporary English composition for the organ, there is still much which is conservative, diatonic writing and which employs only the simplest forms of construction.

Ralph Vaughan Williams (1872-1958) composed Three Preludes founded on Welsh Hymn Tunes (Bryn Calfaria, Rhosymedre, Hyfrydol). The first contains pianistic cadenzas and imitative entries in a fantasy treatment. Rhosymedre, a setting of two stanzas of the tune, is a dignified, flowing arrangement. The Hyfrydol prelude is a stirring, majestic one in which the voices generally march forward in stepwise movement; the piece contains scarcely one accidental, but the lines of the accompaniment are vigorous and frequently syncopated.

Sir Walford Davies (1869-1941) is known for his Solemn Melody, a noble and dignified tune. The two Shaw brothers, Martin (1875-1958) and Geoffrey (1879-1943), have

HISTORICAL BACKGROUND

1900	Elgar Dream of Gerontius
1901-1910	Reign of Edward VII
1901	Shaw Caesar and Cleopatra
1903	Shaw Man and Superman
1904	Barrie Peter Pan
1907-	W. H. Auden
1909	Vaughan Williams Fantasia on a Theme of Tallis
1910	Vaughan Williams Sea Symphony
1910-1936	Reign of George V
1910	Masefield The Tragedy of Pompey the Great
1912	Sinking of the Titanic
1914-1918	World War I
1914-1953	Dylan Thomas
1915	Maugham Of Human Bondage
1919	League of Nations formed
1922	Galsworthy The Forsyte Saga
1924	Shaw Saint Joan
1931	Walton Belshazzar's Feast
1935	Eliot Murder in the Cathedral
1936	Reign of Edward VIII
1936-1952	Reign of George VI
1939-1945	World War II
1945	Britten Peter Grimes
1950	Eliot The Cocktail Party
1952-	Reign of Elizabeth II
1962	Britten War Requiem

---

contributed much to church music. Martin Shaw, one of the editors of the Oxford Book of Carols, wrote a Processional for organ, which contains much parallel chordal writing and leads to a fortissimo harmonization of the hymn-tune associated with the text Praise to the Lord, the Almighty (Lobe den Herren).

Three Liturgical Preludes and Three Liturgical Improvisations came from the pen of George Oldroyd (1886-). Both sets of pieces are improvisatory, tuneful, and contain many meter changes. Harold Darke (1888-) has written A Meditation on Brother James' Air of loose construction, which contains frequent short references to the basic melody.

Herbert Howells (1892-) has composed two sets of Three Psalm Preludes, which are improvisatory, rich

harmonically, rhythmically interesting, and which lend themselves to colorful registration.   These pieces were inspired
by psalm verses.   Howells has dedicated six imaginative
pieces of assorted character to Herbert Sumsion.   Sarabande
for the Morning of Easter and Master Tallis's Testament
come from this group.   Howells' composition technique employs tertial harmonies, flowing melodic lines, moderately
frequent meter changes, and many ingenious divisions of the
rhythmic unit.

Percy W. Whitlock (1903-1946) composed Five Short
Pieces, which are short character pieces.   The Folk Tune
and Scherzo are probably the best known compositions from
the group.   Whitlock's first set of Six Hymn-Preludes contains more variety of musical materials than the second.
Alec Rowley (1892-1958) wrote improvisations and chorale
preludes, which often are restless in nature.   Eric Harding
Thiman (1900-   ) has composed both character pieces and
hymn-tune settings.   His compositions are characterized by
pleasant melody and improvisatory style.   Thiman's Tune
for the Tuba continues the English trumpet voluntary tradition.

The Carillon of Herbert Murrill (1909-1952) is a fan-
fare-toccata which contains shifting meters and rhythms,
which are combined with an interesting pedal part.   Benjamin
Britten's one organ composition is a Prelude and Fugue on
a Theme of Vittoria (1946).   The largamente prelude is only
13 measures long and contains a chant-like, free pedal theme
with sustained chords.   The fugue is in four-part texture
most of the time and later reduced to two-part writing, which
is divided between different voices.   Britten's rhythms change
frequently.   The fugue, conceived in a Romantic style, builds
to a fortissimo climax and closes pianissimo.

The Album of Praise collection contains conventional
pieces by Gordon Jacob (1895-   ), George Dyson (1883-1964),
Norman Gilbert, and Healey Willan (1880-1968).   Peter Hur-
ford (1930-   ), master of the music at the Cathedral and
Abbey Church of St. Albans, contributed an interesting Paean
to the volume.   He has also written a Suite 'Laudate Dominum' in six movements, which was inspired by verses of
scripture.

The most interesting and challenging English organ
composition of today is being written by younger composers
who have become sensitive to contemporary musical advances
and techniques.   John McCabe (1939-   ) is an imaginative

composer who often incorporates jagged rhythms and unusual
subdivisions of the beat.   Parallel chords often have special
articulations indicated.   Traditional styles such as the French
overture and toccata styles are incorporated in fresh ways.
In the Sinfonia, Op. 6 (1961), a passacaglia theme is introduced in $\frac{14}{8}$ time.   Each time the theme is presented it is
altered rhythmically and begins on a different tonal level.

Alleluyas of Simon Preston (1938-) was inspired by
the composition techniques of Messiaen.   The Prelude,
Scherzo and Passacaglia by Kenneth Leighton (1929-) offers
much rhythmic variety and quartal harmonies in both the
prelude and passacaglia;   the scherzo uses the gigue rhythm
as its unifying element.   Leighton's Paean is a march which
is introduced and closed by a section which consists principally of four-note broken chords.

The Exultate of Bryan Kelly (1934-) is strongly
rhythmic and, for the most part, in a regular meter.   The
texture is thin and clear, chords are sometimes treated in
a staccato or syncopated manner, and various articulations
are all important features of the piece.

Parallelisms of both intervals and chords constitute
an important element of the martial Processional by William
Mathias (1934-).   The Toccata alla Giga, Op. 37, by Alun
Hoddinott (1929-) is rhythmically vigorous and contains a
powerful sense of snap and drive within many subdivisions
of $\frac{6}{8}$ time.

Peter Racine Fricker (1920-) has written a clever
suite of Six Short Pieces, which exhibit a sure control of a
modified dodecaphonic system in declamatory, lyric, hymnic,
and free styles.

Canada

Canadian organ composition is closely related to the
English school because of common heritage, taste, and simi-
larity of training.   The most famous composer of church and
organ music who lived in Canada was the English-Canadian
Healey Willan (1880-1968).   Willan's music is traditional and
seemingly untouched by the newer musical styles and techniques of the twentieth century.   Many of his compositions
are well constructed but sometimes lack inspiration and
originality.   The largest portion of Willan's organ composition

ENGLISH ORGAN COMPOSERS SINCE 1900

1870   1890   1910   1930   1950   1970

1870 Walker, Ernest ------- 1949
1871 Buck, Percy Carter -- 1947
1872 Vaughan Williams, Ralph - 1958
1874 Kitson, Charles Herbert 1944
1874 Bairstow, Edward C. - 1946
1875 Ketelbey, Alfred William -- 1959
1875 Shaw, Martin ------------- 1958
1879 Shaw, Geoffrey T. ---- 1943
1879 Bridge, Frank ------- 1941
1879 Ireland, John Nicholson ------- 1962
    1881 Geehl, Henry Ernest ------ 1961
    1883 Dyson, George ----------- 1964
    1883 Harris, William Henry ------- 1973
    1885 Jenkins, Cyril ? (Welsh-Australian)
    1885 Porter, Ambrose P. ---------- 1971
    1886 Dixon, J. H. Reginald -------- 1975
    1886 Oldroyd, George ------ 1951
    1887 Whitehead, Alfred Ernest ----- 1974
    1887 Goldsworthy, William Arthur ?
    1887 Ley, Henry George ------- 1962
    1888 Sceats, Godfrey ?
    1888 Darke, Harold Edwin --------- 1976
    1888 Coleman, Henry Pinwell -- 1965
    1889 Rhodes, Harold Williams ?
    1889 Statham, Heathcote Dicken ----- 1972
    1889 Gibbs, Cecil Armstrong -- 1960
        1890 Bullock, Ernest ----------- 1979
             Dale, Joseph
        1891 Lang, Craig Sellar ------- 1971
        1891 Hunt, Reginald Heber ?
        1892 Howells, Herbert Norman ----- 1983
        1892 Rowley, Alec ----- 1958
        1892 Sorabji, Kaikhosru
        1894 Milner, Arthur Frederick - 1972
        1895 Trevor, Caleb Henry ----- 1976
        1895 Jacob, Gordon P. S.
        1895 Waters, Charles Fredrick
        1896 Maclean, Quentin Stewart M. 1962
        1896 Thalben-Ball, George Thomas (Australian-Eng)
        1896 Slater, Gordon Archbold --- 1979
        1897 Christopher, Cyril Stanley
        1898 Demuth, Norman
        1899 Sumsion, Herbert Whitton
             Wheeldon, Herbert Arthur
             Silver, Alfred J.
            1900 Bush, Alan Dudley
            1900 Thiman, Eric Harding - 1975
            1901 Rubbra, Edmund

ENGLISH ORGAN COMPOSERS SINCE 1900 (continued)

1870	1890	1910	1930	1950	1970

```
1902 Walton, William ---------- 1983
1902 Simkins, Cyril Frank
1903 Watson, Sydney
1903 Whitlock, Percy 1946
1903 Milford, Robin 1959
1903 Taylor, Stainton de Boufflers 1975
1904 Westrup, Jack Allan -- 1975
1904 Downes, Ralph William
1904 Tippett, Michael
1905 Flay, Alfred Leonard
1905 Dykes-Bower, John ------- 1981
1905 Pearson, William Dean
1906 Proctor, Charles
1906 Cooke, Arnold Atkinson
1908 Pritchard, Arthur J.
1908 Woodworth, William
1908 Phillips, Gordon
1909 Butcher, Vernon
1909 Orr, Robin
1909 Emery, Walter James- 1974
1909 Murrill, Herbert 1952
1909 Campbell, Sidney Scholfield 1974
     1911 Scott, Anthony Leonard Winstone
     1911 Ashfield, Robert James
     1912 Gilbert, Norman -- 1975
     1913 Britten, Benjamin - 1976
     1914 Rimmer, Frederick
     1914 Webber, William Southcombe Lloyd
     1915 Searle, Humphrey
     1916 Guest, Douglas Albert
     1916 Wolff, Stanley Drummond
     1917 Smith Brindle, Reginald
     1917 Arnell, Richard
     1917 Jackson, Francis
     1917 Ratcliffe, Desmond
     1918 Cranmer, Philip
     1919 Willcocks, David V.
        1920 Bush, Geoffrey
        1920 Fricker, Peter Racine
        1921 Cruft, Adrian Francis
        1921 Arnold, Malcolm
        1922 Morris, Christopher John
        1922 Smith, Robert (Welsh)
        1922 Hamilton Iain
        1924 Guest, George Howell
        1924 Tomlinson, Ernest
        1925 Milner, Anthony
        1926 Hewitt-Jones, Tony
```

ENGLISH ORGAN COMPOSERS SINCE 1900 (continued)

1870	1890	1910	1930	1950	1970

1926 Wills, Arthur William
1926 Brockless, Brian
1927 Whettam, Graham
1927 Routh, Francis John
1927 Joubert, John
1927 Garlick, Anthony
1927 Barlow, David Frederick 1975
1927 Spooner, Ian
1928 Stevenson, Ronald
1929 Hoddinott, Alun
1929 Leighton, Kenneth
    1930 Hurford, Peter
    1930 Hesford, Michael Bryan
        Williams, Charles Lee
        Rawsthorne, Noel
        Jarvis, Caleb Edward
        Sanders, John Derek
    1931 Holman, Derek
    1931 Williamson, Malcolm (Australian)
    1933 Naylor, Peter
    1934 Davies, Peter Maxwell
    1934 Ridout, Alan Jones
    1934 Dickinson, Peter
    1934 Kelly, Bryan
    1934 Mathias, William James
    1935 Popplewell, Richard John
    1936 Healey, Derek Edward
    1937 Crunden-White, Paul
    1938 Beechey, Gwilym Edward
    1938 Preston, Simon John
    1938 Stoker, Richard
    1939 Harvey, Jonathan Dean
    1939 Standford, Patric John
    1939 McCabe, John
    1939 Steel, Christopher Charles
        1941 Harper, Edward James
        1942 Ferguson, Barry William Cammack
        1944 Drayton, Paul Charles
        1944 Lord, David Malcolm
        1945 Rutter, John
        1948 Berkeley, Michael

lies in hymn-tune settings.   In them there is practically no
change of tonality, the harmonies are bland, and the rhythms
are conventional.

Willan's free organ works include an early Prelude
and Fugue in B Minor and his famous Introduction, Passacaglia and Fugue.   The latter work contains more imaginative and daring writing than his later organ compositions.
Key changes, varying rhythms, and rich harmonies of the
Romantic era mark the work.   There are 18 variations, some
traditional and others theatrical, opulent, rather curiously
juxtaposed.   The fugue is in E-flat minor, and the third section moves to the parallel major key for a stretto over a
pedal point.   The Nobilmente coda utilizes the passacaglia
theme for one final time (the 19th variation) in pedal octaves
which is accompanied by grandiose chords on the manuals.

The Toccata on O Filii et Filiae by Lynwood Farnam
(1885-1930) is a favorite for many Easter congregations.   The
piece contains fast pianistic arpeggios on the manuals with
the theme in pedal octaves;   manual triplet figurations on the
harmonies make up the middle section.

For convenience organ compositions by twentieth-
century Canadian composers can be classified into three
general styles: traditional, moderately contemporary, and
progressive contemporary styles.   Composers who have written in a conventional fashion by using diatonic melodies and
harmonies and simpler forms and rhythms are composers
such as Kenneth Meek (1908-   ), Guy Ducharme, Eugene Hill,
and William France.

The organ works of Frederick Karam (1926-   ) and
Gerald Bales (1919-   ) would be considered contemporary,
but they still contain many features of established forms and
composition techniques such as regular meters and standard
registration practices.   Karam's Divertimento contains a
modal flavor;   in this same piece there is alternation of two
themes, one lyric and the other sprightly.   Bales maintains
interest in his Petite Suite by using such devices as pedal
ostinato passages, mild parallelisms (major triads usually),
and some bitonal chords.   The stately and flowing lines of
Bales' Prelude in E Minor are in a more traditional vein.

Four Canadians who employ more advanced techniques
are François Morel (1926-   ), Keith Bissell (1912-   ), Vernon Murgatroyd, and Maurice Boivin (1918-   ).   All of

HISTORICAL BACKGROUND

1804-1895	Antoine Plamondon, Quebec painter
1810-1871	Paul Kane, painter
1861-1944	Bliss Carman, writer
1867	Confederation of Canada
1869-1944	Stephen Leacock, writer
1873-1932	J. E. H. MacDonald, painter
1879-1941	Emile Nelligan, poet
1882-	A. Y. Jackson, painter
1896	Klondike gold rush began
1914-1918	World War I
1915-	Louis Archambault, sculptor
1920	"Group of Seven" painters formed
1923-	Jean-Paul Riopelle, non-objective artist
1939-1945	World War II
1940	E. J. Pratt Brébeuf and His Brethren
1948	Stratford Festival established
1959	St. Lawrence Seaway opened

CANADIAN ORGAN COMPOSERS: 1870--

1880   1900   1920   1940   1960   1980

```
1877 Crawford, Thomas James ----- 1962 (Scot-Canadian)
   1880 Willan, Healey ------------ 1962 (Eng-Canadian)
   1885 Farnam, Lynwood 1930
   1888 Coutts, George James----- 1962 (Scot-Canadian)
      1891 Egerton, Arthur Henry 1957
      1893 MacMillan, Ernest -------- 1973
         1901 Silvester, Frederick Caton 1966 (Eng-Canadian)
         1902 Brown, Allanson G. Y. (Eng-Canadian)
         1904 Bancroft, Henry Hugh (Eng-Canadian)
         1908 Piché, Paul Bernard
         1908 Meek, Kenneth (Eng-Canadian)
         1909 Hill, Lewis Eugene --- 1976
            Ducharme, Guy; Fox, George; Murgatroyd, Vernon
            1912 France, William Edward; George, Graham; Bissell,
               Keith Warren
            1913 Archer, Violet B.
            1914 Duchow, Marvin
            1915 Drynan, Margaret Isobel Brown
            1918 Boivin, Maurice; Ridout, Godfrey
            1919 Bales, Gerald Albert
               1920 Turner, Robert Comrie
               1921 Fleming, Robert James 1976
               1922 Hatch, Verena
               1926 Morel, François d'Assise; Daveluy, Raymond;
                  Karam, Frederick
               1928 Atkinson, Gordon (Australian-Canadian)
                  1930 Bottenberg, Wolfgang Heinz Otto (Ger-Canadian)
                  1931 Camilleri, Charles Mario (Maltese)
                  1931 Clarke, Frederick Robert Charles
                  1933 Cabena, Harold Barrie
                  1934 Hodkinson, Sydney Philip
```

these men have used metrical indications and parallel treatment of chords (the same type of chord in a series of chords
which appear on different tonal levels).   Murgatroyd placed
a free rhythm section in the middle of the Méditation sur un
Thème Grégorien.   Boivin employed a number of examples
of bitonality in Deux Pièces, two short pieces inspired by
Latin texts (Laetare Jerusalem, Introit for the Fourth Sunday
of Lent, and Ego sum pastor bonus, Preface for the Second
Sunday after Easter).   In the Sonata Keith Bissell utilizes a
style of contemporary counterpoint and both augmentation and
diminution devices.   The Prière (1954) by Morel is the most
advanced harmonically of the pieces mentioned; the composer
uses 11th-chords and chords combining as many as seven different pitches.   Double pedaling and the chant-like melody
(also played by the feet) occur in this mystic piece.

The Canadian organ-building firm of Casavant Frères
has maintained a reputation for instruments of high quality
for many years.   Lawrence L. Phelps, former tonal director
of the Casavant company actively supported the ideals of the
twentieth-century organ reform.   The firm of Gabriel Kney
deserves mention for fine instruments, also.   The specifications of a smaller instrument built along classic lines is
given below.

Wolfville, Nova Scotia, Manning Memorial Chapel,
Acadia University.   Built by Casavant Frères, 1963.

Hauptwerk	Brustwerk	Pedal
Quintaden 16'	Gedackt 8'	Subbass 16'
Prinzipal 8'	Spitzflöte 4'	Prinzipal 8'
Rohrflöte 8'	Prinzipal 2'	Choralbass 4'
Oktav 4'	Quinte 1 1/3'	Mixtur IV (2')
Waldflöte 4'	Sesquialtera II	Fagott 16'
Flachflöte 2'	(2 2/3')	
Mixtur IV (1')	Zimbel II (1/4')	
Trompete 8'	Holzregal 8'	
	Tremulant	

Couplers: Hauptwerk/Pedal;   Brustwerk/Pedal;
Brustwerk/Hauptwerk

Note

1.   Clutton, Cecil, and Austin Niland, The British Organ,

London: B. T. Batsford, 1963; p. 107-118.

Bibliography

Beechey, Gwilym. "Parry and His Organ Music," Musical
    Times, vol. 109, no. 1508 (October 1968), p. 956;
    and vol. 109, no. 1509 (November 1968), p. 1057.
Clutton, Cecil, and Austin Niland. The British Organ. Lon-
    don: B. T. Batsford Ltd. , 1963.
Harverson, Alan. "Britten's Prelude and Fugue," Musical
    Times, vol. 102, no. 1417 (March 1961), p. 175.
Milner, Arthur. "The Organ Sonata of Herbert Howells,"
    Musical Times, vol. 105, no. 1462 (December 1964),
    p. 924.
Phelps, Lawrence I. "A Short History of the Organ Revival,"
    reprinted from Church Music 67.1. St. Louis: Concor-
    dia Pub. House, 1967.
Young, Percy. "A Survey of Contemporary Organ Music:
    England," Church Music 67.2, p. 25.

18. THE LOWLANDS, SCANDINAVIA, SWITZERLAND,
    ITALY, AND CZECHOSLOVAKIA SINCE 1800

Several organ builders from Denmark, the Netherlands, and Switzerland have established enviable reputations for distinguished work in constructing new instruments and in restoring older ones. The ideals of these builders are in concord with the aims of the Orgelbewegung, the organ reform movement of the twentieth century. Sybrand Zachariassen became the head of the Marcussen and Son organ building firm in Aabenraa, Denmark, in 1920. The firm gained renown for restoring instruments, for building excellent organ cases, and for constructing mechanical-action instruments, especially in northern Europe. D. A. Flentrop of Zaandam, the Netherlands, has earned distinction for the same reasons. He has built some splendid instruments of high quality in Europe and America. The firm of Metzler & Söhne, Dietikon, Switzerland, built a superb instrument for St. Peter's in Geneva. Poul-Gerhard Andersen has cooperated with the Metzler firm to build several outstanding organs in Switzerland.

Belgium

Jacques Lemmens founded the modern French organ school. In addition to Guilmant and Widor, Lemmens had other students like Joseph Callaerts (1838-1901) and Alphonse Mailly who became composers of character pieces. Because of Belgium's geographical position between France, the Netherlands, and Germany, it is natural that Belgian organ music would have strong spiritual connections with these other schools of composition.

The three most prominent organ composers of modern Belgium have been Jongen, de Maleingreau, and Peeters. The organ compositions of Joseph Jongen (1873-1953) are closely related to the French school. His pieces have appealing melodies (Chant de May) and interesting rhythmic figures. Jongen's pianistic Toccata is in the tradition of Vierne and Widor.

HISTORICAL BACKGROUND

1831	Belgium became independent
1843-1907	Edvard Grieg
1848	Swiss Constitution
1864	International Red Cross established by Swiss
1870	Unification of Italy established
1890-1948	Reign of Queen Wilhelmina, the Netherlands
1905	Norway became independent
1905-1957	Reign of King Haakon VII, of Norway
1907-1950	Reign of King Gustav V, of Sweden
1912-1947	Reign of King Christian X, of Denmark
1914-1918	World War I
1917	Finland declared independent
1918	Czechoslovakia became independent
1919	League of Nations founded
1934-1951	Reign of King Leopold III, of Belgium
1938	Czechoslovakia dismembered by Munich Pact
1939-1945	World War II
1942	United Nations formed
1947-1972	Reign of King Frederick IX, of Denmark
1948--	Reign of Queen Juliana, the Netherlands
1950--	Reign of King Gustav VI, of Sweden
1951--	Reign of King Baudouin, of Belgium
1951	North Atlantic Treaty Organization founded
1956--	Kekkonen, President of Finland
1957	European Common Market established
1957	Reign of King Olav V, of Norway
1968	Democratization of communism in Czechoslovakia halted by Warsaw Pact powers
1972--	Reign of Queen Margarethe, of Denmark

Paul de Maleingreau (1887-1956) composed several large works which are religious program symphonies similar to the Symphonie-Passion of Dupré. The Symphonie de la Passion, Op. 20, was inspired by the pictorial works of Roger de la Pasture (Vander Weyden); its movements are entitled Prologue, Le Tumulte au Prétoire, Marche au supplice, and O Golgotha! The Symphonie de l'Agneau Mystique, Op. 24, inspired by the pictorial works of Hubert and Jean van Eyck, contains three movements named Images, Rhythmes,

and Nombres. de Maleingreau has also written a Symphonie
de Noël, several Masses, and Opus Sacrum.

Flor Peeters (1903-   ) is famous as a concert organist, teacher, composer, and editor of early organ music,
especially that of the Lowlands. His compositions are a
synthesis of French and Flemish characteristics. English,
American, and Gregorian hymn melodies have been used by
Peeters as the bases for many cantus firmus settings; his
recent series in this genre is entitled Hymn Preludes for the
Liturgical Year, Op. 100, in 24 volumes. The Aria and
Elégie are especially appealing, short melodious works. Archaic and modal harmonies flavor his works as in the 35
Miniatures, Op. 55, and the Suite Modale, Op. 43. Entrata
Festiva, Op. 93, for organ, two trumpets, and two trombones (timpani and unison chorus ad libitum) is a stirring
piece of moderate length, which incorporates the Christus
vincit melody. Peeters also uses programmatic titles such
as Nostalgia and Morning Hymn for some of his works.

Belgian-born Guy Weitz, who resided in London since
early in the twentieth century, composed two organ symphonies. The first symphony is in three movements, each of
which is based on a melody associated with the Virgin Mary,
Regina pacis, Mater dolorosa, and Stella maris. The
Symphony No. 2 is in five movements and includes a passacaglia as one movement. Weitz's writing is well-suited to
the organ and has a strong affinity to French composition
style. [1]

The Netherlands

Contemporary Dutch organ composition is deeply influenced by German and French styles of composition. Dutch
folk-songs and Calvinist psalm-tunes are frequently used as
bases for Dutch cantus firmus organ compositions.

C. F. Hendricks (1861-1923) was a late nineteenth-
century Dutch organ composer. His short, simple pieces
were influenced by French organ works of that period.

Perhaps Hendrik Andriessen (1892-   ) is best known
for his lengthy Toccata and Premier Choral. Andriessen's
organ works have been strongly influenced by the French
school; two of the clearest examples of this French proclivity are shown by manual figurations above pedal themes

BELGIAN ORGAN COMPOSERS: 1800--

1800	1850	1900	1950

    1823 Lemmens, Jacques 1881
    1833 Mailly, Alphonse-Jean-Ernest 1918
    1838 Callaerts, Joseph 1901
        1854 Tinel, Edgar 1912
        1858 Depuydt, Oscar 1925
            1870 Ryelandt, Joseph ---- 1965
            1873 Rasse, François -- 1955
            1873 Jongen, Joseph-Marie 1953
            1875 Dethier, Gaston --- 1958
            1875 Moulaert, Raymond -- 1962
            1877 Dupuis, Albert ------ 1967
                1887 de Maleingreau, Paul 1956
                1890 Schoemaker, Maurice 1964
                1893 Peeters, Emil Aloys Angelica 1974
                1898 Hens, Charles
                1899 Plum, J. M. 1944
                1899 Huybrechts, Albert 1938
                    1903 Woronoff, Wladimir (Russian-Belgian)
                    1903 Peeters, Flor
                    1907 Rosseau, Norbert 1975
                    1909 van Dessel, Lode
                        1910 Eraly, Paul
                        1911 Huybrechts, Lode 1973
                        1914 Froidebise, Pierre 1962
                        1918 de Brabanter, Jos
                        1919 Verschraegen, Gabriel 1981
                            1925 Roelstraete, Herman
                            1929 Kersters, Willem
                                1930 Baervoets, Raymond
                                1935 Roland, Claude-Robert
                                1936 Boesmans, Philippe

SPANISH AND PORTUGUESE ORGAN COMPOSERS: 19th-20th CENTURIES

1800	1850	1900	1950

    1812 Emilio, Manuel 1871
                1872 Torres, Eduardo 1934
                1880 Otaño, José Maria Nemesio 1956
                1882 Urteaga, Luis
                1884 Beobide, José Maria
                1885 Arabaolaza, Gaspar de
                1887 Valdès, Julio
                1888 Erausquin, José Antonio de
                    1912 Montsalvatge Bassols, Xavier
                        1930 Castillo, Manuel
                        1930 Halffter, Cristóbal
                        1932 Raxach, Enrique
                        1935 Soler, Josep

and a harmonic palette similar to that of Vierne. The Toccata by Marius Monnikendam (1896-) is a brilliant and
rhythmic work dedicated to Charles Tournemire. An insis-
tent, monotonous quarternote tread is the unifying rhythmic
feature of Monnikendam's Cortège. His compositions are
characterized by a definite tonal center, interesting harmonies,
dissonances used for color, modality, and frequent use of
parallel fourths.

The Concert Etude, Op. 104 (1963) by Anthon van der
Horst (1899-1965) is an intense, dramatic, and virtuoso work,
especially for the pedal technique. This piece is in tripartite form and contains a contrasting middle section in a quiet
mood. Toccata in modo conjuncto (1943), Orgel Partita op
Ps. 8 (1946), and Concerto, Op. 58 (1954) are three larger
compositions by the Amsterdam Conservatorium teacher.

Cor Kee (1900-) is famous for his course in improvisation at the Haarlem Summer Academy for Organists.
The styles of his composition range extend from the conservative, tonal writing of his earliest period to the 12-tone
writing which he practices today. Kee has composed 17 settings of Calvinist psalm-tunes, which are divided into three
volumes. These pieces are tonal, contain meter changes,
and many varieties of rhythmic divisions of the beat. These
pieces also follow several of the general types of chorale-
prelude writing such as fantasy, solo melody and accompaniment, and manualiter settings. Carefully designated articulations, the use of key signatures but few accidentals, scant
ornamentation, and changing tempi also characterize these
works. Drie Inventionen (1967) and Reeks-veranderingen
(Variations on a Tone-Row) (1966/1967), examples of Kee's
more recent writing, contain the following characteristics:
constantly changing rhythms and tempos, no tonal center,
tiny melodic fragments, unusual stop combinations, frequent
stop changes, lean texture, and intensely dissonant chords.

Piet Kee (1927-), son of Cor Kee, has written a
contemporary chorale fantasia on Wachet auf (Wake, Awake)
and a chorale prelude on O Sacred Head Now Wounded (1964).
The first of these two pieces contains a number of toccata
elements and has the chorale melody moving from one voice
to another (sometimes identified as "migrant" form of
chorale prelude). Triptych on Psalm 86 (Chorale, Canon,
Toccata) (1964) makes use of much more dissonance and
free counterpoint. The rhythms are not complex, although
they do change from measure to measure. Piet Kee has

ORGAN COMPOSERS OF THE NETHERLANDS: 1860--

```
1860      1880      1900      1920      1940      1960      1980

1861 Hendricks, C. F. ----------------- 1923
1861 Kruijs, Marius van t' ----------- 1919
1865 Petri, Willem --------------------------------- 1950
  1877 Zwart, Jan ------------------ 1937
  1878 Zagwijn, Henri ------------------------------------- 1954
    1880 Bonset, Jacobus ?
    1881 Dresden, Sem -------------------------------------- 1957
    1880 Bunk, Gerard ?
    1888 Van den Siegtenhorst-Meyer, B. ---------------- 1953
       1892 Andriessen, Hendrik
       1895 Voormolen, Alexander
       1895 King, Harold Charles
       1896 Monnikendam, Marius --------------------------------------- 1977
       1897 Vranken, Jaap ------------------------- 1956
       1898 Mulder, Ernest Willem ----------------- 1959
       1899 van der Horst, Anthon ----------------------- 1965
          1900 Kee, Cor
          1900 Schouten, Hennie ------------------------------------- 1976
          1902 Bijster, Jacob --------------------- 1958
          1903 Nieland, Jan ---------------------------- 1963
          1905 Orthel, Léon
          1906 Hoogewoud, Han
          1906 Baaren, Kees van ------------------------------------- 1970
          1907 Badings, Henk
          1907 Felderof, Jan
          1908 Stougie, K
          1909 Pouwels, Jan
          1909 de Braal, Andries
          1909 Mudde, Willem-Federik-Antonius
```

1910 Nieland, Hermann
1910 Weegenhuise, Johan Eduard
1911 Koetsier, Jan
1911 Mul, Jan Johan -------- 1971
1912 Strategier, Hermann
1913 Koert, Hans van
1916 Toebosch, Louis
1917 de Klerk, Albert
1918 Niël, Matty
1918 van Dijk, Jan
1919 Maessen, Antoon
1919 Post, Piet
1920 Vogel, Willem
1922 Franken, Willem (Wim)
1925 Andriessen, Jurriaan
1927 Kee, Piet
1927 Dijker, Mathieu
1929 Bartelink, Bernard
1930 Dragt, Jaap
1930 Kox, Hans
1931 Brons, Carel T.
1931 Spaink, Pierre Abbink François
1932 Marez Oyens, Tera de
1934 Bruynèl, Ton
1934 Bois, Rob du
1934 Straesser, Joep
1935 Booren, Jo van den
1937 Welmers, Jan
1938 Vriend, Jan
1938 Amerongen, Jan van
1939 Manneke, Daan
1939 Temmingh, Henk
1943 Bank, Jacques
1943 Ruiter, Wim de
1947 Schoonebeck, Kees
1948 Goorhuis, Rob

also composed a series of short manualiter settings of the
tune associated with the English text "God Himself Is with
Us" (Arnsberg, a hymn-tune by Neander).

Jacob Bijster (1902-   ), an outstanding Dutch orchestral composer, writes in a conventional Romantic style.   The
forms he uses in his organ works are the passacaglia, partita, fantasy, and fugue.   Another leading Dutch contemporary
organ composer is Henk Badings (1907-   ), who was the director of the Royal Conservatory at the Hague.   His music,
like that of Bijster, is Romantic with little dissonance.   One
of his unusual compositions is the Passacaglia for organ and
timpani.   Badings has employed such forms as the prelude
and fugue, canzona, toccata, and concerto.

Partita, Op. 41, No. 1 (1954) for English horn and
organ manuals alone by Jan Koetsier (1911-   ) is an effective
work for organ and a solo instrument.   The piece incorporates
the chorale tune Wie schön leuchtet der Morgenstern ("How
Brightly Shines the Morning Star").   Koetsier has also composed the Twelve Preludes and Fugues (1946) in a contemporary contrapuntal idiom.   These pieces are short, and the
texture is principally that of a trio.   There is one prelude
and fugue for each of the 12 chromatic tones.

Two contemporary Dutch organ composers who have
been active in Utrecht are Hermann Strategier (1912-   ) and
Albert de Klerk (1917-   ).   Strategier's Toccatina and de
Klerk's Ten Pieces in two volumes are moderately difficult.

Denmark

Martin Radeck (died 1684), one of the earliest Danish
organ composers, is represented by a partita on Jesus
Christus unser Heiland ("Jesus Christ our Saviour).   The
Danes also claim Buxtehude as one of their most famous
musicians because he lived in Denmark for approximately
the first half of his life, before he moved to Lübeck, Germany.   Another organ composer associated with the North
German Organ School was Melchior Schildt, who served
Christian IV of Denmark from 1626-1629.

Johann Peter Emilius Hartmann (1805-1900) and his
son-in-law Niels Wilhelm Gade (1817-1890) are the chief
Danish organ composers of the nineteenth century.   Hartmann
composed free works such as fantasias, marches, a sonata,

DANISH ORGAN COMPOSERS

1600	1700	1800	1850	1900	1950

ca. 1610 Lorentz 1689

1805 Hartmann, J. P. E. 1900
1817 Gade, Niels W. 1890
1835 Krygell, J. A. 1915
1848 Malling, Otto 1915
1865 Nielsen, Carl 1931
1876 Emborg, Jens Laursøn 1957
1879 Rung-Keller, Paul S. ?
1888 Raastad, Niels Otto ?
1888 Schierbeck, Poul J. O. 1949
1889 Senstius, Kai Helmer 1966
1892 Jeppesen, Knud 1974
1893 Thomsen, Peter (American-Danish)
1893 Langgaard, Rued I. 1952
1898 Weis, Carl Flemming
1900 Sandberg Nielsen, O. 1941
1903 Møller, Svend-Ove 1949
1903 Bjerre, Jens
1906 Christensen, Bernhard
1906 Viderø, Finn
1909 Holmboe, Vagn
1912 Andersen, Aksel
1919 Kayser, Leif
1919 Bentzon, Niels Viggo
1922 Thybo, Leif
1927 Lewkovitch, Bernhard
1928 Høgenhaven Jensen, Knud
1929 Bjerno, Erling D.
1929 Nielsen, Tage
1931 Nørholm, Ib
1932 Nørgaard, Per
1935 Lorentzen, Bent
1936 Norby, Erik

POLISH COMPOSERS

1500	1600	1700	1800	1900

Sowa, Jakub
Leopolita, Marcin
Mikolaj z Krakowa (Jan z Lublin)
Rohaczewski, Andrzej
1708 Janitsch, J. G. 1763
1792 Zöllner, K. H. 1836
1821 Lewandowski, L. 1894
1902 Gniot, Walerian
1903 Janacek, Karel ------------1974
1909 Dziewulska, Maria
1910 Chajes, Julius
1912 Juroský, Simon ------ 1963
1916 Paciorkiewicz, Tadeusz
1919 Haubenstock-Ramati, Roman
1922 Machl, Tadeusz
1924 Pietrzak, Bernard
1933 Górecki, Henryk Mikolaj
1936 Hawel, Jan Wincenty
1941 Glinkowski, Aleksander

and character pieces in the Romantic tradition.   Gade's organ
compositions include three "tone-pieces" and four works based
on chorale melodies.   Other nineteenth-century Danish organ
composers were G. Matteson-Hansen, his son Hans, and Otto
Valdemar Malling (1848-1915), who wrote character pieces
with religious programs (Shepherds in the Field, Easter
Morn).

Perhaps the most famous organ composition by a later
Danish composer is the Commotio by Carl August Nielsen
(1865-1931), who is better known for his orchestral works.
The Commotio is one continuous movement which suggests
perpetual motion, even in slower passages.   Tonal centers
frequently shift and are rarely established.   The writing is
always metrical and contains a use of cross-rhythms such
as six notes against four.   Articulations are carefully indicated, and, although the piece is difficult, there are no unusual technical demands.

Other Danish composers of the same period who wrote
shorter works for the organ were Paul S. Rung-Keller
(1879-), Niels Otto Raastad (1888-), Bernhard Christensen (1906-), and Otto Sandberg Nielsen (1900-1941).   The
compositions of Jens L. Emborg (1876-) resemble those
of Reger and Karg-Elert in style.   Knud Jeppesen (1892-)
and Finn Viderø (1906-) are two famous Danish musicolo-
gists and teachers who have written chorale settings in a
traditional vein.

After Nielsen's death musical composition in Denmark
was guided by the works and teaching of the late Romanticist
Rued Langgaard (1893-1952).   Leif Kayser (1919-), Niels
Viggo Bentzon (1919-), and Knud Høgenhaven (1928-) are
the principal Danish composers of 12-tone music for the organ.   The compositions of Leif Thybo (1922-) and Svend-
Ove Møller (1903-1949) contain lean, contrapuntal lines, thin
textures, quartal harmony, and irregular meters.   The
Sonata 1969 of Leif Kayser features metrical rhythms and
even divisions of the beats;   the tonality also shifts frequently.

Two younger Danish organ composers are Ib Nørholm
(1931-) and Per Nørgaard (1932-).   The Partita Concertante, Op. 23, by Nørgaard is in three movements: Fantasia, Canto variato, and Toccata.   The writing is linear
and atonal.   Although the notes are metrically distributed in
the measures, they are so complex rhythmically that the
passages are rare when a regular pulse can be felt.   Much

of the composition is played high on the manuals and the few
dynamic alterations are strongly contrasting.   Constant
changes in harmony and rhythms give Nørgaard's music a
restless character.

Sweden

For the most part Swedish organ compositions are
metrical and tonal;   few organ compositions have appeared
in more advanced twentieth-century techniques.   Swedish organ composers have usually employed traditional forms such
as cantus firmus compositions based on Swedish hymn-tunes[2]
or plainsong,[3] and preludes (or fantasias) and fugues.[4]   Gunnar Thyrestam's Preludium och Fuga No. 2 (1947) contains
a rhapsodic, sectional prelude followed by a fugue which has
a rather square-cut subject eight measures long, which is
first sounded in the pedal part.   The Triptyk (1951) of Valdemar Söderholm (1909-   ) contains a short toccata, a chromatic Adagio, and rhythmic Allegro energico, which employs
an active pedal part.

One of Sweden's leading twentieth-century composers
is Hilding Rosenberg.   His Fantasia e Fuga (1941) begins
with an arresting rhythmic theme which contrasts strongly
with the second theme, which is constructed of sixteenth-
note triplets;   the subject of the fugue is a lyric one, which
eventually leads to a manual cadenza.   Rosenberg's Praeludium e Fuga (1948) is poetic and pastoral in nature.   Rosenberg's harmonic palette remains triadic for the most part.

Bengt Hambraeus (1928-), a pupil of Messiaen, is
one Swedish composer who uses a serial technique in organ
composition.   Stig Gustav Schönberg (1933-   ) wrote a Toccata Concertante (1954) which is moderately long, strongly
rhythmic, principally for manuals, and contains a Calmato
middle section.   Schönberg's Lacrimae Domini (1958) is a
tone-poem of 18 minutes' duration.   At the beginning its
brooding principal theme is presented alone in the pedals.
The piece contains several sections of contrasting character:
brilliant toccata parts, an extremely chromatic, pensive middle section, a short fugal portion, and a broad Grave section
at the end.

SWEDISH ORGAN COMPOSERS

```
1850            1900            1950
```

1841 Andree, Elfrida ---------- 1929
  1853 Sjögren, Johann G. E. 1918
    1867 Hägg, Gustaf Wilhelm 1925
      1879 Olsson, Otto Emanuel --------- 1964
        1882 Fryklöf, H. 1919
        1884 Wikander, David ------ 1955
        1886 Bengtsson, Gustav -------- 1965
        1886 Nordqvist, Gustav Lazarus 1949
        1887 Lindberg, Oskar ------ 1955
        1887 Atterberg, Kurt Magnus ------- 1974
        1889 Berg, Gottfrid
          1892 Rosenberg, Hilding
          1894 Ahlen, Waldemar
          1894 Runbäck, Albert
          1895 Cedarwall, Harald 1952
          1898 Olson, Daniel
            1900 Thyrestam, Gunnar Olof
            1902 Eriksson, Nils ------- 1978
            1903 Hallnäs, Hilding
            1903 Lundborg, Gösta
            1905 Olsson, Thure V. - 1960
            1906 Carlmann, Gustav 1958
            1908 Sörenson, Torsten
            1909 Söderholm, Valdemar
              1910 Koch, Sigurd Christian Erland von
              1910 Lindroth, Henry
              1919 Johansson, Sven-Eric
              1919 Naumann, Siegfried
              1919 Bäck, Sven-Erik
                1920 Carlid, Göte 1953
                1920 Nilsson, Torsten
                1927 Eklund, Hans
                1928 Hambraeus, Bengt
                  1932 Hedwall, Lennart
                  1933 Schönberg, Stig Gustav
                  1934 Welin, Karl-Erik
                  1938 Hemberg, Eskil
                  1939 Forsberg, Roland
                    1940 Morthenson, Jan W.
```

RUSSIAN/SOVIET ORGAN COMPOSERS

```
1850            1900            1950
```

```
    1881 Strimer, Joseph ---------- 1962
      1890 Kushnarev, Khristofor Stepanovich 1960
        1901 Starokadomsky, Mikhail 1954
        1906 Shostakovitch, Dmitri - 1975
        1909 Mushel, Georgi Alexandrovitch
          1919 Shaverzashvili, Alexander Vassilievitch
            1932 Slonimsky, Sergei Mikhailovitch
            1935 Arro, Edgar Alexandrovitch
            1939 Tishchenko, Boris Ivanovitch
              1941 Kikta, Valeri Grigorievitch
```
```

Norway

The present-day Norwegian school of organ composition seems to be rather conservative, content to continue in simple, diatonic lines and harmony. Even the compositions of the mid-twentieth century have a mild, pastoral character, which is underlined by uncomplicated rhythms and metrical writing. Some Norwegian cantus firmus compositions have been based on plainsong[5] and carols.[6] Knut Nystedt (1915-) and Conrad Baden (1908-) are leading contemporary Norwegian composers who have utilized established organ forms and styles such as the pastorale, toccata, and chaconne.

Finland

One example of Finnish contributions to contemporary organ literature is Ta Tou Theou, Op. 30, by Einojuhani Rautavaara (1928-). This fantasy was inspired by sacred texts and was written in 1966 for the dedication of the new Marcussen organ in the Helsinki Cathedral. The free form of toccata has appealed to other Finns such as Sulo Salonen (1899-), Erkki Salmenhaara, and Jarmo Parvainen (1928-).

Switzerland

Swiss organ composers tend to write in styles similar to the German or French schools. Otto Barblan (1860-1943) was probably the first Swiss composer of modern times to have written much for the organ. Barblan wrote in a Romantic style similar to that of Reger and, like Reger, employed forms such as the chaconne, toccata, fugue, and passacaglia, in addition to smaller character pieces and religious adagios.

Frank Martin (1890-) has composed a Passacaille for organ solo and a Sonata da Chiesa (1938) for either viola d'amore or flute and organ. Martin's writing contains elements of French Impressionism and Franck's style, but his writing is more linear than that usually associated with those styles.

The organ compositions of Walther Geiser (1897-) are Germanic in tendency,[7] while those of his contemporary Albert Moeschinger (1897-) have been influenced by both

NORWEGIAN ORGAN COMPOSERS: 19th-20th CENTURIES

1800	1850	1900	1950	1980

1812 Lindeman, L. M. 1887
    1845 Cappelen, Christian
        1881 Eggen, Arne -- 1955
        1887 Valen, Fartein Olaf 1952
        1893 Isólfsson, Páll ----- 1974 (Icelandic)
        1895 Sandvold, Arild
        1901 Kjellsby, Erling - 1976
        1906 Nielsen, Ludvig
        1908 Baden, Conrad
            1911 Karlsen, Rolf Kåre
            1915 Nystedt, Knut
            1916 Johnsen, Halvard
            1919 Sommerfeldt, Øistein
            1919 Fongaard, Björn
                1924 Hovland, Egil
                1930 Elgarøy, Jan
                1939 Saeverud, Ketil
                1947 Karlsen, Kjell Mørk

FINNISH ORGAN COMPOSERS

1860	1900	1940	1980

1865 Sibelius, Jean J. J. C. ------ 1957
    1891 Raitio, Väninö 1945
    1898 Salonen, Sulo
        1905 Kuusisto, Taneli
            1911 Bergman, Erik
            1914 Johansson, Bengt
            1918 Stenius, Torsten
            1918 Sipilä, Eero ------ 1972
                1921 Kokkonen, Joonas
                1928 Rautavaara, Einojuhani
                1928 Parvainen, Jarmo Uolevi
                1928 Mononen, Sakari
                    1933 Kuusisto, Ilkka Taneli
                    1934 Linjama, Jouko Jaakko Armas

German Romanticism and French Impressionism.

Paul Müller-Zürich (1898-   ) has composed a quantity of organ works in larger forms (toccata, fantasy and fugue, canzone, concerto) and for other instruments with organ. Since 1950 he has written chorale toccatas and fantasies on Ein' feste Burg ("A Mighty Fortress"), Wie schön leuchtet ("How Brightly Shines the Morning Star"), Ach Gott vom Himmel ("O God in Heaven"), and Christ ist erstanden ("Christ is arisen") for organ, two trumpets, and two trombones.   His organ chorales and chorale preludes date from 1959.   Henri Gagnebin (1886-   ) has also written for the combination of organ and other instruments[8] in addition to his organ solo works.

Mysticism, numerical symbolism, and polymodality play a part in the works of Willy Burkhard (1900-1955), a pupil of Karg-Elert.   Many of the organ works by this famous Swiss composer of the first half of the twentieth century are based on chorale melodies;   the Choral-Triptychon (1953) is one of his major works in the chorale field.   Rudolf Moser (1892-1960), Bernhard Reichel (1901-   ), and Adolf Brunner (1901-   ) have also contributed to chorale-based literature for the organ.

Italy

The principal Italian composer of organ pieces about the turn of the twentieth century was Marco Enrico Bossi (1861-1925), an important Italian symphony composer, conservatory director, and concert performer who toured in both Europe and America.   Bossi's organ compositions are post-Romantic in style.[9]   His Alleluia is similar to mid-nineteenth-century French works of the Romantic era;   the piece exhibits contrapuntal writing and composition devices of that period.   Bossi also wrote two sonatas for the organ.

Ottorino Respighi (1879-1936), the brilliant orchestrator and composer of The Pines of Rome and The Fountains of Rome, wrote a Preludio for organ which combines chromatic harmonies with contrapuntal imitations and figures. This piece closes with a quick flourish in octaves and large fortissimo chords.   Alfredo Casella (1883-1947) composed a Concerto Romano for organ and orchestra which had its first performance in New York on March 11, 1927.

SWISS ORGAN COMPOSERS: 1800--

        1850   1900   1950

1808 Hess, Ernst 1863
         1860 Barblan, Otto ------------ 1943
            1876 Vretblad, Viktor Patrik --- 1953
               1883 Mottu, Alexandre - 1943
               1886 Gagnebin, Henri (Belgian-Swiss)
                  1890 Martin, Frank ------------ 1974
                  1892 Moser, Rudolf -------- 1960
                  1894 Roesgen-Champion, Marguerite 1976
                  1896 Kuhn, Max
                  1897 Geiser, Walther
                  1897 Moeschinger, Albert
                  1898 Müller-Zürich, Paul
                  1899 Wieruszowski, Lili (German-Swiss)
                     1900 Blum, Robert
                     1900 Burkhard, Willy 1950
                     1901 Beck, Conrad
                     1901 Reichel, Bernhard
                     1901 Brunner, Adolf
                     1904 Baum, Alfred
                     1904 Ammann, Benno
                     1906 Wolff, Hellmuth Christian
                        1911 d'Alessandro, R. 1959
                        1911 Studer, Hans
                        1912 Jenny, Albert
                        1913 Jaeggi, Oswald 1963
                        1913 Segond, Pierre
                        1914 Ducommun, Samuel
                        1917 Hildenbrand, Siegfried
                        1918 Vollenweider, Hans
                        1919 Zahner, Bruno
                             Zbinden, Julien-Francois
                             Rogg, Lionel
                        1921 Wehrle, Heinz
                        1922 Pfiffner, Ernst
                        1922 Wildberger, Jacques
                        1924 Huber, Klaus
                        1926 Heer, Emil
                        1929 Vogler, Ernst
                           1931 Kelterborn, Rudolf
                           1942 Bovet, Guy

Pietro Yon (1886-1943), the composer of Gesu Bambino and organist of St. Patrick's Cathedral, New York City, for 17 years, composed in the nineteenth-century Romantic style with conventional harmonies and simple forms. The organ works of Oreste Ravanello also derive their principal musical style from that same period.

Czechoslovakia

The modern Czech organ school is an outgrowth of the musical traditions of Smetana and Dvořák, whose primary interest lay in the orchestral medium. Both of these men composed a few organ works in polyphonic style early in their careers. Leoš Janáček (1854-1928), Vítězslav Novák, and Josef Suk were the leading Czech teachers of composition in the early part of the twentieth century. Janáček, as an organ composer, is chiefly known for the demanding Postludium from the Glagolithic Mass. In that same period several virtuoso organist-teachers[10] were instrumental in restoring interest in concert organ music in Czechoslovakia.

Czech organ composers have drawn upon a number of different sources for bases of cantus firmus compositions such as Czech sacred songs (Miloslav Krejčí), folk songs (Otto Albert Tichý), Christmas carols (Josef Blatný), and chorales (František Michálek, Bedřich Wiedermann). Romantic, orchestral qualities and the improvisatory spirit are also very strong in Czech organ music.[11] Mid-twentieth-century composers continued utilizing polyphonic forms such as chaconne,[12] fantasy,[13] and prelude and fugue (or toccata).[14]

A few observations about some of the Czech organ music of the 1960's can be drawn from works by six composers who wrote compositions in conjunction with the Second International Organ Competition at the Music Festival in Prague in 1966. In Laudes Petr Eben (1929-   ) uses standard metrical indications and divides the beat into rhythms made up of notes of small denomination, sometimes in complex juxtapositions.[15] Other devices used by Eben in the same piece are double pedaling, polytonalities, and quick changes for three manuals.

Karel Reiner (1910-   ) in the first (Moderato. Energico) of Three Preludes employs a preponderance of small intervals (half-steps and whole-steps) within a third in

ITALIAN ORGAN COMPOSERS: 1800--

1800	1820	1840	1860	1880	1900	1920	1940	1960	1980

1819 Gambini, Carlo Andrea 1865
       1861 Bossi, Marco Enrico 1925
       1864 Leoni, Franco ------------ 1949
       1866 Busoni, Ferrucio B. 1924
       1867 Fino, Giocondo -------------- 1950
         1871 Ravanello, Oreste - 1938
         1872 Perosi, Lorenzo ---------- 1956
         1875 Fano, Guido Alberto ---------- 1961
         1877 Cappelletti, Arrigo ?
         1879 Respighi, Ottorino - 1936
           1883 Casella, Alfredo -- 1947
           1885 Mauro-Cottone, M. 1938
           1886 Yon, Pietro ------ 1943 (Italian-American)
           1887 Manari, Raffaele 1933
             1893 Somma, Bonaventura -- 1960
             1895 Castelnuovo-Tedesco, M. 1969
               1906 Germani, Fernando
               Bellandi, N. Carlo
               1911 Rota, Nino
               1911 Sorensina, Alberto
               1913 Bresgen, Cesar
                 1920 Chailly, Luciano
                 1925 Berio, Luciano
                 1929 Tagliavini, Luigi Ferdinando
                 1932 Castiglioni, Niccolò
                 1937 Corghi, Azio

HUNGARIAN ORGAN COMPOSERS

1500	1600	1700	1800	1900

1507 Bacfarc 1576
      1643 Wohlmuth 1724
      1656 Croner 1740
      Zarewutius
         174? Zimmermann 1781
         1742 Novotny 1773
         1748 Rigler, Ferenc Pál
           1801 Müller, Adolf 1886
             1843 Bella, Ján Levoslav 1936
             1877 Perényi, Géza 1954
             1882 Kodaly, Zoltán 1967
             1890 Jemnitz, Sandor 1963
               1903 Kadosa, Pal
               1905 Farkas, Ferenc
               1906 Gárdonyi, Zoltán
               Imre, Sulyok
               1915 Huzella, Elek
               1916 Schiske, Karl 1969
               1917 Maros, Rudolf
                 1932 Koloss, István
                 1934 Károlyi, Pál
                 1934 Durkó, Zsolt
                 1940 Sáry, László

CZECHOSLOVAKIAN ORGAN COMPOSERS: 1750--

1800   1850   1900   1950

1756 Kopřiwal 1785
  1786 Pitsch, Karel F. 1858
    1807 Führer, R. J. N. 1861
      1852 Musil, František 1908
        1859 Foerster, Josef Bohuslav --------- 1951
          1865 Martinu, Bohuslav ----------- 1959
            1872 Moyzes, Mikuláš ----- 1944
              1882 Vycpálek, Ladislav -------- 1969
                1883 Wiedermann, Bedrich Antonin 1951
                  1890 Tichý, Otto Albert
                  1892 Kvapil, Jaroslav -- 1958
                  1893 Zelinka, Jan Evangelista 1969
                  1893 Hába, Alois -------------- 1973
                  1893 Chlubna, Osvald ---------- 1971
                  1895 Michálek, František 1951
                  1896 Brož, František
                       Blatný, Josef
                    1901 Hlobil, Emil
                    1905 Babušek, František 1954
                    1906 Vačkár, Dalibor (Yugoslavian)
                    1908 Kabeláč, Miloslav
                    1908 Suchoň, Eugen
                      1910 Tittel, Ernst - 1969
                      1910 Reiner, Karel
                      1910 Slavický, Klement
                      1911 Očenáš, Andrej
                      1913 Sokola, Miloš
                      1914 Kardoš, Dezider
                      1915 Hanus, Jan
                        1920 Janáček, Bedrich
                        1921 Ramovš, Primož
                        1921 Ferenczy, Oto
                        1922 Ropek, Jiri
                        1922 Macha, Otmar
                        1923 Kalabis, Viktor
                        1924 Rezáč, Ivan
                        1925 Zimmer, Jan
                        1928 Istvan, Miloslav
                        1928 Sluka, Luboš
                        1929 Eben, Petr
                          1930 Dadák, Jaromír
                          1930 Odstrčil, Karel
                          1931 Neumann, Věroslav
                          1932 Zeljenka, Ilja
                          1932 Kopelent, Marek
                          1935 Teml, Jiři
                          1935 Pololáník, Zdeněk
                          1941 Loudová, Ivana

constructing his melodies.   Reiner also utilizes polytonal chords in parallel motion, frequent meter changes, and sudden dynamic alterations or fast crescendos and dimenuendos in the same prelude.   In the second prelude (Sostenuto) the first thematic idea carried out in several voices is that of a written-out mordent used melodically (another reference to Reiner's idiomatic use of melodies constructed of small intervals).   This prelude also contains some nine-note chords, each note on a different pitch.   Prelude III (Allegro Assai) utilizes very frequent meter changes and practically constant use of triplet eighth-notes is the unifying rhythmic element.

The works of Otmar Mácha (1922-   ), Klement Slavický (1910-   ), and Miloš Sokola (1913-   ) are more traditional in approach than those just considered, although their compositions are definitely contemporary in nature.   The Mourning Toccata (Mácha) and Passacaglia Quasi Toccata on the Theme B-A-C-H (Sokola) are metrical throughout.   The Passacaglia is evenly constructed upon a triplet figure;   the coda begins with a pedal cadenza and ends on rolled chords in which most of the pitches are different.   Rapid meter changes[16] and chord tones of all different pitches occur frequently in the Slavický Invocation.

The use of the most advanced twentieth-century composition style in these six pieces from the mid-'60's is that of Miloslav Kabeláč (1908-   ) in his Four Preludes.   These pieces call for three manuals and pedal, each at a different dynamic level.   The only registration suggestions are the pitch level desired by the composer (e. g. +4' -1').   The tempo is very carefully indicated, and the rhythmic unit is shown by dotted lines arranged at regular intervals (e. g. , 1. 8 cm. apart, 1. 35 cm. , 2. 03 cm.), which specify precisely where each note or chord is played.   If notes are held, a horizontal heavy line indicates duration by the length of the line, and tone-clusters are the rule rather than the exception in these pieces.

Notes

1.   Several Belgian organ composers moved to the United States: Gaston Dethier, Charles Courboin (organist of St. Patrick's Cathedral, New York City), August Maekelberghe (Organist of St. John's Episcopal Church, Detroit), and Camil van Hulse, who resides in Arizona.

2. Berg: Koralpartita over Lov Vare Dig, o Jesu Krist;
   Lindberg: Fyra Orgelkoraler; Wikander: Passacaglia
   över koralen "Jag Ville Lova och Prisa."
3. Runbäck: Sequentia Pentecostes "Veni sancte spiritus."
4. Daniel Olson (1898-   ), Otto Olsson (1879-1964), Hilding
   Rosenberg (1892-   ), Gunnar Thyrestam (1900-   ),
   Sven-Eric Johannsson (1919-   ).
5. Sandvold: Två gregorianska melodier.
6. Nielsen: Fantasia pastorale (1946).
7. Chorale preludes, at least two fantasies, and a Sonatine,
   Op. 26 (1939).
8. Sonata da Chiesa, per la Pasqua, for trumpet and organ.
9. Siciliana, Resignation.
10. Josef Klička (1855-1937), Josef Bohuslav Foerster (1859-
    1951), Eduard Tregler (1868-1932), Bedřich Antonín
    Wiedermann (1883-1951), and František Michálek (1895-
    1951).
11. Example: Jaroslav Kvapil: Fantasy in E Minor (1932).
12. Example: Vladimír Hawlík (1955).
13. Example: Alois Hába, Op. 75 (1951); Miloslav Kabeláč,
    Op. 32 (1957).
14. Example: František Broz (1949); Emil Hlobil (1948).
15. One example: ten 32nd-notes against seven 16th-notes.
16. $\frac{12}{16}$ $\frac{8}{16}$ $\frac{11}{16}$ $\frac{10}{16}$ $\frac{8}{16}$ $\frac{5}{16}$ $\frac{6}{4}$ $\frac{8}{16}$ $\frac{9}{4}$

Bibliography

Gibbs, Alan. "Carl Nielsen's 'Commotio'," Musical Times,
   vol. 104, no. 1441 (March 1963), p. 208.
Lade, John. "The Organ Music of Flor Peeters," Musical
   Times, vol. 109, no. 1505 (July 1968), p. 667.
Peeters, Flor. "The Belgian Organ School," Sixth Music
   Book. London: Hinrichsen Edition Ltd., 1950; p. 270-
   274.
Phelphs, Lawrence I. "A Short History of the Organ Revival,"
   reprinted from Church Music 67.1. St. Louis: Con-
   cordia Pub. House, 1967.
Spelman, Leslie P. "20th Century Netherlands Organ Music,"
   Music/The A.G.O. and R.C.C.O. Magazine, vol. 4,
   no. 9 (September 1970), p. 35.
Wickline, Homer. "Flor Peeters' Organ Works Are Intended
   to Serve Noble Art," Diapason (September 1947), p. 22.

19.   AMERICAN ORGAN MUSIC: 1700-1970

   Section I: Through 1900

      Organ music in America was slow to attain what we
would consider today a respectable standard.   For many
years the primitive conditions in the new country forbade
most artistic efforts.   Music of most kinds was forbidden in
some forms of worship.   Psalms were practically the only
kind of music allowed by the Puritans.   If organ music was
allowed in worship, its principal (and sometimes only) function was to accompany congregational singing, and sometimes
short organ introductions and interludes were permitted in
connection with hymn-singing.   Organs were costly to have
made in Europe and to ship across the ocean.   Even if there
were organs, few organists were trained to play them.   Episcopal churches were the principal kind of church which installed organs as an adjunct to worship.   Other churches to
use organ music were Roman Catholic, Lutheran, Reformed, and
Moravian churches.   Up until 1800 there were no more than
20 organs in New England churches.   The rest of the country
had about the same number in proportion to the population.[1]

      English practices, tradition, and taste predominated
in early America.   Voluntaries were improvised, and the
works of Stanley, Greene, Boyce, Felton, and Arne were
used.   Transcriptions for the organ of such things as Handel
choruses and Scotch airs were frequently played.   William
Selby (1738-1798) was an Englishman who became a merchant
in America with a lively interest in music.   Selby, as the
organist of King's Chapel, Boston, gave concerts which included some of his own compositions.   He wrote Voluntaries
or Fugues for Organ or Harpsichord and a Concerto for
Organ or Harpsichord.[2]

      During the first half of the nineteenth century, music
in the church improved gradually because there was a general
reaction against the florid "fuguing tunes" of William Billings
and the frivolous, secular types of music which had crept
into church use.   Lowell Mason (1792-1872) wrote hundreds

HISTORICAL BACKGROUND

1780	Cornwallis surrendered at Yorktown
1785	Jefferson designed the capitol of Virginia
1787	American Constitutional Convention
1789-1794	Washington, President of the United States
1791	Paine Rights of Man
1791	Bill of Rights
1793	Whitney invented the cotton gin
1803	Louisiana Purchase
1804-1806	Lewis and Clark expedition to the Pacific
1807	Robert Fulton built steamboat
1809-1849	Edgar Allan Poe
1812-1814	War of 1812
1819	Florida purchased from Spain
1823	Monroe Doctrine
1825	Opening of the Erie Canal
1826-1864	Stephen Collins Foster
1826	Cooper Last of the Mohicans
1834	McCormick patented reaper
1837	Morse invented telegraph
1846	Mexican-American War
1848	California gold rush
1850	Hawthorne Scarlet Letter
1850	Longfellow Evangeline
1852	Stowe Uncle Tom's Cabin
1853	Peery opened Japan to world trade
1854	Thoreau Walden
1855	Whitman Leaves of Grass
1857	Currier and Ives published prints
1861-1865	Civil War
1867	Alaska purchased from Russia
1871	Emerson Essays
1876	Bell invented telephone
1877/78	Edison invented microphone, phonograph, and introduced incandescent lamp
1884	Mark Twain Huckleberry Finn
1896	Edward MacDowell Indian Suite
1897	Sousa Stars and Stripes Forever
1898	Spanish-American War

of hymn-tunes such as <u>Bethany</u>, <u>Olivet</u>, and <u>Missionary Hymn</u>.
He also introduced music teaching into the public schools
and organized teachers' conventions, which later became music festivals.   Mason was an organist and directed church
choirs in Savannah, Georgia, and later in Boston.

During the period between 1825 and 1850 so many
organs were built in America that there were not enough
trained organists to play them.   The first organ recitals in
America contained many types of music such as transcribed
vocal arias and choruses, transcribed harpsichord music,
band marches, ballroom waltzes, and improvisations on
popular airs.   Dudley Buck (1839-1909) was probably the
first prominent American organist to play organ recitals with
any frequency.   His own works included <u>Concert Variations
on the Star Spangled Banner</u>, Op. 23, a transcription of the
<u>William Tell Overture</u>, Op. 37, and <u>The Last Rose of Sum-
mer, Varied</u>, Op. 59.

After the Civil War hymn introductions and interludes
were still used and transcriptions were still popular, but
preludes and postludes were regularly played at church services.   Works by Batiste, Lemmens, and Smart were added
to those by Dudley Buck, John H. Willcox (1827-1875), and
George W. Chadwick (1854-1931).   Recitalists often included
dramatic improvisations in their programs. [3]

Many German musicians came to the United States
during the nineteenth century and had a profound effect upon
music in this country.   One of the first to come and live in
America was Karl Theodore Pachelbel (a son of Johann
Pachelbel), who visited Boston in 1732 or 1733.   During the
latter half of the nineteenth century many leading American
musicians such as Dudley Buck, John Knowles Paine (1839-
1906), George Chadwick, Horatio Parker (1863-1919), and
James H. Rogers (1857-1940) pursued musical studies in
Europe with teachers such as Liszt, Moscheles, Rheinberger,
Guilmant, and Widor.   In 1860 Paine composed his <u>Variations
on Austria</u>, which contains the theme, four variations, and
a fugue.   Professor Horatio Parker of Yale University was
one of the leading nineteenth-century American composers of
organ music.   Many of Parker's works are character pieces
with titles such as <u>Wedding Song</u> and <u>Triumphal March</u>, but
he also wrote music similar to Mendelssohn's <u>Songs without
Words</u> and the works of his teacher Rheinberger in forms
such as fugue and canon.

AMERICAN ORGANISTS AND ORGAN COMPOSERS

1750	1800	1850	1900	1940

1737 Hopkinson, Francis 1791
1738 Selby, William 1798 (English-American)
  1745 Jackson, George K. 1823 (English-American)
(1746 Billings, William 1800)
  1747 Taylor, Rayner --- 1825
   1756 Reinagle, Alexander 1809 (English-American)
   1757 Read, Daniel ----- 1836
    1768 Carr, Benjamin 1831
     1770 Hewitt, James 1827 (English-American)
  ca. 1770 Atwell, Richard ?
    1776 Schetky, George 1792 (Scot-American)
    1779 Taylor, Samuel Priestly - 1875
     1781 Heinrich, Anthony Philipp 1861
      1792 Mason, Lowell -----1872
      1795 Zeuner, Charles 1857 (German-American)
       1807 Moore, John W. ---- 1887
        1811 Beckel, James Cox after 1887
        1815 Zundel, John ---- 1882 (German-American)
        1817 Emerick, Albert G. 1878?
        1818 Jackson, Samuel P. 1885 (German-American)
     before 1820 Johnson, Artemus Nixon after 1892
        fl. 1822 Getze, Jacob Alfred 1870?
        1825 Bristow, George Frederick 1898
        1825 Cutler, Henry Stephen - 1902
        1827 Southard, Lucien H. 1881
        1827 Willcox, John H. 1875
         1835 Seward, Theodore Frelinghuysen ?
         1835 Darling, John Augustus ?
         1836 Hopkins, Charles Jerome 1898
         (1837 Lang, Benjamin --- 1909)
         1837 Jarvis, Charles H., Jr. 1895
         1838 Thayer, Whitney Eugene 1889
         1839 Buck, Dudley ----- 1909
         1839 Paine, John Knowles 1906
          Hommann, Charles
          Loud, Thomas (English-American)
         (1840 Whiting, George Elbridge 1923)
         (1841 Warren, Samuel Prowse 1915)
         1842 Whitney, Samuel Brenton 1914
         (1846 Gilchrist, William 1916)
        fl. 1847 Reimer, Louis 1859
        (1848 Gleason, Frederick 1903)
         fl. 1850 Darley, Francis T. Sully 1900
          1851 Eddy, Hiram Clarence --- 1937
          1853 Dunham, Henry Morton 1929
          1853 Foote, Arthur ----------- 1937
          1854 Chadwick, George ------- 1931
          1856 Bird, Arthur -------- 1923
          1856 Brewer, John Hyatt ----- 1931
          1856 Burdett, George Albert ?
          1856 Stewart, Humphrey John - 1932
          1857 Rogers, James Hotchkiss ---- 1940
          1858 Shelley, Harry Rowe -------- 1947
           1861 Andrews, George Whitfield 1932
           1861 Woodman, Raymond H. --- 1943
           1861 Truette, Everette Ellsworth 1933
           1861 Whiting, Arthur Battell 1936
           1862 Baldwin, Samuel Atkinson - 1949
           1863 Parker, Horatio 1919

Note: Names in parentheses are of non-organ composers influential in organ performance and composition.

AMERICAN ORGAN COMPOSERS

1850   1900   1950

```
1863 Middleschulte, Wilhelm (German) ----- 1943
1865 Carl, William Crane ---------------- 1944
1867 Beach, Amy Marcy Cheney ---------- 1944
1867 Noble, Thomas Tertius (English-American) - 1953
1867 Douglas, Charles Winfred ----------- 1944
1869 Stebbins, George Waring ------- 1930
      1870 Coerne, Louis Adolphe 1922
      1871 Nevin, Arthur ---------------- 1943
      1872 Palmer, Courtlandt ?
      1872 Borowski, Felix (English-American) -- 1956
      1872 Spencer, S. Reid -------------- 1945
      1873 Dickinson, Clarence --------------------- 1969
      1873 Whitmer, T. Carl ?
      1874 Ives, Charles ---------------------- 1954
      1874 Demarest, Clifford ------------- 1946
      1875 Oetting, William H. ---------------------- 1969
      1876 Kinder, Ralph --------------------- 1952
      1877 Frysinger, J. Frank ---------------- 1954
      1878 Farjeon, Harry --------------- 1948
      1879 Matthews, Harvey Alexander -------------------- 1973
            1880 Bloch, Ernest ----------------- 1959
            1880 DeLamarter, Eric ------------- 1953
            1880 Montani, Nicola A. ------- 1948
            1880 Dieckmann, Charles William --------- 1963
            1880 Russell, George Alexander ----- 1953
            1881 Gaul, Harvey Bartlett ----- 1945
            1882 Howe, Mary ------------------------ 1964
            1882 Bingham, Seth Daniels -------------------- 1972
            1882 Becker, Rene Louis (French-American) 1956
            1883 Federlein, Gottfried Harrison --- 1952
                  Pelissier, Victor
            1884 Titcomb, Everett ------------------ 1968
            1884 Dunn, James Philip -- 1936
            1885 Shure, Ralph Deane --------------------------- 1980
            1885 Riegger, Wallingford ---------------- 1961
            1886 Becker, John J. -------------------- 1961
            1886 Lundquist, Matthew Nathanael -------- 1964
            1886 Biggs, Richard Keys ---------------- 1962
            1887 Diggle, Roland ----------------- 1954
            1887 Schmutz, Albert Daniel
            1887 Barnes, Edwin Shippen --------- 1958
            1888 Martin, Miles I'A. -------- 1949
            1888 Tuthill, Burnet
                  1890 Kramer, A. Walter ------------ 1969
                  1890 Thompson, Van Denman -------- 1969
                  1890 Clokey, Joseph Waddell -------- 1960
                  1890 James, Philip ---------------------- 1975
                  1891 Snow, Francis Warren --------- 1961
                  1891 Grandjany, Marcel ------------------ 1975
                  1891 Jacobi, Frederick -------- 1952
                  1891 Baumgartner, H. Leroy -------- 1969
                  1891 Donovan, Richard Frank ------------- 1970
                  1892 Whitford, Homer Pasco -------------------- 1980
                  1892 Candlyn, T. Frederick H. (Eng-Amer) 1964
                  1892 Nevin, Gordon Balch - 1943
                  1893 Moore, Douglas Stuart --------- 1969
                  1893 Coke-Jephcott, Norman (Eng-Amer) 1962
                  1894 Sinzheimer, Max (Ger-Amer) -------- 1977
```

AMERICAN ORGAN COMPOSERS (continued)

	1900	1950	1980

1894 Piston, Walter H. -- 1976
1894 Wagenaar, Bernard (Dutch-Amer) ------------------------- 1971
1894 Bennett, Robert Russell -------------------------------------- 1981
1895 Still, William Grant ------------------------------------- 1978
1895 Sowerby, Leo ------------------------------------- 1968
1895 McKinley, Carl --------------------------------- 1966
1895 Simonds, Bruce
1896 Sessions, Roger H.
1896 Weinberger, Jaromir (Czech-Amer) ---------------- 1967
1896 Hanson, Howard -- 1981
1896 Thomson, Virgil
1896 Pasquet, Jean
1897 Cowell, Henry Dixon ---------------------------- 1965
1897 van Hulse, Camil (Belgian-American)
1897 Porter, William Quincy ------------------------- 1966
1898 Harris, Roy
1898 Elwell, Herbert -- 1974
1898 Campbell-Watson, Frank ------------------------------------- 1980
1898 Owen, Blythe
1898 Grieb, Herbert C. -- 1973
1899 McKay, George Frederick ------------------------------ 1970
1899 Thompson, Randall
1899 Tcherepnin, Alexander (Russian-American) ---------------- 1977
1899 Buszin, Walter Edwin ------------------------------------ 1973
      1900 Edmundson, Garth ----------------------------- 1971
      1900 Copland, Aaron
      1900 Freed, Isador (Russian-American) -------- 1960
      1901 Schreiner, Alexander
      1902 Watters, Clarence E.
      1903 Fisk, Beatrice Hatton -------------------------- 1977
      1903 Fischer, Irwin
      1903 Giannini, Vittorio ------------------------ 1966
      1904 Parrish, Carl -------------------------- 1965
      1904 Oncley, Alma
      1904 Mader, Clarence Victor -------------------- 1971
      1904 Inch, Herbert
      1905 Friedell, Harold ------------------ 1958
      1905 Fromm, Herbert (German-American)
      1906 Finney, Ross Lee; Kettering, Eunice L.; Lockwood, Normand
      1908 Stevens, Halsey; Woodward, Henry Lynde; Verrall, John;
            Bitgood, Roberta; Casner, Myron
      1909 Bender, Jan (Dutch/German-American); Whitney, Maurice C.
      1909 Bedell, Robert Leech ---------------------------- 1974
            1910 Barber, Samuel --------------------------------- 1981
            1910 Berlinski, Herman (German-American)
            1910 Crandell, Robert ------------------------ 1976
            1910 Hilty, Everett Jay; Roff, Joseph; Noehren, Robert
            1911 Arbatsky, Yury (Russian-American); Canning, Thomas;
                 Hovhaness, Alan; Sifler, Paul J. (Yugoslavian-American)
            1912 Lafford, Lindsay (English-American); Fleischer, Heinrich
                 (German-American); Barlow, Wayne; Roberts, Myron J.
            1913 Read, Gardner; Dello Joio, Norman; Kennan, Kent
                 Wheeler; Sateren, Leland B.; Elmore, Robert H.
            1914 Kroeger, William; Faxon, Nancy Plummer; Haines,
                 Edmund Thomas; Bunjes, Paul; Kubik, Gail; Effinger,
                 Cecil; Held, Wilbur; Lenel, Ludwig (French-American)
            1915 Persichetti, Vincent
            1915 Huston, John ------------------------- 1975

Romantic clichés were used by Parker and his contemporaries, but their works were a great improvement upon the hundreds of transcriptions and cheap pseudo-organ music absorbed by church congregations and the audiences at theaters and municipal auditoriums about the turn of the twentieth century. For many years orchestral organs were popular, and the music performed on these instruments had saccharine tunes which could be easily remembered, foot-tapping rhythms, and often earth-shaking volume.

19.   Section II: Twentieth Century

Fortunately a number of factors have improved the general levels of musical taste of not only the American organist, but of the organ builder, and of those who hear organ music frequently.   The American Guild of Organists has labored valiantly since 1896 to raise standards of organ and church choral music.   Universities and colleges have secured fine teachers, who now train splendid performers and composers of both recital and church organ music.

A great exchange of organ music between America and Europe has taken place, and many organ recitalists, both American and European, have crossed the Atlantic to perform music of their own countries.   Many Americans have studied organ playing and organ literature in Germany, France, Belgium, the Netherlands, Austria, Italy, and England.   Many leading European musicians such as Schoenberg, Milhaud, Stravinsky, and Hindemith have come to America to live and teach.

The great improvements in communication media-- television, radio, and recordings--have increased appreciation of music in general and of organ music in particular. The ease with which organ music is published and distributed today has also been a large contributing factor to an awareness of better organ music.

Organ Building in the United States

During the early part of the eighteenth century colonists of German background, who lived in Pennsylvania and

HISTORICAL BACKGROUND

1903	Wright brothers' first successful flight
1905	Einstein Theory of Relativity
1906	San Francisco earthquake and fire
1909	Frank Lloyd Wright Robie House, Chicago
1914	Robert Frost North of Boston
1914-1918	World War I
1915	Charles Ives Concord Sonata
1918	Cather My Antonia
1919	League of Nations founded
1922	James Joyce Ulysses
1924	Gerschwin Rhapsody in Blue
1925	F. Scott Fitzgerald The Great Gatsby
1926	Hemingway The Sun Also Rises
1927	Lindbergh flew alone across the Atlantic
1928	First commercial talking films
1928	Benét John Brown's Body
1929	Thomas Wolfe Look Homeward, Angel
1930	Grant Wood American Gothic
1931	Eugene O'Neill Mourning Becomes Electra
1933-1945	Roosevelt President
1934	Virgil Thomson Four Saints in Three Acts
1935	Gerschwin Porgy and Bess
1939-1945	World War II
1939	Roy Harris Third Symphony
1939	John Steinbeck The Grapes of Wrath
1942	United Nations formed
1944	Aaron Copland Appalachian Spring
1945-1953	Truman President
1947	Williams Streetcar Named Desire
1949	Barber Knoxville: Summer of 1915
1949	Arthur Miller Death of a Salesman
1950	Menotti The Consul
1950-1953	Korean War
1950	Stravinsky The Rake's Progress
1951	NATO formed
1953-1961	Eisenhower President
1958	First American satellite in orbit
1961	Viet Nam involvement began
1961	Eliot Carter Double Concerto
1961-1963	Kennedy President
1961	Berlin War raised
1961	First space flights flown by man
1963-1969	Johnson President
1969	Apollo 11 landed Americans on the moon
1969-	Nixon President

neighboring sections of the country, imported small chamber
instruments from Germany.   David Tannenberg (1728-1804)
was the principal organ builder of the German tradition in
Pennsylvania.   English organs were ordered for Anglican
churches in Virginia, New York, and New England.   Organs
of the English type were built in the New York and Boston
areas.

Leading American organ builders of the early nineteenth century were George Jardine, Henry Erben, and the
Hook brothers.   After 1850 the Romantic movement made its
influence felt.   The two prominent builders of this period
were Hilborne Roosevelt and George Hutchings. [4]

John T. Austin and Ernest M. Skinner were two outstanding American builders of the early twentieth century.
Their organs, like those of Roosevelt and Hutchings, were
expressions of the Romantic movement in organ building which
was still in full swing.   The English engineer Robert Hope
Jones made strong inroads against the performance of legiti-
mate organ literature on real pipe organs with two of his
accomplishments, the theater organ (conceived totally in an
orchestral way for amusement and popular music) and the
unit organ, the effects of both achievements which have been
very difficult to overcome. [5]

Although Americans were aware of Albert Schweitzer's
search for a truer performance of Bach through his prefaces
to the Widor-Schweitzer edition of Bach's organ works, the
tonal and mechanical conceptions of the organ reform movements in Europe did not make much headway until organ
builders in America themselves became aware of the wide
difference between what they were building and what kind of
instrument had, in fact, been able to produce the best results
in the performance of classic organ literature.   The credit
for awakening the American organ world to the organ reform
can be given to concert organists such as Lynwood Farnam,
Melville Smith, E. Power Biggs, and Robert Noehren, and
to organ builders such as Walter Holtkamp and the Englishman G. Donald Harrison of the Aeolian-Skinner Company.
Both Holtkamp and Harrison independently studied the construction practices, voicing techniques, and tonal designs of
old European master organ builders and adopted practices
which were harmonious with their own aesthetic ideals.   They
were thus able to produce instruments much superior to those
of the earlier part of the twentieth century. [6]

Herman Schlicker, the German-born builder who established his firm in Buffalo, New York, has made many
fine contributions to the art of organ building in America.
He has encouraged the use of mechanical action and has ably
designed instruments for the true literature of the organ.

Since the late 1940's many mature and student organists have been able to observe the finest European organs
first-hand and have demanded that American builders produce
instruments of similar quality. A number of foreign firms,
which have subscribed to the ideals of the organ reform
movement such as von Beckerath, Walcker, Flentrop, Rieger, and Casavant, have built some splendid instruments in
America. Some smaller builders in New England such as
Charles Fisk and Fritz Noack have also supported the principles of the organ reform. Larger firms such as Schantz,
Austin, and Möller have adopted to various degrees some of
the guidelines of the European organ reform. Surely the
wide interest in a return to the high ideals of the organ reform movement augers well for the musical art of the organ
and its literature in America. [7]

There are at least six different types of organ music
which have been written in America during the twentieth century thus far. These types may be identified as program
music for recital use, an eclectic style which combines two
or more rather traditional stylistic elements, French, English, and German (neo-Baroque) oriented works, and, finally,
twentieth-century techniques, which include newer styles of
composition such as serial, chance (aleatory), atonal, jazz,
and combinations of organ with tapes. Some composers have
adopted several different styles for different purposes; other
composers have chosen one style or technique and have consistently remained within one style or perhaps have developed
their own personal adaptation of the style.

Program music

Under the Romantic influence, many organ transcriptions and character pieces were written by American organ
composers toward the end of the nineteenth and well into the
twentieth century. Their colorful titles suggested a program
for the imagination of the listener. These pieces were intended for concert use or for the amusement of the organist,
not for church services. Two of the chief exponents of
character pieces were Harvey B. Gaul (1881-1945) (Easter

AMERICAN ORGAN COMPOSERS (continued)

	1920	1950	1970

```
1916 Kohs, Ellis B.
1916 Ellis, Merrill
1916 Jordan, Alice
1916 Walter, Samuel
1917 Ward, Robert Eugene
1917 Kay, Ulysses S.
1917 Purvis, Richard
1917 Keller, Homer
1918 Ossewaarde, Jack Herman
1918 Bouman, Paul
1918 Wright, M. Searle
1918 Cook, John (English-American)
1918 Dallin, Leon
1919 Manz, Paul O.
1919 Williams, David H. (Welsh-American)
1919 Young, Gordon
1919 Nelhybel, Vaclav (Czech-American)
1919 Lovelace, Austin Cole
1919 Kenins, Talivaldis (Latvian-American)
1919 Crane, Robert
             1920 LaMontaine, John
             1920 Wienhorst, Richard
             1920 Cooper, William Benjamin
             1921 Goode, Jack C.
             1921 Wyton, Alec (English-American)
             1921 White, Louie --------------------------------- 1979
             1921 Dirksen, Richard W.
             1921 Pfautsch, Lloyd
             1921 Strandberg, Newton
             1922 Brand, Gerhard (German-American)
             1922 Johnson, David N.
             1922 Foss, Lucas
             1923 Bohnhorst, Frank ---------------- 1956
 20th century: King, Larry Peyton
             Kolb, Barbara
             Huston, Scott
             Proulx, Richard
             Richner, Thomas
             Welsh, Wilmer Haydon
             1923 Bristol, Lee Hastings, Jr. -------------------- 1979
             1923 Pinkham, Daniel
             1923 Bassett, Leslie
             1923 Rorem, Ned
             1923 Diemente, Edward
             1923 Karlén, Robert A.
             1924 Brandon, George
             1924 Krapf, Gerhard (German-American)
             1924 Beale, James
             1924 Birkby, Arthur Alfred
             1924 Hudson, Richard Albert
             1924 Parris, Robert
             1924 Sandloff, Peter
             1925 Gehring, Philip
             1925 Ochse, Orpha Caroline
             1925 Schuller, Gunter
             1925 Engel, James
             1926 Rohlig, Harald (German-American)
             1926 Arnold, Corliss R.
```

AMERICAN ORGAN COMPOSERS (continued)

1930   1960

1926 Moe, Daniel
1926 Coleman, Charles DeWitt
1926 Cooper, Paul
1926 Cundick, Robert Milton
1926 Johns, Donald Charles
1926 Goemanne, Noel (Belgian-American)
1926 Pelz, Walter L.
1926 Richter, Marga
1926 Schmidt, William
1927 Zes, Tikey A.
1927 Walker, Alan D.
1927 Cacioppo, George
1927 Diemer, Emma Lou
1927 Erb, Donald
1927 Kremer, Rudolph Joseph
1927 Goossen, Jacob Frederic
1927 Smart, David William
1927 Peek, Richard
1928 Adler, Samuel (German-American)
1928 Berry, Wallace
1928 Owens, Sam Batt
1928 Sydeman, William T.
1929 Hancock, Eugene W. W.
1929 Schalk, Carl
1929 Beck, Theodore
1929 Wyner, Yehudi (Canadian)
1929 Simmons, Morgan F.
1929 Thomas, Paul Lindsley
1929 Groom, Lester H.
1929 DaCosta, Noel George
              1930 Arnatt, Ronald (English-American)
              1930 Felciano, Richard
              1930 Bielawa, Herbert W.
              1930 Boeringer, James L.
              1930 Gottlieb, Jack
              1930 Hamill, Paul Robert
              1930 Copley, R. Evan
              1930 Scoggin, Robert E.
              1931 Gehrenbeck, David M.
              1931 Gieschen, Thomas
              1931 Stearns, Peter Pindar
              1931 Uehlein, Christopher M.
              1932 Stout, Alan
              1932 Jones, Robert W.
              1932 Kemner, Gerald
              1932 Coe, Kenton
              1932 Powell, Robert J.
              1932 Tallis, James H. -------------------- 1969
              1932 Wetzler, Robert Paul
              1932 Withrow, Scott S.
              1932 Zaninelli, Luigi
              1933 Long, Page C.
              1933 Watson, Walter Robert
              1934 Busarow, Donald A.
              1934 Hancock, Gerre
              1934 Anderson, Robert T.
              1934 Baker, Philip E.
              1934 Hebble, Robert C.

AMERICAN ORGAN COMPOSERS (continued)

1940   1980

```
1934 Earls, Paul
1934 Smith, Lani
1934 Staplin, Carl Bayard
1934 Tulan, Frederick Thomas
1934 Wehr, David A.
1934 Wood, Dale
1935 Susa, Conrad
1936 Ore, Charles William
1936 Schwartz, Elliott S.
1936 Wolford, Darwin
1937 Ferris, William
1937 Weaver, John B.
1937 White, Gary C.
1938 Haan, Raymond H.
1938 Hampton, G. Calvin
1938 Hutcheson, Jere
1938 Bolcom, William E.
1938 Wuorinen, Charles
1939 Norris, Kevin Edward
1939 Lowenberg, Kenneth D.
1939 Moore, Carman
            1940 Pillin, Boris William
            1940 Swift, Robert F.
            1940 Toensing, Richard
            1941 Perrera, Ronald C.
            1941 Martin, Gilbert M.
            1941 Hill, Jackson
            1941 Curtis-Smith, Curtis O.
            1941 Newman, Anthony
            1942 Near, Gerald
            1942 Young, Michael E.
            1942 Stewart, Richard N.
            1942 Cuckson, Robert (Australian)
            1942 Moevs, Robert Walter
            1942 Klausmeyer, Peter Ballard
            1942 Ashdown, Franklin
            1943 Burcham, Wayne
            1943 Burton, Stephen Douglas
            1943 Morris, Robert Daniel (English-American)
            1943 Schwantner, Joseph
            1944 Albright, William
            1944 Shackleford, Rudy
            1944 Snyder, Randall
            1945 Hegarty, David H.
            1945 Peck, Russell
            1946 Isele, David Clark
            1946 Stover, Harold
            1947 Janson, Thomas
            1947 Lovinfosse, Dennis M.
            1947 Schack, David A.
            1948 Smith, Stuart
            1949 Schneider, William John
                    1951 Schober, Brian
                    1952 Drumwright, George W., Jr.
```

Morning on Mt. Rubidoux, Daguerreotype of an Old Mother)
and Joseph Waddell Clokey (1890-1960) (Dripping Spring,
Twilight Moth, The Kettle Boils, Grandfather's Wooden Leg).
As only one example of the taste of audiences and of the
performers of the earliest third of the twentieth century it
has been observed that many organists could not resist the
temptation to include Powell Weaver's The Squirrel on their
recitals.   One illustration of lush Romantic harmonies and
an orchestral conception of organ composition is that of
Richard Purvis (1917-   ), whose Seven Chorale Preludes on
Tunes found in American Hymnals have been popular with
organists who prefer organ music in this vein.

     Several leading musicians have written organ music
of a higher artistic level than that of the early nineteenth
century which has programmatic titles and which is intended
for recital use.   Dr. Seth Bingham (1882-1972) included two
such pieces (Black Cherries, Forgotten Graves) in his Pastoral Psalms.   His Roulade and Rhythmic Trumpet from the
Baroques suite have provided lighthearted and cheerful music
for many organ programs.   The Carnival suite by Robert
Crandell (1910-   ) contains four movements, each of which
depicts one of four characters in Italian comedy: Pulcinella,
Harlequin, Columbina, and the clowns Giangurgolo and Co-
viello.

     Garth Edmundson (1900-1971) also composed music of
this type (March of the Magi, from Christmas Suite No. 1).
Eric DeLamarter (1880-1953) and Leo Sowerby (1895-1968),
two famous Chicago composers, gave colorful titles to some
of their compositions: Festival Prelude in Honor of St.
Louis, King of France (DeLamarter) and Madrigal, Jubilee,
and Comes Autumn Time (Sowerby).   The Bible Poems and
Religious Preludes of Czech-American Jaromir Weinberger
(1896-1967) are suites of short, programmatic pieces inspired by Biblical texts.   These pieces are through-composed;
their rich harmonies and rhapsodic writing call for colorful
registrations.

Eclectic Style

     Many American organ composers have formed individ-
ual styles which are eclectic in nature and which continue
rather traditional composition practices and conventional uses
of the organ's resources.   Dr. Clarence Dickinson (1873-
1969), a founder of the School of Sacred Music at Union

Theological Seminary, New York City, based his works on
German Romanticism of the Mendelssohnian type (The Joy of
the Redeemed, a setting of the hymn-tune O Quanta Qualia).
Carl McKinley (1895-1966), H. Leroy Baumgartner (1891-
1969), and G. Winston Cassler (1906-) have set hymn or
chorale melodies in somewhat customary ways.   George
Frederick McKay (1899-1970) (Benedictions) and Myron Ro-
berts (1912-) (Homage to Perotin, Prelude and Trumpetings)
have each put his own stamp of individuality on their compositions which were constructed of traditional elements.

French Style

     French composition practices have made a strong im-
pression upon many American organ composers.   Bruce
Simonds (1895-), former dean of the School of Music at
Yale University, chose to write his two plainsong settings in
an impressionistic style.   Seth Bingham and Garth Edmundson
were only two Americans who adopted the French toccata type
somewhat resembling those of Vierne and Widor for some of
their pieces (Bingham: Toccata on Leonie;   Edmundson:
Gargoyles, Vom Himmel hoch).   It is interesting to observe
the style changes which occur in the organ works of Philip
James (1890-) between his Méditation à Sainte Clotilde
(published in 1924) in Franckian style;   Fête (published in
1924), a joyous, full-bodied work;   and the Galarnad (published in 1949), which approaches 12-tone writing in sections.

English Style

     A substantial number of American organist-composers
associated with the Episcopal Church exhibited a marked preference for an English type of composition of the last half of
the nineteenth century.   This style might be characterized in
a very general way by conventional harmonies in unsurprising
progressions, uncomplicated rhythms, and standard organ
registration practices.   Sometimes this style of writing follows a loosely structured, improvisatory fashion.   These composers have often set hymn-tunes and plainsong melodies and
free-accompaniments for congregational singing.   Dr. T.
Tertius Noble (1867-1953), an English cathedral organist who
served at St. Thomas Church, New York City, wrote many
hymn-tune settings.   T. Frederick H. Candlyn (1892-1964),
Dr. Noble's successor at St. Thomas Church, composed
arrangements of plainsong melodies (Divinum Mysterium,

Sursum Corda) and dignified pieces of the English trumpet
tune genre.   Other distinguished organ composers in the English school include Everett Titcomb (1884-1968), Harold Frie-
dell (1905-1958), Winfred Douglas (1867-1944), and M. Searle
Wright (1918-   ).   David N. Johnson (1922-   ) has composed
several Trumpet Tunes patterned after the English trumpet
tunes which alternate a melody played on the solo trumpet
stop with a harmonized version of the same melody.

German Style

A Germanic, neo-Baroque style has been expressed by
composers within the Lutheran church tradition.   The chorale
and hymn settings of these composers employ the well-
established polyphonic forms and contrapuntal devices of the
German schools of the seventeenth and eighteenth centuries
and combine them with contemporary conceptions of harmony
and melody.   Some of the most practical and interesting
church melody arrangements are the Chorale Improvisations
by Paul Manz (1919-   ).   The Four Organ Chorales by Ludwig Lenel (1914-   ) are much more complex.   Jan Bender
(1909-   ) is an important contributor to this contrapuntal
school of organ works.   The Voluntaries on the Hymn of the
Week by Wayne Barlow (1912-   ) were composed in similar
character for use in the Lutheran Church.

Two Baroque forms which have been employed as
means of expression by twentieth-century American organ
composers are the passacaglia and the fugue.   Composers
who have used the passacaglia type are Douglas Moore (1893-
1969), Ellis B. Kohs (1916-   ), Leo Sowerby, Virgil Thomson (1896-   ), Gardner Read (1913-   ), and Searle Wright.
Only a few of those who have used the fugue form are Robert
Noehren (1910-   ), Cecil Effinger (1914-   ), and Homer Keller (1917-   ).

Twentieth-Century Techniques

Seth Bingham introduced such musical devices as a
prominent use of fourths, delayed parallel intervals, unpre-
pared and unresolved discords, cross-relations and false-
relations, bi-tonalisms, augmented and diminished intervallic
leaps, and consecutive and hidden fifths into his Thirty-six
Hymn and Carol Canons in Free Style, Op. 52.   Bingham's
use of these devices, unexpected harmonies, and surprising

rhythmic arrangements in his hymn-tune settings anticipated
similar methods of writing by other organ composers.

Some composers have chosen sturdy, folk hymn-tunes,
and white spirituals from the South from shaped-note collections such as The Sacred Harp as their cantus firmus material.   Gardner Read (1913-   ) has a collection of Eight Preludes on Old Southern Hymns, Op. 90, sometimes sprightly,
sometimes melancholy pieces, which often employ contrapuntal
elements.   In 1946 Richard F. Donovan (1891-   ) wrote two
contemporary settings of the tunes Land of Rest and Christian
Union.   Samuel Barber (1910-   ) selected Wondrous Love for
a set of variations, Op. 34, in addition to his own organ
transcription of his Silent Night arrangement from Die Natali,
Op. 37.

Charles Ives (1874-1954), the eccentric but highly
original composer who anticipated many contemporary composition techniques, wrote his amusing and bizarre Variations
on America in 1891.   It is composed of an introduction,
chorale, and five variations, to which he made polytonal
additions in 1894.

Virgil Thomson (1896-   ) employed lean contrapuntal
lines for his arrangement of Divinum Mysterium in his
Pastorale on a Christmas Plainsong.   Thomson's Pange lingua
is much more elaborate and contains triple-pedaling, intricate
alternation between manuals, polytonalities, many parallel
seconds, and complex rhythmic figures.

The name of Leo Sowerby would probably be the first
mentioned as the most prominent American organ composer
of the mid-twentieth century.   Sowerby was associated with
St. James Cathedral, Chicago, for a major portion of his
life.   He was deeply interested in the music of the church,
often in demand for Episcopal church music conferences, and
was one of the music editors of the Hymnal 1940.   His 29
cantus firmus (principally hymn-tune) settings are generally
post-Romantic in style.   String and orchestral reed stops are
often indicated in the registration suggestions of the composer.
Sowerby usually placed the tune in a different range and in
varying qualities of sound for each stanza of the arrangement.
The harmonizations are warm and unashamedly chromatic in
nature.   Probably the best-known collection of Sowerby's
hymn-tune settings is the Meditations on Communion Hymns.
One of his best hymn-preludes is the Prelude on Malabar,
which he based on David McK. Williams' hymn-tune and

wrote for inclusion in the Modern Anthology, which was edited
by Williams.   In the Malabar prelude, Sowerby employed the
same technique which had proved effective in so many chorale
preludes of the Baroque period, that of using the melodic
elements of the basic material (in this case, the hymn-tune
phrases) in imitation, in sequences, and in anticipation of the
solo treatment of the melody phrase.   Toward the end of this
same prelude Sowerby builds to a splendid climax by the
gradual addition of stops and by playing the hymn-tune melody
in octave chords.   H. W. Gray, the music publishing firm
with which Sowerby had a close relationship, published one-
third of Sowerby's hymn preludes in a series in 1956.   The
settings of Deus tuorum militum and Sine nomine are vigor-
ously martial and aggressive.

        Roughly three-fourths of Sowerby's organ compositions
were designed for concert and recital use.   A number of
free works of moderate length, which were popular in the
late 1930's and 1940's, exhibit Sowerby's use of such traditional forms, devices, and techniques as variations on an
original theme (Arioso, Requiescat in pace), ostinato (Carillon), and use of a rhythmic motive as a unifying factor
(Fanfare).   Much chromaticism is also a recurring characteristic in some of his earlier pieces.   Comes Autumn Time
is a colorful and strongly rhythmic orchestral overture which
Sowerby arranged for organ; the piece, which is conceived
in sonata-allegro form, was inspired by some lines of the
poet Bliss Carman.   The Toccata (1940) is one of Sowerby's
best pieces of moderate length.   Deft use of manual changes
for echo effects, addition or periodic elimination of the pedal
part to strengthen the listeners' understanding of the construction (sonata-allegro form), and a technically challenging part
for the manuals are features of this work.

        Sowerby's largest single work for organ solo is the
Symphony in G Major (1930), which was dedicated to the
Canadian organ virtuoso Lynwood Farnam.   The first of
three movements (Very broadly) is highly unified by the frequent appearance of the principal theme in many guises;
even the second theme is closely related to the principal
theme.   The second movement (Fast and sinister) has often
been used alone as a recital number.   The thematic material
is in two segments, one chordal segment in the rhythm ♩♩♩
and the other an eighth-note figure which leaps upward in
the intervals of fourths and fifths to and within the range of
an octave.   The pedal part is active and often sounds thematic material under manual figurations.   The final movement

is in the form of a passacaglia (Slowly), which is built upon an eight-measure melody. The 33 variations contain a wide variety of rhythmic, harmonic, and contrapuntal effects, which attest to Sowerby's great command of musical materials. Another large variation work is Pageant (1931), a pedal concerto-extravaganza designed to exhibit the pedaling prowess of Sowerby's friend Fernando Germani, the Italian organ virtuoso. The theme-tune has the lilt and mood of folk music, a characteristic of many of Dr. Sowerby's compositions.

The Suite (1933-1934) contains examples of Sowerby's two principal composition styles. The well-known Fantasy for Flute Stops in tripartite form employs a dry, contemporary, contrapuntal style, which features dissonance for its color and both melodies and harmonies built upon seconds, fourths, and fifths. In contrast the Air with Variations from the same Suite features extreme chromaticism, frequent syncopation, and shifting and quartal harmonies in subjective expression. The registrations call for the use of Romantic and orchestral colors such as soft strings, clarinet, English horn, flute with tremolo, and gradual crescendos and diminuendos by addition or retiring of stops or the use of the Crescendo pedal.

The Sinfonia Brevis (1965) was one of Sowerby's last major compositions for organ solo. The Sinfonia contains three movements which are cyclic since themes for the first and third movements were drawn from the second movement, which Sowerby had completed first and had originally planned as a single piece.

Dr. Sowerby contributed generously to literature for the organ with other instruments in groups or alone. Probably the three most popular of his works in this type were the Poem (viola and organ) (1942), Ballade (English horn and organ) (1949), and Festival Musick (two trumpets, two trombones, kettledrums, and organ) (1953). Two of Sowerby's best composition pupils are Jack C. Goode (1921-) and Gerald Near (1942-).

Specifications of the organ at St. James Cathedral are given below as the resources of the instrument were when Sowerby was the organist and choirmaster from 1927-1962.

Chicago, St. James Cathedral.
Built by Austin Organ Co. , 1920.

Great

Double Open Diapason 16'
Principal Diapason 8'
Second Open Diapason 8'
Doppel Flute 8'
Gemshorn 8'
Gemshorn Celeste 8'
Octave 4'
Harmonic Flute 4'
Trumpet 8'
Chimes

Choir

Open Diapason 8'
Concert Flute 8'
Unda Maris 8'
Dulciana 8'
Flute d'Amour 4'
Flautina 2'
Clarinet 8'
Tremulant

Pedal

Resultant 32'
Open Diapason 16'
Violone 16'
Bourdon 16'
Second Bourdon 16'
Gross Flute 8'
Tuba Profunda 16'
Harmonic Tuba 8'
Contra Fagotto 16'

Swell

Bourdon 16'
Open Diapason 8'
Stopped Diapason 8'
Viole d'Orchestre 8'
Echo Salicional 8'
Vox Celeste 8'
Flauto Traverso 4'
Piccolo 2'
Dolce Cornet III
Contra Fagotto 16'
Cornopean 8'
Oboe 8'
Vox Humana 8'
Tremulant

Solo

Flauto Major 8'
Stentorphone 8'
Gross Gamba 8'
Gamba Celeste 8'
Flute Ouverte 4'
Tuba Profunda 16'
Harmonic Tuba 8'
Harmonic Tuba 4'
Cor Anglais 8'
Chimes

One of the best examples of the use of the serial technique in American organ compositions is the Chromatic Study on the Name of Bach by Walter Piston (1894-   ). The tone-row is reversed while the second voice presents the row in its original order. This process is repeated when the third and fourth parts enter. Piston has also contributed the Prelude and Allegro to instrumental ensemble literature for organ and strings.

The Chorale No. 1 is a striking piece written by
Roger Sessions (1896-   ), which employs rhapsodic writing
in sophisticated rhythms.   The Sonata, Op. 86 (1961), by
Vincent Persichetti (1915-   ) is an atonal work which is
technically challenging.   Persichetti has also composed a
three-movement Sonatine, Op. 11, for pedals alone.   A number of other famous American composers who are usually
associated with musical media other than the organ who have
written a few pieces for the organ include Henry Cowell
(1897-1965), Aaron Copland (1900-   ), Quincy Porter (1897-
1966), and Norman Dello Joio (1913-   ).

The jazz element has not been used very much in
organ literature, but Robert Russell Bennett (1894-   ) did
employ some jazz rhythms in his Sonata, as did Robert El-
more (1913-   ) in his Rhythmic Suite (Rhumba).

The newer technique of chance (aleatory) music was
used by Lucas Foss (1922-   ) in his Etudes for Organ, in
which tone-clusters are juxtaposed with a hymn-tune, a
combination which might seem strange to traditionalists.   The
use of tapes with organ has made Richard Felciano (1930-   )
one of the pioneers in another twentieth-century attempt to
find new means of musical expression.

A few of the outstanding American works on a larger
scale for organ with other instruments are Howard Hanson's
Concerto for Organ, Strings and Harp, Op. 22, No. 3, Nor-
mand Lockwood's Concerto for Organ and Brass Quartet,
Seth Bingham's Connecticut Suite, Samuel Barber's Toccata
Festiva for organ, strings, trumpet, and timpani, and Daniel
Pinkham's two Concertantes.

Notes

1.   John Tasker Howard, Our American Music, New York:
     Thomas Y. Crowell Co. , 1946;   p. 20.
2.   Ibid. , p. 137-140.
3.   The "Thunder Storm" (often with lighting effects) and
     the "Midnight Fire Alarm" (produced in one New York
     church with real firemen) are described by Barbara
     Owen in "American Organ Music and Playing, from
     1700," Organ Institute Quarterly, vol. 10, no. 3
     (Autumn 1963), p. 12.
4.   Barbara Jane Owen, "Organ: History," Harvard Diction-
     ary of Music, 2nd ed. , Cambridge, Mass. : Harvard

University Press, 1969; p. 618-619.
5. Ibid. , p. 619
6. Lawrence I. Phelps, "A Short History of the Organ Revival," reprinted from Church Music, St. Louis: Concordia Pub. House, 1967; p. 10-15.
7. Ibid. , p. 17-20.

Bibliography

Amacker, Marianne. "The Chorale Preludes of Leo Sowerby,"
   The Diapason (August 1970), p. 20-21.
Armstrong, William H. Organs for America: The Life and
   Work of David Tannenberg. Philadelphia: University of
   Pennsylvania Press, 1967.
Barnes, William Harrison. The Contemporary American
   Organ: Its Evolution, Design and Construction, 8th ed.
   Glen Rock, N. J. : J. Fischer, 1964.
Cowell, Henry, and Sidney Cowell. Charles Ives and His
   Music. New York: Oxford University Press, 1955.
Gallo, William K. "Dudley Buck--the Organist," Diapason
   (November 1971), p. 22-24.
Howard, John Tasker. Our American Music. New York:
   Thomas Y. Crowell Co. , 1946.
Osborne, William. "Five New England Gentlemen," Music/
   The A. G. O. and R. C. C. O. Magazine, vol. III, no. 8
   (August 1969), p. 27-29.
Owen, Barbara Jane. "American Organ Music and Playing,
   from 1700," Organ Institute Quarterly, vol. 10, no. 3
   (Autumn 1963).
_____. "Organ: History," Harvard Dictionary of Music,
   2nd ed. Cambridge, Mass. : Harvard University Press,
   1969.
Phelps, Lawrence I. "A Short History of the Organ Revival,"
   reprinted from Church Music 67. 1. St. Louis: Concor-
   dia Pub. House, 1967.

APPENDIX: ORGAN WORKS OF BACH

Containing a table of the pagination in standard editions
(with cross-references to BWV numbers and chronologies of
Wolfgang Schmieder and Hermann Keller)

Works Cited

Bach-Gesellschaft. Johann Sebastian Bachs Werke, 47 vols.
    Leipzig: Breitkopf und Härtel, 1851-1926. Reprint, Ann
    Arbor, Mich.: J. W. Edwards, 1947.

Bower, John Dykes, and Walter Emery, Sir Frederick
    Bridge, James Higgs, Sir Ivor Atkins, et al., eds.
    The Organ Works of J. S. Bach, 19 vols. London:
    Novello and Co., n. d.

Dupré, Marcel, ed. Oeuvres Complètes pour Orgue de
    J. S. Bach, 12 vols. Paris: S. Bornemann, Editeur,
    1938-1941.

Griepenkerl, Friedrich Conrad, and Ferdinand Roitzsch, eds.
    Johann Sebastian Bachs Kompositionen für die Orgel, 9 vols.
    Frankfurt: C. F. Peters Corp., n. d. Johann Sebastian Bach
    Orgelwerke, 9 vols., Copenhagen: Wilhelm Hansen Forlag,
    n. d., is the same edition. This same edition is also pub-
    lished as Johann Sebastian Bach Complete Organ Works, 9
    vols. New York: Edwin F. Kalmus, 1947. A later edition
    of one volume is Vol. IX, Neue Ausgabe, Hermann Keller,
    ed., New York: C. F. Peters Corp., 1950. The Orgel-
    büchlein in Bach's original, autograph order is published by
    C. F. Peters Corp. as a separate volume.

J. S. Bach: The Complete Organ Works, from the "Bach-
    Gesellschaft" edition. New York: Lea Pocket Scores,
    n. d.

Johann-Sebastian-Bach-Institut Göttingen and vom Bach-Archiv
    Leipzig. Neue Ausgabe Sämtlicher Werke, to be pub-
    lished in 75 vols. Kassel, Germany: Bärenreiter Ver-
    lag, 1954 [in progress]. Organ music is found in the
    three following volumes: Die Orgelchoräle aus der
    Leipziger Originalhandschrift, Hans Klotz, ed., BA 5009,
    1958; Die Einzeln überlieferten Orgelchoräle, Hans
    Klotz, ed., BA 5017, 1961; Präludien, Toccaten, Fan-
    tasien und Fugen II, Frühfassungen und Variaten zu I
    und II, Deitrich Kilan, ed., BA 5025, 1964.

Lohmann, Heinz, ed. : Sämtliche Orgelwerke, 10 vols. ,
  Wiesbaden: Breitkopf & Härtel.
Riemenschneider, Albert, ed.   Eighteen Large Chorales for
  the Organ by Johann Sebastian Bach, Bryn Mawr, Pa. :
  Oliver Ditson Co. (Theodore Presser Co. , Distributors),
  1952.
Riemenschneider, Albert, ed.   The Liturgical Year (Orgel-
  büchlein) by Johann Sebastian Bach, Philadelphia: Oliver
  Ditson Co. (Theodore Presser Co. , Distributors), 1933.
Riemenschneider, Albert, ed.   Six Organ Chorals (Schübler)
  by Johann Sebastian Bach, Philadelphia: Oliver Ditson
  Co. (Theodore Presser Co. , Distributors), 1942.
Widor, Charles-Marie, and Albert Schweitzer, eds.   Johann
  Sebastian Bach: Complete Organ Works, vols. 1-5, New
  York: G. Schirmer, Inc. , 1912;   reprint, 1940-1941.
  The remaining volumes are published as: Johann Sebas-
  tian Bach; Complete Organ Works, Vols. 6-8, Edouard
  Nies-Berger and Albert Schweitzer, eds.   New York:
  G. Schirmer, Inc. , 1954-1967.

SCHMIEDER INDEX* TABLE OF BACH ORGAN WORKS

Order of Groups Within the Index

Index Numbers	Composition Groups or Titles
525-530	Six trio sonatas
531-552	Larger preludes and fugues
553-560	Eight "Little" Preludes and Fugues
561-566	Fantasias, toccatas, and fugues
567-582	Single preludes, fantasias, fugues, Passacaglia
583-591	Trios, Aria, Canzona, Allabreve, Pastorale, Harmonic Labyrinth
592-598	Six concerti, Pedal Exercitum
599-644	Orgelbüchlein
645-650	Six Chorales (Schübler)
651-668	Great Eighteen Chorales
669-689	Clavierübung, Part III
690-713a	Kirnberger's collection of chorales
714-740	Miscellaneous chorale settings
741-765	Youthful chorales and chorales of questionable authenticity
766-771	Chorale Partitas

[Note to table following: editions are indicated at heads of columns by symbols of publishers' names--see Key following. Blank spaces in table indicate that the edition is in process. A colon separates volume number from page number--25:17 signifies vol. 25, page 17.]

Key to Publishers' Symbols

Bach G	Bach Gesellschaft
Lea	Lea
P/K/H	Peters/Kalmus/Hansen
P. Or	Peters Orgelbüchlein
Schir	G. Schirmer
Born	Bornemann
Novel	Novello
Br. H.	Breitkopf und Härtel
Bären	Bärenreiter (NBA)
Dit	Ditson
Schm. C	Schmieder chronology
Kel. C	Keller chronology

Abbreviations Used

arr.	arranged	incompl.	incomplete
attrib.	attributed to	mvt	movement
ca.	circa	no.	number
chor.	chorale or chorales	Orgelbüchl.	Orgelbüchlein
Clavierüb.	Clavierübung	pt	part
coll.	collection	transcrip.	transcription
comp.	composed by	unfin.	unfinished
d. a.	doubtful authenticity	variat.	variations
dbl	double	w/	with

*Wolfgang Schmieder, Thematisch-Systematisches Verzeichnis der Musikalischen Werke von Johann Sebastian Bach, Leipzig: Breitkopf & Härtel, 1950. The title of this catalog is often abbreviated BWV (Bach-Werke-Verzeichnis) or S. (Schmieder).

BWV no.	Chorale Collection & No. w/in Coll.	Title	Bach G	Lea
649	6 'Schübler' Chor. 5	Ach bleib bei uns	25:71	6:13
692	Kirnberger coll. 3	Ach Gott und Herr (J. G. Walther)	40:4	3:4
693	Kirnberger coll. 4	Ach Gott und Herr (J. G. Walther)	40:5	3:5
714		Ach Gott und Herr (canon)	40:43	3:43
741		Ach Gott vom Himmel sieh darein (attrib. J. C. Bach)	40:167	
742		Ach Herr, mich armen Sünder (d. a.)	40:	
743		Ach, was ist doch (d. a.)		
770	partita	Ach, was soll ich	40:189	
644	Orgelbüchl. 46	Ach wie nichtig	25:60	2:60
589		Allabreve (D Major)	38:131	7:57
643	Orgelbüchl. 45	Alle Menschen	25:59	2:59
711	Kirnberger coll. 22	Allein Gott (bicinium) (attrib. Bernhard Bach)	40:34	3:34
717		Allein Gott (12/8)	40:47	3:47
675	Clavierüb. Pt III 7	Allein Gott (F Major)	3:197	1:31
676	Clavierüb. Pt III 8	Allein Gott (6/8)	3:199	1:33
664	18 Chor. 14	Allein Gott (A Major)	25:130	6:72
663	18 Chor. 13	Allein Gott (3/2)	25:125	6:67
662	18 Chor. 12	Allein Gott (coloratura)	25:122	6:64
677	Clavierüb. Pt III 9	Allein Gott (manualiter fughetta)	3:205	1:205
716		Allein Gott (fugue)	40:45	3:45
715		Allein Gott (chor. w/ interludes)	40:44	3:44
771		Allein Gott (d. a.) (variat.)	40:195	
653b		An Wasserflüssen Babylon (5-pt dbl pedal)	40:49	6:32
653	18 Chor. 3	An Wasserflüssen Babylon	25:92	6:34
587		Aria in F Major (after François Couperin)	38:22	
744		Auf meinen lieben Gott (d. a.)	40:170	
745		Aus der Tiefe rufe (attrib. to Johann Christoff Bach)	40:171	
686	Clavierüb. Pt III 18	Aus tiefer Not (6-pt dbl pedal)	3:229	1:63
687	Clavierüb. Pt III 19	Aus tiefer Not (4-pt manualiter) Canonic Variations (see Vom Himmel hoch, BWV 769)	3:232	1:66
588		Canzona in D Minor	38:126	7:52
766	partita	Christ, der du bist	40:107	2:61
670	Clavierüb. Pt III 2	Christe, aller Welt (manualiter)	3:186	1:20
673	Clavierüb. Pt III 5	Christe, aller Welt (manualiter)	3:194	1:28
619	Orgelbüchl. 21	Christe, du Lamm	25:30	2:30
627	Orgelbüchl. 29	Christ ist erstanden	25:40	2:40
746		Christ ist erstanden (comp. J. K. F. Fischer)	40:173	
718		Christ lag (Fantasia)	40:52	3:52
625	Orgelbüchl. 27	Christ lag	25:38	2:38
695	Kirnberger coll. 6	Christ lag (3/8 manualiter)	40:10	3:10
611	Orgelbüchl. 13	Christum wir sollen	25:15	2:15
696	Kirnberger coll. 7	Christum wir sollen (Fughetta)	40:13	3:13
684	Clavierüb. Pt III 16	Christ, unser Herr, zum Jordan (C Minor pedaliter)	3:224	1:58
685	Clavierüb. Pt III 17	Christ, unser Herr, zum Jordan (manualiter)	3:228	1:62
620	Orgelbüchl. 22	Christus, der uns selig macht	25:30	2:30
747		Christus, der uns selig macht	40:177	
592		Concerto in G Major (after J. Ernst)	38:149	7:73
593		Concerto in A Minor (after Vivaldi)	38:158	7:82
594		Concerto in C Major (after Vivaldi)	38:171	7:95
595		Concerto in C Major (1 mvt) (after Johann Ernst)	38:196	7:120

P&K/H	P. Or	Schir	Born	Novel	Br. H	Bären	Dit	Schm. C.	Kel. C.
6:4		8:9	10:12	16:10	8:114		70	ca1746	1746/47
		6:18	11:1	18:1	-	3:			
6:3		6:19	11:2	18:2	-	3:			
9:41		6:20	11:3	18:3	9:1	3:3		?	n. d.
K/H9:48									
9:42		6:109	12:50		9:2	3:4			
K/H9:67					-	3:			
P --					10:2			1703/07	
K/H9:68									
9:68		8:114	10:71		10:4			1700/02	n. d.
5:2	55	7:60	7:66	15:123	7:66	1:	137	1717	1717
8:72		1:18	6:60	2:26	4:86			ca1709	1708/17
5:2	54	7:59	7:65	15:121	7:65	1:	134	1717	1717
6:6		6:23	11:9	18:5	9:5	3:11			
6:8		6:27	11:12	18:11	9:11	3:8			n. d.
6:10		7:72	8:28	16:39	8:26	4:30		1739	1739
6:12		7:74	8:31	16:40	8:28	4:33		1739	1739
6:17		8:64	9:63	17:66	7:143	2:79, 179		1746/50	1750
6:22		8:60	9:58	17:60	7:136	2:72, 172		1746/50	1750
6:26		8:56	9:54	17:56	7:131	2:67, 168		1746/50	1750
6:29		7:79	8:38	16:41	8:34	4:41		1739	1739
6:30		6:21	11:6	18:7	9:9	3:			Weimar
9:45		6:1	11:4	18:4	9:8	3:14		1703/07	1703/07
		8:122	10:82		10:60	3:		ca1705	
6:32		6:29	11:15	18:13	7:171				1720
6:34		8:27	9:17	17:18	7:87	2:22, 130, 133		1746/50	1750
9:16			6:55	12:112	6:107	8:82		1723/30	1723/29
K/H9:44									
9:46		6:109	12:53		9:13				
K/H9:48									
9:47		6:110	12:54		10:14				
K/H9:63									
6:36		7:100	8:70	16:68	8:64	4:74		1739	1739
6:38		7:103	8:74	16:72	8:68	4:78		1739	1739
						1:			
4:58		2:71	6:64	2:34	4:81			ca1709	1708/17
5:60		8:78		19:36	10:18	1:		ca1700	n. d.
7:20		7:63	8:14	16:30	8:14	4:18		1739	1739
7:27		7:70	8:24	16:37	8:23	4:28		1739	1739
5:3	27	7:30	7:34	15:61	7:32	1:	65	1717	1717
5:4	36	7:40	7:45	15:83	7:44	1:	90	1717	1717
		6:110	12:57		-				
K/H6:40		6:31	11:19	18:19	9:18	3:16		bef. 1703	n. d.
5:7	34	7:38	7:43	15:79	7:42	1:	84	1717	1717
6:43		6:34	11:24	18:16	9:15	3:20		1708/17	n. d.
5:8	17	7:15	7:18	15:33	7:18	1:	36	1717	1717
5:9		6:36	11:27	18:23	9:22	3:23		1708/17	Weimar?
6:46		7:96	8:64	16:62	8:58	4:68		1739	1739
6:49		7:99	8:69	16:67	8:62	4:73		1739	1739
5:10	28	7:30	7:35	15:64	7:33	1:	67	1717	1717
K/H9:74					9:23			1708/17	
8:2		5:2	6:1	11:1	5:40	8:56		1716/17	1708/17
8:10		5:12	6:10	11:10	5:49	8:16		1716/17	1708/17
8:22		5:26	6:22	11:24	5:62	8:30		1716/17	1708/17
8:44		5:52	6:43	11:49	5:84	8:65		1716/17	1708/17

BWV no.	Chorale Collection & No. w/in Coll.	Title	Bach G	Lea
596		Concerto in D Minor (after Vivaldi)		
597		Concerto in E-flat Major		
621	Orgelbüchl. 23	Da Jesus an dem Kreuze	25:32	2:32
614	Orgelbüchl. 16	Das alte Jahr	25:19	2:19
702	Kirnberger coll. 13	Das Jesulein soll (d. a.)	40:20	3:20
605	Orgelbüchl. 7	Der Tag, der ist so	25:8	2:8
719		Der Tag, der ist so (d. a.)	40:55	3:55
635	Orgelbüchl. 37	Dies sind die heil'gen	25:50	2:50
678	Clavierüb. Pt III 10	Dies sind die heil'gen (pedaliter)	3:206	1:40
679	Clavierüb. Pt III 11	Dies sind die heil'gen (manualiter fughetta)	3:210	1:44
705	Kirnberger coll.	Durch Adams Fall (d. a.)	40:23	3:23
637	Orgelbüchl. 39	Durch Adams Fall	25:53	2:53
		Eight Little Preludes and Fugues(see Preludes and Fugues, Eight Little		
720		Ein' feste Burg	40:57	3:57
721		Erbarm' dich mein (d. a.)	40:60	3:60
629	Orgelbüchl. 31	Erschienen ist	25:45	2:45
628	Orgelbüchl. 30	Erstanden ist	25:44	2:44
638	Orgelbüchl. 40	Es ist das Heil	25:54	2:54
571		Fantasia in G Major (Concerto, 4/4)	38:67	8:67
572		Fantasia in G Major (12/8)	38:75	8:75
570		Fantasia in C Major	38:62	8:62
563		Fantasia in B Minor con imitazione	38:59	8:59
562		Fantasia in C Minor (fugue unfin.)	38:64	8:64
573		Fantasia in C Major (unfin.)	38:209	
561		Fantasia and Fugue in A Minor	38:48	8:48
537		Fantasia and Fugue in C Minor	15:129	5:129
542		Fantasia and Fugue in G Minor (Great)	15:177	5:177
-		Fugue in C Major	36:159	
946		Fugue in C Major		
Anh. 90		Fugue in C Major (pedal flügel)	38:213	
574		Fugue in C Minor (Legrenzi)	38:94	8:94
575		Fugue in C Minor	38:101	8:101
562		Fugue in C Minor (incompl.)		
580		Fugue in D Major	38:215	
576		Fugue in G Major (4/4)	38:106	8:106
577		Fugue in G Major (12/8) ('Gigue')	38:111)	8:111
581		Fugue in G Major	not listed	
579		Fugue in B Minor (Corelli)	38:121	8:121
578		Fugue in G Minor ('Little')	38:116	8:116
		Fugue in G Minor (Cantata 131)	38:217	
722		Gelobet seist du (chor. w/interludes)	40:62	3:62
697	Kirnberger coll. 8	Gelobet seist du (fughetta)	40:14	3:14
604	Orgelbüchl. 6	Gelobet seist du	25:7	2:7
723		Gelobet seist du	40:63	3:63
748		Gott der Vater, wohn (J. C. Bach or J. G. Walther)	40:177	
703	Kirnberger coll. 14	Gottes Sohn ist kommen	40:21	3:21
600	Orgelbüchl. 2	Gottes Sohn ist kommen	25:4	2:4
724		Gottes Sohn ist kommen	40:65	3:65
613	Orgelbüchl. 15	Helft mir Gott's Güte	25:18	2:18
698	Kirnberger coll. 9	Herr Christ, der ein'ge (fughetta)	40:15	3:15
601	Orgelbüchl. 3	Herr Christ, der ein'ge	25:5	2:5
725		Herr Gott, dich loben (5 pt)	40:66	3:66
617	Orgelbüchl. 19	Herr Gott, nun schleuss	25:26	2:26
726		Herr Jesu Christ, dich (chor. w/interludes)	40:72	3:72

P&K/H	P. Or	Schir	Born	Novel	Br. H	Bären	Dit	Schm. C.	Kel. C.
P. E. 3002					-	8:3		1716/17	1708/17
K/H9:30					6:100				
5:11	29	7:32	7:37	15:67	7:35	1:	71	1717	1717
5:12	20	7:19	7:24	15:43	7:22	1:	45	1717	1717
9:49		6:37	11:28	18:24	9:26	3:		1703/07	Weimar?
K/H--									
5:13	11	7:8	7:9	15:18	7:8	1:	16	1717	1717
		6:38	11:30	18:26	9:28			?	Weimar?
5:14	46	7:50	7:56	15:105	7:56	1:	112	1717	1717
6:50		7:80	8:40	16:42	8:35	4:42		1739	1739
6:54		7:84	8:46	16:47	8:42	4:49		1739	1739
6:56		6:39	11:32	18:28	9:30	3:			?
5:15	48	7:53	7:59	15:109	7:59	1:	119	1717	1717
6:58		6:41	11:34	18:30	9:32	3:24		1709	1709
		6:44	11:38	18:35	9:36	3:28		bef. 1703	n. d.
5:17	40	7:45	7:50	15:91	7:49	1:	98	1717	1717
5:16	39	7:44	7:49	15:89	7:48	1:	96	1717	1717
5:18	49	7:54	7:60	15:111	7:60	1:	122	1717	1717
9:11		1:34	5:84	12:75	-			1705/06	1700/05
K/H9:25									
4:62		1:46	5:76	9:168	5:16			1705/06	1708/17
8:78		1:2	5:71	12:92	5:2	6:16		ca1709	1700/05
9:1		1:110	5:91	12:71	5:24	6:68		ca1710	1700/05
4:70		3:29	5:73	3:57	5:4	5:54		1712/16	1700/23?
			6:75		-	6:18		1722	1717/23?
9:19		1:86	3:18	12:60	2:76	5:47		ca. 1710	
K/H9:3									
3:55		3:20	3:1	3:76	2:68			ca.1716	
2:20		4:40	3:8	8:127	2:56	5:167		1708/09	1717/23
8:80					-			ca1720	fugue:1720
				12:100	-				
			5:34		-				
4:40		1:10	5:41	10:230	4:51	6:19, 82		1708/09	1700/05
4:54			5:37	12:95	4:58	6:26		1703/04	1700/05
			6:76		-				
K/H9:22			5:47	12:83	-				
9:28		1:56	5:50	12:86	4:62			?	1700/05
K/H9:12									
9:4		1:62	6:66	12:55	4:67			1705/06	1700/05
K/H9:18									
					-				
4:50		1:114	5:67	3:60	4:76	6:71		ca.1709	1708/17
4:46		2:104	5:63	3:84	4:72	6:55		ca.1709	1708/17
8:85			5:60	2:41	-			?	1708/17
5:102		6:3	11:40	18:37	9:39	3:30,31		1703/07	1703/07
5:20		6:46	11:44	18:38	9:38	3:32		1708/17	Weimar?
5:19	10	7:7	7:8	15:15	7:7	1:	14	1717	1717
6:61		6:47	11:42	18:39	9:40			?	?
6:62		6:112	12:61		-				
5:22		6:49	11:45	18:41	9:43	3:34		1708/17	Weimar?
5:20	6	7:3	7:3	15:5	7:2	1:	5	1717	1717
6:64		6:50	11:46	18:42	9:42	3:33		?	?
5:23	19	7:18	7:22	15:39	7:21	1:	42	1717	1717
5:25		6:51	11:48	18:43	9:44	3:35		1708/17	Weimar?
5:24	7	7:4	7:5	15:9	7:4	1:	8	1717	1717
6:65		6:4	11:49	18:44	9:47	3:36		?	1703/07
5:26	24	7:26	7:30	15:53	7:27	1:	57	1717	1717
P 9:50		6:9	11:59	18:52	9:56	3:45		?	1703/07
K/H--									

BWV no.	Chorale Collection & No. w/in Coll.	Title	Bach G	Lea
749		Herr Jesu Christ, dich		
632	Orgelbüchl. 34	Herr Jesu Christ, dich	25:48	2:48
709	Kirnberger coll. 20	Herr Jesu Christ, dich (coloratura)	40:30	3:30
655	18 Chor. 5	Herr Jesu Christ, dich (trio in G Major)	25:98	6:40
750		Herr Jesu Christ, mein's Lebens Licht		
727		Herzlich tut mich verlangen	40:73	3:73
630	Orgelbüchl. 32	Heut triumphiret	25:46	2:46
624	Orgelbüchl. 26	Hilf Gott, dass mir's	25:36	2:36
707	Kirnberger coll. 18	Ich hab mein Sach (d. a.)	40:26	3:26
708	Kirnberger coll. 19	Ich hab mein Sach (d. a.)		
639	Orgelbüchl. 41	Ich ruf' zu dir	25:55	2:55
640	Orgelbüchl. 42	In dich hab ich	25:56	2:56
712	Kirnberger coll. 23	In dich hab ich (major melody)	40:36	3:36
615	Orgelbüchl. 17	In dir ist Freude	25:20	2:20
751		In dulci jubilo (trio in G Major, d. a.)		
729		In dulci jubilo (A Major)	40:74	3:74
608	Orgelbüchl. 10	In dulci jubilo (canon)	25:12	2:12
752		Jesu, der du meine Seele (per canonem) (d. a.)		
610	Orgelbüchl. 12	Jesu, meine Freude	25:14	2:14
753		Jesu, meine Freude (incompl.)	40:163	
713	Kirnberger coll. 24	Jesu, meine Freude (fantasia)	40:38	3:38
626	Orgelbüchl. 28	Jesus Christus, unser Heiland	25:39	2:39
688	Clavierüb. Pt III 20	Jesus Christus, unser Heiland, der von uns (cantus firmus in pedal)	3:234	1:68
689	Clavierüb. Pt III 21	Jesus Christus, unser Heiland, der von uns(manualiter fugue in F Minor)	3:239	1:73
665	18 Chor. 15	Jesus Christus, unser Heiland, der von uns (pedaliter, in E Minor)	25:136	6:78
666	18 Chor. 16	Jesus Christus, unser Heiland, der von uns (manualiter, in E Minor)	25:140	6:82
728		Jesus, meine Zuversicht	40:74	3:74
		Kleines harmonisches Labyrinth (see Little harmonic labyrinth)		
631	Orgelbüchl. 33	Komm, Gott, Schöpfer	25:47	2:47
667	18 Chor. 17	Komm, Gott, Schöpfer	25:142	6:84
651	18 Chor. 1	Komm, heiliger Geist (fantasia)	25:79	6:21
652	18 Chor. 2	Komm, heiliger Geist (G Major)	25:86	6:28
650	6 'Schübler' Chor. 6	Kommst du nun	25:74	6:16
671	Clavierüb. Pt III 3	Kyrie, Gott, heiligen Geist	3:190	1:24
674	Clavierüb. Pt III 6	Kyrie, Gott, heiligen Geist	3:196	1:30
669	Clavierüb. Pt III 1	Kyrie, Gott Vater	3:184	1:18
672	Clavierüb. Pt III 4	Kyrie, Gott Vater (manualiter)	3:194	1:28
633	Orgelbüchl. 35	Liebster Jesu, wir sind hier	25:49	2:49
634	Orgelbüchl. 36	Liebster Jesu, wir sind hier		
706	Kirnberger coll. 17	Liebster Jesu, wir	40:25	3:25
730		Liebster Jesu, wir sind(G Major, d.a)	40:76	3:76
731		Liebster Jesu, wir sind(coloratura, d. a.)	40:77	3:77
754		Liebster Jesu (d. a.)		
591		Little harmonic labyrinth	38:225	
		Lobe den Herren(see Kommst du nun)		
704	Kirnberger coll. 15	Lob sei dem allmächtigen Gott	40:22	3:22
602	Orgelbüchl. 4	Lob sei dem allmächtigen Gott	25:13	2:13
732		Lobt Gott, ihr Christen (E Major)	40:78	3:78
609	Orgelbüchl. 11	Lobt Gott, ihr Christen	25:13	2:13
733		Magnificat, Fugue on	40:79	3:79
648	6 'Schübler' Chor. 4	Meine Seele erhebt	25:70	6:12
616	Orgelbüchl. 18	Mit Fried und Freud	25:24	2:24

P&K/H	P. Or	Schir	Born	Novel	Br. H	Bären	Dit	Schm. C.	Kel. C.
					-				1696/99
5:28	44	7:48	7:54	15:99	7:53	1:	107	1717	1717
5:28		6:52	11:60	18:50	9:54	3:43		1708/17	early
6:70		8:34	9:24	17:26	7:96	2:31,140	30	1746/50	1750
					-			1695/03	1696/99
5:30		6:54	11:62	18:53	9:57	3:46		?	Weimar
5:30	40	7:46	7:51	15:94	7:50	1:	101	1717	1717
5:32	32	7:36	7:41	15:76	7:40	1:	80	1717	1717
6:74		6:55	11:64	18:55	9:59	3:			?
		6:10	11:70	18:58	9:64				
5:33	50	7:55	7:61	15:113	7:61	1:	124	1717	1717
5:35	41	7:56	7:62	15:115	7:62	1:	127	1717	1717
6:94		6:65	11:75	18:59	9:65	3:48		1708/17	early
5:36	21	7:20	7:25	15:45	7:23	1:	48	1717	1717
P 9:50		6:59			9:69			1695/03	?
K/H9:65									
5:103		6:12	11:71	18:61	9:67	3:50,52		1703/07	1703/07
5:38	14	7:12	7:14	15:26	7:14	1:	25,27	1717	1717
					-				
5:34	16	7:14	7:17	15:31	7:17	1:	33	1717	1717
5:112		6:64	12:78		-				
6:78		6:61	11:78	18:64	9:71	3:54		1708/17	1723
5:34	35	7:39	7:44	15:81	7:43	1:		1717	1717
6:82		7:105	8:77	16:74	8:72	4:81		1739	1739
6:92		7:110	8:82	16:80	8:78	4:89		1739	1739
6:87		8:69	9:71	17:74	7:151	2:87,187	86	1746/50	1750
6:90		8:72	9:76	17:79	7:155	2:91,191		1746/50	1750
5:103		6:64	11:83	18:69	9:75	3:58		1722	?
7:86	42	7:47	7:53	15:97	7:57	1:	105	1717	1717
7:2		8:74	9:79	17:82	7:159	2:94,194	96	1746/50	1750
7:4		8:15	9:1	17:1	7:68	2:3,117	2	1746/50	1750
7:10		8:21	9:10	17:10	7:77	2:13,121	12	1746/50	1750
7:16		8:12	10:14	16:14	8:118		87	ca1746	1746/47
7:23		7:66	8:18	16:33	8:18	4:22		1739	1739
7:28		7:71	8:26	16:38	8:24	4:29		1739	1739
7:18		7:61	8:11	16:28	8:12	4:16		1739	1739
7:28		7:69	8:23	16:36	8:22	4:27		1739	1739
5:40	45	7:49	7:55	15:102	7:55	1:	110	1717	1717
		7:50		15:101	7:54		111		
5:39		6:14	12:1	18:72	9:76	3:59		1708/17	Weimar
5:105		6:67	12:2	18:70	9:77	3:60			1703/07
5:105		6:68	12:3	18:71	9:78	3:61			
K/H9:50					9:79				
P 9:34			6:58		-				
K/H9:16									
5:41		6:69	12:5	18:73	9:81	3:62		1708/17	Weimar?
5:40	8	7:5	7:6	15:11	7:5	1:	10	1717	1717
5:106		6:15	12:4	18:74	9:82	3:63,64		1703/07	1703/07
5:42	15	7:13	7:16	15:29	7:16	1:	31	1717	1717
7:29		6:70	12:6	18:75	9:83	3:65		?	Weimar
7:33		8:8	10:10	16:8	8:112		57	ca1746	1746/47
5:42	23	7:24	7:28	15:50	7:25	1:	54	1717	1717

BWV no.	Chorale Collection & No. w/ in Coll.	Title	Bach G	Lea
657	18 Chor. 7	Nun danket alle Gott	25:108	6:50
755		Nun freut euch (fughetta, d. a.)		
734		Nun freut euch (Es ist gewisslich) trio, cantus firmus in pedal)	40:84	3:84
699	Kirnberger coll. 10	Nun komm der Heiden Heiland (fughetta)	40:16	3:16
599	Orgelbüchl. 1	Nun komm der Heiden Heiland	25:3	2:3
659	18 Chor. 9	Nun komm der Heiden Heiland (coloratura)	25:114	6:56
660	18 Chor. 10	Nun komm der Heiden Heiland (trio)	25:116	6:58
661	18 Chor. 11	Nun komm der Heiden Heiland (cantus firmus in pedal)	25:118	6:60
756		Nun ruhen alle Wälder		
767	partita	O Gott, du frommer	40:114	2:68
757		O Herre Gott, dein (d. a.)		
		O Lamm Gottes unschuldig(manualiter)		
618	Orgelbüchl. 20	O Lamm Gottes unschuldig	25:28	2:28
656	18 Chor. 6	O Lamm Gottes unschuldig	25:102	6:44
622	Orgelbüchl. 24	O Mensch, bewein	25:33	2:33
758		O Vater, allmächtiger Gott (3 verses, d. a.)	40:179	
582		Passacaglia and Fugue in C Minor	15:289	7:39
590		Pastorale in F Major	38:135	7:61
598		Pedal Exercise (Exercitium)	38:210	8:126
943		Prelude in C Major (manualiter)	36:134	
567		Prelude in C Major (3/4)	38:84	8:84
568		Prelude in G Major	38:85	8:85
569		Prelude in A Minor (3/4)	38:89	8:89
531		Prelude and Fugue in C Major ('Fanfare')	15:81	4:81
545		Prelude and Fugue in C Major	15:121	5:212
547		Prelude and Fugue in C Major (9/8)	15:228	5:228
549		Prelude and Fugue in C Minor	38:3	8:3
546		Prelude and Fugue in C Minor('Great')	15:218	5:218
532		Prelude and Fugue in D Major	15:88	4:88
539		Prelude and Fugue in D Minor ('Fiddle Fugue')	15:148	5:148
552	Clavierüb. Pt III	Prelude and Fugue in E-flat Major	3:173	P 1:7 F 1:88
548		Prelude and Fugue in E Minor('Wedge')	15:236	5:236
533		Prelude and Fugue in E Minor ('Cathedral')	15:100	4:100
534		Prelude and Fugue in F Minor	15:104	4:104
550		Prelude and Fugue in G Major (3/2)	38:9	8:9
541		Prelude and Fugue in G Major('Great')	15:169	5:169
535		Prelude and Fugue in G Minor	15:112	4:112
536		Prelude and Fugue in A Major	15:120	4:120
543		Prelude and Fugue in A Minor('Great')	15:189	5:189
944		Prelude and Fugue in A Minor		
551		Prelude and Fugue in A Minor	38:17	8:17
544		Prelude and Fugue in B Minor('Great')	15:199	5:199
553-560		Preludes and Fugues, Eight Little	38:23	8:23
603	Orgelbüchl. 5	Puer natus	25:6	2:6
654	18 Chor. 4	Schmücke dich	25:95	6:37
759		Schmücke dich (attrib. J. C. Bach or G. A. Homilius)	40:181	

P&K/H	P. Or	Schir	Born	Novel	Br. H	Bären	Dit	Schm. C.	Kel. C.
7:34		8:44	9:36	17:40	7:111	2:46	45	1746/50	1750
P 9:52		6:77			-			1695/03	n. d.
K/H9:70									
7:36		6:75	12:12	18:80	9:91	3:70		1703/07	n. d.
5:45		6:79	12:15	18:83	9:94	3:73		1708/17	Weimar?
5:44	5	7:2	7:2	15:3	7:1	1:	3	1717	1717
7:38		8:48	9:43	17:46	7:118	2:55,157	54	1746/50	1750
7:40		8:50	9:46	17:49	7:122	2:59,160	58	1746/50	1750
7:42		8:52	9:49	17:52	7:126	2:62,164	62	1746/50	1750
					-			1695/03	1696/99
5:68		8:84	10:26	19:44	10:26	1:		ca1700	n. d.
P --					-				
K/H9:66									
						3:74			
5:46	26	7:28	7:32	15:58	7:30	1:	61	1717	1717
7:45		8:38	9:30	17:32	7:103	2:38,146	36	1746/50	1750
5:48	30	7:33	7:38	15:69	7:36	1:	74	1717	1717
		6:113	12:64		9:98				
1:76		4:91	2:65	10:214	6:2			1716/17	1717/23
1:88		2:96	6:68	12:102	5:28			1703/07	1708/17
P 9:40			6:78					1700/03	1700/05
K/H--									
8:76				12:94				?	
8:77		2:56	5:26	12:91	4:41			1709	
8:82		1:42	5:27	2:30	4:42	6:51		1708	1700/05
4:72		1:104	5:30	10:238	4:46	6:59		ca1709	1700/05
4:2		2:48	1:1	7:74	4:2	5:3		ca1709	1700/05
						6:77(var)			
2:2		3:2	1:9	3:70	1:2	5:10		P ca1730	1723/29
						5:20		F 1716/17	
2:46		3:8	1:15	9:156	1:19	6:101(var)		ca1744	1730/40
4:36		1:4	1:36	2:48	4:10	5:30		ca1703/04	1700/05
2:36		3:34	1:25	7:64	1:8	5:35		P ca1730	1730/40
						5:58;6:95		F ca1716	
4:16		2:57	1:41	6:10	2:18	(Fugue var)		ca1709	1706/08
						5:70			
3:42		2:76	1:52	9:150	2:			1724/25	1717/23
						P 4:2			
3:2		3:61	P 8:1	P 16:19	2:2	F 4:105		1739	1739
			F 8:85	F 16:83					
				(both 6:28)		5:94			
2:64		3:84	1:63	8:98	1:41	5:90;6:106(var)		1727/36	1730/40
3:88		3:80	1:59	2:44	3:76			ca1709	1706/08
						5:130			
2:29		4:20	2:1	6:24	2:38	5:138		ca1716	1708/17
4:9		1:68	2:17	7:80	3:67	5:146		ca1709	1708/17
2:7		4:30	2:9	8:112	1:	5:157;6:109(var)		1724/25	1723/29
3:48		1:76	2:24	8:120	2:46	5:180;6:114(var)		ca1709	1708/17
2:14		4:54	2:31	3:64	1:	5:186;6:121(var)		ca1716	1708/17
2:54		4:62	2:38	7:42	1:30			ca1709	1717/23
					-	6:63			
3:84		1:98	2:48	10:208	3:80	5:198		bef. 1706	1700/06
2:78		4:76	2:53	7:52	1:58			1727/36	1730/40
P 8:48-71		2:2-31	5:1-25	1:	4:16ff.	1:		bef. 1710 attrib. Krebs	
5:50	9	7:6	7:7	15:13	7:6	2:26,136	12	1717	1717
7:50		8:30	9:20	17:22	7:91		25	1746/50	1750
		6:114	12:68		-				

BWV no.	Chorale Collection & No. w/in Coll.	Title	Bach G	Lea
768	partita	Sei gegrüsset	40:122	2:76
529		Sonata in C Major	15:50	4:50
526		Sonata in C Minor	15:13	4:13
527		Sonata in D Minor	15:26	4:26
525		Sonata in E-flat Major	15:3	4:3
528		Sonata in E Minor	15:40	4:40
530		Sonata in G Major	15:66	4:66
566		Toccata in E Major (also in C Major)	15:276	7:26
565		Toccata and Fugue in D Minor	15:267	7:17
564		Toccata, Adagio and Fugue	15:253	7:3
540		Toccata and Fugue in F Major	15:154	5:154
538		Toccata and Fugue in D Minor ('Dorian')	15:136	5:136
586		Trio in G Major (Telemann) transcription		
584		Trio in G Minor	33:110	
585		Trio in C Minor	38:219	
583		Trio in D Minor	38:143	7:69
1027a		Trio in G Major (transcrip.)		
735		Valet will ich(B-flat Major)(fantasia)	40:86	3:86
736		Valet will ich (D Major) (cantus firmus in pedal)	40:90	3:90
762		Vater unser (d.a., coloratura)		
760		Vater unser (attrib. J. C. Bach)	40:183	
636	Orgelbüchl. 38	Vater unser	25:52	2:52
761		Vater unser (attrib. J. C. Bach or Georg Böhm)	40:184	
737		Vater unser (4/2)	40:96	3:96
682	Clavierüb. Pt III 14	Vater unser (E Minor) (5 pt)	3:217	1:51
683	Clavierüb. Pt III 15	Vater unser (manualiter)	3:223	1:57
738		Vom Himmel hoch (D Major) (12/8)	40:97	3:97
701	Kirnberger coll. 12	Vom Himmel hoch (fughetta)	40:19	3:19
606	Orgelbüchl. 8	Vom Himmel hoch	25:9	2:9
700	Kirnberger coll. 11	Vom Himmel hoch (cantus firmus in pedal)	40:17	3:17
769		Vom Himmel hoch (Canonic variat.)	40:137	2:91
607	Orgelbüchl. 9	Vom Himmel kam	25:10	2:10
658	18 Chor. 8	Von Gott will ich	25:112	6:54
668	18 Chor. 18	Vor deinen Thron	25:145	6:87
645	6 'Schübler' Chor. 1	Wachet auf	25:63	6:5
696		Was fürchst du (see Christum, wir sollen)		
641	Orgelbüchl. 43	Wenn wir in höchsten Nöthen sein	25:57	2:57
		Wenn wir (see Vor deinen Thron)		
642	Orgelbüchl. 44	Wer nur den lieben Gott	25:58	2:58
690	Kirnberger coll. 1	Wer nur den lieben Gott (3/4, manualiter)	40:3	3:3
691	Kirnberger coll. 2	Wer nur den lieben Gott (coloratura)	40:4	3:4
647	6 'Schübler' Chor. 3	Wer nur den lieben Gott (C Minor)	25:68	6:10
764		Wie schön leuchtet (fragment)		
739		Wie schön leuchtet (d.a.)	40:99	3:99
763		Wie schön leuchtet (d.a.)		
710	Kirnberger coll. 21	Wir Christenleut (trio, attrib. J. L. Krebs)	40:32	3:32
612	Orgelbüchl. 14	Wir Christenleut	25:16	2:16

P&K/H	P. Or	Schir	Born	Novel	Br. H	Bären	Dit	Schm. C.	Kel. C.
5:76		8:92	10:37	19:55	10:38	1:		ca1700 and 1707/17	n. d.
1:46		5:111	4:44	5:134	6:48			after 1727	1723/28
1:11		5:70	4:10	4:97	6:11			after 1727	1723/28
1:24		5:84	4:22	4:110	6:24			after 1727	1723/28
1:2		5:58	4:1	4:88	6:2			after 1727	1723/28
1:36		5:98	4:34	5:124	6:38			after 1727/	1723/28
1:63		5:130	4:61	5:151	6:65			after 1727	1723/28
3:94 (3:62)		1:22	3:63	8:88	3:20	6:40		ca1707	1706/08
4:27		2:84	3:43	6:2	3:58	6:31		ca1709	1706/08
3:72		2:32	3:29	9:137	3:45	6:3		ca1709	1708/17
3:16		4:2	3:73	9:176	3:2	5:112		ca1716	1717/23
3:30		3:47	3:51	10:196	3:32	5:76		P 1727/36 F 1716/17?	1717/23
P -- K/H9:42					6:90	8:78		1723/30	1723/29
					-			1723/25	
P 9:36 K/H9:38			6:48	12:108	6:84	8:73			
4:76		5:143	6:52	2:54	6:78			1717/23	1723/28
P 9:8 K/H9:35					6:94			1723/30	1723/29
7:53		6:80	12:16	19:2	9:102	3:77,81		1703/07	1703/07
7:56		6:84	12:20	19:7	9:106	3:84		?	n. d.
P -- K/H9:72		6:90			9:112				
		6:116	12:70		-				
5:52	47	7:53	7:58	15:107	7:58	1:	116	1717	1717
P 9:54 K/H--		6:117	12:72		-				
7:66		6:88	12:26	19:12	9:111	3:90		?	n. d.
7:60		7:90	8:55	16:53	8:49	4:58		1739	1739
5:51		7:95	8:62	16:61	8:56	4:66		1739	1739
5:106		6:17	12:28	19:19	9:118	3:94		1703/07	1703/07
7:67		6:92	12:32	19:14	9:116	3:96		1708/17	Leipzig?
5:52	12	7:10	1:11	15:21	7:10	1:	19	1717	1717
7:68		6:94	12:30	19:16	9:114	3:92		1708/17	early
5:92		8:106	10:58	19:73	8:142	2:98,197		1746/47	1746
5:54	12	7:10	7:12	15:23	7:12	1:	22	1717	1717
7:70		8:46	9:40	17:43	7:114	2:51,154	50	1746/50	1750
7:74		8:76	9:82	17:85	7:163	2:113,212	100	1746/50	1750
7:72		8:2	10:2	16:1	8:100 9:22		11	ca1746	1746/47
5:55	52	7:57	7:63	15:117	7:63	1:	128	1717	1717
5:57	53	7:58	7:64	15:119	7:64	1:	131	1717	1717
5:56		6:18 6:96	12:34	19:21	9:120	3:98		1708/17	?
5:56		6:97	12:35	19:22	9:122	3:98		1725	?
7:76		8:6	10:8	16:6	8:108		41	ca1746	1746/47
		6:102	12:79		-				
P 9:56 K/H--		6:98	12:36	19:23	9:123			1703/07	1703/07
P -- K/H9:49					-				
P 9:60 K/H--		6:103	12:42	19:28	9:128	3:100			
5:58	18	7:16	7:20	15:36	7:20	1:	39	1717	1717

BWV no.	Chorale Collection & No. w/in Coll.	Title	Bach G	Lea
623	Orgelbüchl. 25	Wir danken dir	25:35	2:35
		Wir danken dir (Sinfonia arr. Dupré from Cantata 29)		
765		Wir glauben all (4/2, d. a.)	40:187	
680	Clavierüb. Pt III 12	Wir glauben all (fugue)	3:212	1:46
681	Clavierüb. Pt III 13	Wir glauben all (manualiter)	3:216	1:50
740		Wir glauben all	40:103	
		Wir müssen durch (Sinfonia arr. Dupré from Cantata 146)		
646	6 'Schübler' Chor. 2	Wo soll ich fliehen	25:66	6:8
694	Kirnberger coll. 5	Wo soll ich fliehen (G Minor) (cantus firmus in pedal)	40:6	3:6
802		Duetto I	3:242	
803		Duetto II	3:245	
804		Duetto III	3:248	
805		Duetto IV	3:251	

P&K/H	P. Or	Schir	Born	Novel	Br. H	Bären	Dit	Schm. C.	Kel. C.
5:59	32	7:35	7:40	15:73	7:39	1:	78	1717	1717
			12:81						
P 9:62		6:120	12:75		9:131				
K/H9:51									
7:78		7:86	8:49	2:38,16:49	8:44	4:52		1739	1739
7:82		7:89	8:54	16:52	8:48	4:57		1739	1739
7:82		6:121	12:44	19:30	9:133			?	n. d.
					-				
7:84		8:4	10:5	16:4	8:104		27	ca1746	1746/47
P 9:64		6:105	12:46	19:32	9:135	3:103		1708/17	early
K/H9:57						4:92			
						4:96			
						4:99			
						4:102			

INDEX